Jason Salkey is a British actor, a regular on screens, big and small, for over thirty years. In 1992 he landed the part of Rifleman Harris in a drama based on Bernard Cornwell's Sharpe novels, a show that lasted five seasons and was eventually screened across the globe. His memoir, *From Crimea with Love*, is his first book. He lives in London with his wife and son.

www.riflemanharris.co.uk

FROM CRIMEA
WITH LOVE

Misadventures in the Making of

SHARPE'S RIFLES

JASON SALKEY

unbound

First published in 2021
This paperback edition first published in 2022

Unbound
Level 1, Devonshire House, One Mayfair Place, London W1J 8AJ
www.unbound.com
All rights reserved

Text Design by PDQ Digital Media Solutions Ltd.

A CIP record for this book is available from the British Library

ISBN 978-1-80018-183-0 (paperback)
ISBN 978-1-78352-957-5 (hardback)
ISBN 978-1-78352-958-2 (ebook)

Printed in Great Britain by Clays Ltd, Elcograf S.p.A

1 3 5 7 9 8 6 4 2

This book is dedicated to my dad, my mum and my love from the Crimea.

CONTENTS

FOREWORD

My first encounter with the *Sharpe* film crew was in Ukraine. I had flown from London to Simferopol (universally known as Simplyawful) with Muir Sutherland, one of the two producers of Sharpe Film, and we were accompanied by two actors joining the cast and a heap of equipment. At Simplyawful's airport we were met by an interpreter, a minivan and a lorry. The latter was swiftly loaded with all the equipment, but three men in black leather jackets informed our interpreter that it could not leave the airport. Muir, sitting in the minivan, slid open a window and, in his stentorian Scottish voice, demanded to know why not. The interpreter, a scared and skinny young man, nervously informed us that the three leather-jacketed thugs were from the local mafia and were demanding a bribe.

It was long after nightfall and Muir was eager to leave. 'How much?' he demanded.

'A lot!' the young interpreter stammered.

'How much!' Muir demanded again.

There was a pause. The interpreter plainly feared the wrath to come, but finally, in a tremulous voice, he managed to answer. 'Ten dollars!'

'Oh, for Christ's sake!' Muir roared, fished out his wallet and handed the interpreter a $10 bill. He slammed the window shut and then, as the interpreter carried the money away, yanked it open again. 'And I want a receipt!' he bellowed. He got one, too.

So began a most extraordinary experience and one, I confess, I approached with some trepidation. All the amazing people who were in the Ukraine crew were there because of my creation, Richard Sharpe, which meant the ultimate blame lay with me. Besides, I had long had mental images of my characters like Sharpe, Harper, Hagman and Hakeswill, and now I would have those conceptions challenged by actors. I need not have worried. I was welcomed warmly by the film crew and, as I watched them perform, realised that far from clashing with my mental images they added extraordinary value to what I had imagined.

Yet, as Jason Salkey says, Rifleman Harris was not my creation. He was added to the Chosen Men by the production team and I suspect his name was taken from history. In August 1806 a young man called Benjamin Harris joined the 2nd Battalion of the 95th Rifles. He was a shepherd's son from Dorset and, unusually, joined the army from patriotic motives. The Duke of Wellington, who knew his troops well, reckoned that most men joined from desperation: 'Some of our men enlist from having got bastard children, some for minor offences, many more for drink... and it really is wonderful that we should have made them the fine fellows they are.' Harris was different. He had joined the Militia, the equivalent of today's Territorial Army, in 1803 with the ambition to serve his country, but the Militia did not serve abroad and abroad, of course, was where the army met Britain's enemies, and so Benjamin Harris transferred to the 95th, where his ambition to fight for his country was amply rewarded. He served in the expedition to Copenhagen in 1807, then fought in Portugal at the battles of Obidos, Rolica and Vimeiro, had the misfortune to be in Sir John Moore's army in the retreat to Corunna, and the even greater misfortune to be part of the Walcheren Expedition in 1809. He was invalided from the army in 1814 and took up the trade of cobbler, working as a bootmaker in Soho's Richmond Street.

He also left a memoir, one of the finest that emerged from the Napoleonic Wars, and reading Jason Salkey's memoir of recreating that war with the Sharpe Film unit I was struck by the similarities. Benjamin Harris's recollections are rife with descriptions of discomfort, bad food, sickness and wild, drunken celebrations. Welcome to Sharpe Film! The conditions under which they filmed the series were often atrocious, the food inedible and the hangovers constant, yet they succeeded in making episode after episode, and all of an astonishing high quality. Despite all the problems there was a dedication and determination which drove the filming onwards and Jason who, in *Sharpe's Havoc*, I described as 'ever-cheerful', was an important part of that. He is, essentially, an optimistic and generous character who meets hardship with humour and he was richly rewarded by meeting the delicious Natasha in Ukraine. Lucky man! He also kept a diary which forms the basis of this book; an entertaining, ever-cheerful account of how a TV series is made.

I wish I had invented Rifleman Harris, though I am guilty of killing him off at Waterloo. I did incorporate him in the books after the film unit created him, and always saw Jason in my mind's eye as I wrote him, just as I saw Sean Bean as Sharpe after I first saw him on film. Sharpe was lucky that so many brilliant actors came to recreate his adventures and I was fortunate to visit them in Ukraine, Portugal and Turkey. To me, an intruder on their sets, it still seemed a glamorous endeavour, though Jason's memoir offers a very different perspective. Yet, despite all the discomforts, I suspect Jason would echo Benjamin Harris, who wrote, 'I enjoyed life more while on active service than I have ever done since, and I look back upon my time spent in the fields of the Peninsula as the only part worthy of remembrance.'

Bernard Cornwell

PREFACE

The truth is that more than half of *Sharpe* wasn't shot on the Crimean Peninsula; Turkey, England and Portugal also provided backdrops for eight of the fourteen original episodes. However, in the end everything comes back to the Crimea. The Crimean *Sharpe*s are indelibly etched upon my mind for multiple reasons; first and foremost are the flesh and blood evidence of my three Crimean tours, my wife Natasha and our son Daniel. Secondly, the incredible bond the unit formed as a result of the adversity we faced in the early weeks – and beyond – of our inaugural foray into the Crimea. Lastly the freak injury to our lead actor that caused his removal from the role, paving the way for Sean Bean to take the part of Sharpe. Certainly, there were countless other tales and secrets I had no idea about, but from day one of my time on *Sharpe* I was determined to remember every twist and turn and to commit all to memory as I knew people would be astonished by what we experienced. I had always gravitated to non-fiction, documentary-style books, particularly the insiders' take on things, so writing about my experiences shooting a film in the chaos of the newly disintegrated Soviet Union seemed appropriate.

EARLY YEARS AND LEFT-LEANING DAD

Growing up in 1970s London I had ambitions either to appear on *Top of the Pops*, run out for Chelsea on *Match of the Day* or be a regular on stage and screen. In tandem with that superficial triumvirate was a desire to write a book, just like my novelist dad. My father, Andrew Salkey, was a poet, novelist, journalist and broadcaster. He moved to England from Jamaica in the early fifties, first becoming an English teacher at a London secondary school by day and nightclub manager by night while working on his desired profession: writing. Pretty soon he left teaching to be a freelance journalist/broadcaster for the BBC World Service, Caribbean section, moving on to having his first books published in the late fifties. He eventually settled in New England with a tenure at Hampshire College, a liberal arts school in Amherst, Massachusetts.

Creative writers in the sixties and seventies tended to be left leaning and my father was no exception. In the late sixties I remember going to a Soviet Union expo in London's Earl's Court; breaking the monotony of heroic tractors, tributes to socialism and sputniks were shouts of anger. I looked up to see two men daubing anti-Soviet slogans above the wall of a huge, shiny tractor exhibit. Why were these nasty people protesting against the heroic socialists of the Soviet Union? The walls of my dad's study were lined with books and filled with Marxist-Socialist imagery: Cuba, the Soviet Union, Vietnam, Allende, represented in books, posters and magazines. We even had a Kremlin ashtray and a mini bag of sand from the Bay of Pigs. This was the household I grew up in as a young kid.

It was all a bit contrary to the image of the Soviet system we had in the West. The contrast became even starker in 1976 when my family moved to the USA, where I lived until 1985. Living within the borders of the communist system's main rival, you don't get a lot of sympathy for the commie cause. Soviet moves to suppress the 1968 Prague Spring, along with Hungary '56, the Berlin Wall, Afghanistan and the downing of the Korean airliner in '83, Ronald Reagan's reference to the Soviet Union as the Evil Empire seemed justified. In October 1983, in the aftermath of the US invasion of Grenada, a telegram arrived from the writers of Cuba dramatically urging Dad to rally sympathetic voices within the left-wing American literary community to oppose such actions as they feared Cuba could be next. As if all the left-leaning sympathies of my father weren't enough, I grew up on a street in London called Moscow Road – not deliberately chosen by my dad. It seemed that by a perverse form of destiny I would one day have some sort of association with Russia.

PRE-*SHARPE* CAREER

After university I feared a stateside acting career would be severely hampered by the lack of a Green Card; we'd been in America for almost ten years, but my dad hadn't fancied elevating our resident alien status. There was also the thought that US casting directors seemed to cast Brits only as butlers or psychopaths; I decided to return to London to begin my career, starting from scratch with no UK drama-school connections or associations. I figured the chances of getting a job in front of the camera were slim as there seemed to be a dearth of actors with ginger dreadlocks and imperfect teeth up on the screen, so my sights were set on proscenium arches.

After jobs in schools' theatre, fringe theatre and national tours I acquired my first proper agent. I immediately went up a league, securing a small part in a BBC drama and landing a commercial campaign for Miller Lite beer. The impact of the commercial was aided greatly by its use of the Hollies 1969 song 'He Ain't Heavy, He's My Brother', which, re-released, spent two weeks at the top of the charts thanks to the commercial's heavy rotation. It was a perfect storm of maximum exposure. At the time I was also playing a spear-carrier alongside a cast of Shakespearian luminaries in Derek Jacobi's *Richards II* and *III*. I understudied Pete Postlethwaite as well as appearing with him in a couple of scenes. I was getting seen by all the top casting directors; I started to audition for bigger projects, especially big-budget American movies. Due to my time spent stateside I could muster a convincing East Coast accent, garnering roles in the 1989 *Batman* movie, playing a paper boy – my role was eventually cut and given to the Joker as producers decided to expand Jack Nicholson's role – *Memphis Belle*, playing an airman, and a CIA operative in *The Russia House*.

THE *SHARPE* ERA

By the summer of 1992 I was starting to feel as though my barely developed career was hitting a plateau. One morning – Monday 6 July to be precise – I was watching the Wimbledon final delayed by a day due to exceptionally heavy rain. I'd fallen behind on my income tax; high repeat fees from the Miller Lite commercial meant high taxes. Not only was I in arrears, but I'd missed an instalment of the rescheduled payments. I was up shit creek with no rainy-day money and no jobs lined up. Little did I know the serve volley was about to be interrupted by a call from my agent bringing news far more exciting than an extra day's play at Wimbledon: several weeks work on something called *Sharpe*.

My audition for *Sharpe* had been on 12 May; as it was now the first week of July, fantasies of scoring a regular role on an attractive-sounding job in the former Soviet Union had long-since faded. My meeting with the first director of *Sharpe*, Jim Goddard, was unremarkable. I'd not been sent a script and I'd avoided reading any of the *Sharpe* novels, so I didn't know what to expect. Customarily you read a prepared text provided on the day, or at the very least someone from production chats with you about the project while taping you on a handy cam. At my *Sharpe* audition we had done none of the above. In a cramped, narrow room, I sat across from the imposing figure of Jim Goddard, a well-established director known mostly to me as the man who directed Madonna and Sean Penn in *Shanghai Surprise*.

He sat on a high stool gently lobbing questions my way; we barely talked about the job or the background to *Sharpe* and there was certainly no mention of the former Soviet Union, it was almost a cryptic chat. Particular interest was shown in my father, author of thirty novels, anthologies and books of poetry. I had no inkling Jim's interest in my dad would prove significant. Leaving the casting I had no clue if I had got the job; it was time to put it very far to the back of my mind. So, when I got the call confirming the sixteen-week engagement in Russia, I was mostly happy for the work and the ability to pay my overdue tax bill. What I couldn't possibly have foretold was that the phone call would set off a chain of events that changed my life forever.

With the role in the bag, I bought the novels from which the first series scripts were adapted: *Sharpe's Rifles*, *Sharpe's Eagle* and *Sharpe's Gold*; after devouring *Rifles* I slipped heavily under the spell of the world Bernard Cornwell had created. In addition to the excellent *Sharpe* novels I read the book that inspired the character I was to play, *The Recollections of Rifleman Harris*, an unglamorous, recounted memoir of life in the British Army during the Napoleonic Wars, that is my direct inspiration for writing this account of my journey through *Sharpe*. Harris is not a Bernard Cornwell invention and hadn't featured in the books until the advent of the television show. Taking a cue from my Peninsular War namesake, I was determined to remember and document my experiences with a written diary and photo journal for however long the adventure lasted. The newly disintegrated Soviet Union struck me as a perfect backdrop for my story. Of course, I wasn't anticipating facing anything as scary and brutal as the original Harris – or so I thought – but I believed documenting my upcoming experiences to be a good idea, especially if *Sharpe* ever became a success.

The journey to bring *Sharpe* to the point of principal photography was a rocky, protracted ride. Initially Muir Sutherland and his first producer, Kenny McBain, drew up a budget for the cost of a three-episode shoot in Spain. This proved prohibitive for ITV. Muir then scouted much of Europe, including Montenegro in the former Yugoslavia, to shoot *Sharpe*, a notion quickly abandoned when war broke out. As the Balkan door closed, so the rusty iron curtain began to fall away and eyes turned to Ukraine, Crimea to be exact, home of the Soviet film industry. In the weeks leading up to departure all the old stereotypes of sputniks, matryoshkas (Russian dolls), ballet dancers and an upside-down alphabet danced though my mind.

WHAT HAVE I GOT MYSELF INTO?

The thought of flying to Moscow sparked off fantasies of standing in Red Square, sipping vodka with former KGB honeytrap beauties, watching decommissioned ICBMs roll past. Fairly quickly I was disabused of that particular fantasy when I was told we were actually shooting in southern Ukraine; shortly after that, the reality of day-to-day existence in the newly broken-up Soviet Union began to dawn. Four days after my agent's call, I went through the labyrinthine process of getting a Russian visa, followed later by a physical with the physician to the film industry, Dr Gaynor. Then it was inoculations against hepatitis A and typhoid; the *pièce de résistance* was a letter from the Sharpe Film production secretary telling us what to be prepared for, including the immortal words 'bring your own toilet paper'. For sixteen weeks?

My costume fitting with two-time Oscar winner John Mollo shone a little more light on the location we were due to descend upon; we'd be on the Black Sea coast, which bore an uncanny resemblance to parts of the Iberian Peninsula. John was also a bit of a Crimean War buff, thrilled that we'd be so close to the valley where the Charge of the Light Brigade took place in 1854 and that after perestroika we could possibly be some of the first Brits to visit the battlefields in seventy-one years. At least now, after my costume fitting, my imminent arrival in the Crimea didn't seem as mysterious and formidable; my main focus wouldn't be how much toilet paper I'd need for sixteen weeks.

SHARPE'S BEGINNINGS

Early on I learned that Paul McGann was to be cast as Sharpe; I'd been acquainted with him for a few years, having met him in 1986 at Arabella Weir's birthday party in Camden, so the prospect of actually working with him was thrilling. As a relative novice to the book, I at first thought nothing of the dissimilarity between the description of Sharpe in *Rifles* and Paul McGann. So what if Sharpe was scarred, six foot four with jet-black hair and a cockney accent? It wouldn't be the last time Bernard's original depiction of Sharpe would be at odds with the actor portraying him. Paul's pedigree wasn't in question – he had starred in a BBC production of *The Monocled Mutineer* and co-starred in the cult film *Withnail and I* – so the fact that we had a high-profile actor in the lead role augured well.

In late July we gathered in the basement of St Saviour's Church on Warwick Avenue, west London, for a read-through. I sat between fellow actor John Tams and a man dressed in clothing I could only say was not of this era. He didn't say a word and when not perusing the script he gazed dreamily off into the distance; this was Richard Moore, our military adviser. Dressed in full 95th Rifles uniform minus the pack straps, water bottle and shako, he even had his Baker rifle, sheathed in what I thought was a fishing rod holder, which it appeared he had carried in on the London Underground. Needless to say, I immediately questioned the sanity of this chap, especially when he started stoking his clay pipe. Though I might have thought him bonkers back then, he was to become my guru, the man who taught me how to be a Chosen Man. If I for even one second look like a true Rifleman on screen then it's down to Richard. Sitting between him and John Tams it seems I'd made a prophetic choice of seat that day.

In the next two weeks before departing for Ukraine, Richard led us through several classroom sessions followed by training in the field, where we were drilled in every aspect of being a 95th Rifleman. In the classroom we were tutored in the basics of the Peninsula campaign; we covered firing positions: standing, crouched, prone. We learned to load, care for and love our Baker rifle, the instrument that defined our special status. One afternoon after returning from lunch we discovered the church basement in darkness; thinking nothing of it, I reached for the light switch. As the fluorescent strip flickered into life the click of a weapon cocking could be heard coming from the corner of the room. It was Richard crouched in a recess, rifle trained on a bunch of oblivious actors, uttering words that stuck with me down the years: 'Chosen Men never get ambushed.' I loved it. He was a bigger method actor than De Niro; you couldn't see the join. Richard was *on* all the time. He was a true inspiration, his teaching started me believing that the Chosen few were invincible, superheroes making the appeal of *Sharpe* that much greater.

During Chosen Man School, the six regulars began the process of getting to know each other, feeling each other out and setting patterns of behaviour that would last through the years. I remember those first few days. Daragh O'Malley, an imposing figure at the best of times, always sat fidgeting with his pack of Rothmans. Sitting quietly 'keeping his powder dry' in what was to become a familiar mode was John Tams. An accomplished talent in his own right, he had, I was to learn, been lighting up the folk scene for years and had no need to stand out or act cool. The younger guns consisted of Mike Mears, Lyndon Davies, Paul Trussell and me; we were an eclectic mix possessed of disparate energies essential to the chemistry that would eventually create what we now know and love as the Chosen Men.

It came time to begin shooting *Rifles* in a derelict fifteenth-century mansion near Stamford called Apethorpe Manor. The Chosen Men were peripheral in the way the scenes were shot, leaving me in no doubt our parts were pretty insignificant; we could almost have been extras. But I knew that it was sixteen weeks' work in a profession that had 98 per cent unemployment, with the added bonus of it being shot in an exotic location. What was impossible to know then was that in four months' time we'd be shooting the scene all over again in a different country with a different actor in the lead. And even more impossible to foresee the catalogue of catastrophic events experienced by the Sharpe Film unit over the final four and a half months of 1992.

1

INTO THE WILD RED YONDER

On 10 August 1992 we gathered at Heathrow for the flight to Moscow; Aeroflot was our first taste of perestroika Russia, an experience that did little to disprove our western prejudices. After landing at Sheremetyevo we shuffled through the draconian customs and immigration checks, me getting stern looks from the official as he leafed through my papers with particular attention paid to how much hard currency we were bringing in. With that rather intimidating introduction to Russia, we crossed to the domestic terminal to board an even shabbier plane sat on the tarmac alongside rows of aircraft and the husks of helicopters left to the elements to rust. The interminably long wait on the ground gave us lots of time to wonder what the hell we'd got ourselves into, before we eventually took off for the Crimean capital, Simferopol.

It was an inauspicious start to our Crimean campaign, and we hadn't even reached Ukraine yet. Worse was to come as we decamped to the 'Gateway of the Crimea', Simferopol. Or 'Simplyawful', as we came to nickname it, a destination we would learn to know and loathe. Located in the heart of the Crimea, it's the scientific, financial and cultural centre of the region; the name Simferopol comes from the Greek meaning 'city of usefulness', though we found it useful only as an exit for getting the hell back home quickly.

That hot, sticky evening we stepped off the plane at Simferopol International, finding Ukraine at a time of great optimism and upheaval, but we had little idea of the impact that upheaval would have on us. Finally, we arrived at the main hotel in the Crimean capital, the Moscow Hotel. I settled in my room, halfway down the musty fourth-floor corridor. A room of modest size, it had an overwhelmingly green bathroom equipped with a funny little toilet bowl that had a platform for examining your 'leavings'. Hanging on a rudimentary roll was rough, brown toilet paper, no worse than the crinkly, waxy 'tracing paper' we scraped our little bumholes on at school in the seventies. I guessed this was why the production office had felt the need to advise us to stock up on good old western loo roll. One level up from my room was an unpretentious residents' bar serving funky Soviet beer, tins of nuts from Germany, vicious vodka, very drinkable Crimean champagne, water chock full of minerals and a mild, white cheese weighed out on an old-school grocer's scale; the damage was totted up on an even older-school abacus. If you wanted to escape the built-up heat of a Simferopol night you could always take your life in your hands sitting on the bar's balcony, no doubt superbly constructed back in the Khrushchev era, but now looking distinctly decayed.

Relieved at finally arriving after so much build-up, we held a party in my room. All the major runners and riders, including the show's star, the director and executive producer, Malcolm Craddock, were at some point crammed into my room during the course of the night. Director Jim, a huge man in every sense of the word, led the way in the overindulgence, setting the standard for outrageous partying from day one, a pace that would impact the production early in the shoot; and if the director's destructive urges didn't do us in then our gun-toting security might, one of whom drunkenly pulled a gun on me in the early hours as I tried to walk off the fourth floor. I was merely having a mosey around the establishment, unaware I was committing a crime; the guard were perhaps a little zealous in his reaction to me ignoring him, but in his mind he was merely protecting me from what lay beyond the hotel. His sober colleague dissuaded him from holding me at gunpoint, but for this incident to happen on the first night of our stay didn't bode well. Were we really going to have to look over our shoulders for the entire sixteen weeks?

The following morning, once we had shaken off our hangovers and started to adjust to the three-hour time difference, a group of us embarked on a walking tour downtown. As we strolled along, Julian Fellowes (Major Dunnett) entertained us with charming, witty banter interrupted only by a stream of local money changers, who assumed (rightly) that we would have hard currency. The encounters were so numerous it seemed to be a national pastime. Production had told us to be careful who we converted our US dollar per diems with, directing us to exchange our bucks into the local currency at 'the various banks' in Simferopol. Easier said than done, since banks were still quite hard to identify in the post-communist world of the early nineties where all shops and banks looked very similar. Naturally the man on the street offered a better rate than any official source, but in theory we were taking our lives into our hands, especially as it was our first day 'in country'. Early in the tour we were constantly on the prowl for the best exchange rate, no matter how kosher or otherwise; bragging rights could be claimed by sniffing out the most generous exchange. Dollars could buy goods on the black market but for settling your hotel phone bill – if you were lucky enough to get an outside line – or for official shop purchases, coupons were the order of the day. In 1992, Ukrainian currency was the *karbovanets*, which had replaced the ubiquitous Russian rouble, but Crimeans referred to them as *coupony*, so we called them coupons. In 1996, after much hyperinflation, the *karbovanets* became the *hryvnia*, which it remains to this day.

Our initial taste of Simferopol didn't impress us much, hindered as we were by having zero Russian between us beyond 'da' and 'nyet', and with no knowledge of the Cyrillic alphabet we had no idea what anything was. No local lingo was needed, however, to recognise the many tributes to Lenin which we assumed would soon be taken down, destined for a Soviet-era theme park. Another uniquely Soviet phenomenon was the street vendors selling a drink called kvass, made from fermented rye bread. It sounded utterly unappealing, so I declined the temptation of kvass, probably one of the best decisions I made as those who did imbibe paid dearly with gastrointestinal problems.

In fact, the film unit began experiencing stomach troubles within the first week of our tour. It may have been the kvass, it could have been the water, it also could have been the minimal hygiene standards observed in the hotel kitchen. Alarm bells rang upon entering the dining hall one afternoon to see they had already laid the cucumber salad starters for dinner in the stifling heat of the day. I found the butter served up was rancid more often than not. Production flew out two film caterers from the UK to do our location food as well as to help the hotel's chef shape the food to our needs; the only problem being they arrived without a mobile kitchen, proposing to cook our meals at the hotel and courier them up to location.

After a couple of days acclimatising, our first day of filming in Crimea arrived; we gathered at the hotel entrance for our transport expecting to see a fleet of comfortable air-conditioned cars. Instead what greeted us were clapped-out minivans with no seat belts, unpleasantly hard seating with quaint little curtains across passengers' windows. I did notice the executive producers and Russian co-producers sped smoothly to work in Volgas, a Russian-made four-door, mid-size car. The proles were left to travel in steerage; it seemed the pre-revolution status quo was alive and well on Sharpe Film. The Chosen Men travelling together within the confines of our sardine can on wheels did serve to strengthen the connection between us, galvanising the bond that would aid us in times of crisis; a bond that manifested itself on screen as well.

On the drive to location we discovered the curtains' usefulness – keeping the ferocious sun from roasting the vehicle's interior, proving there was a little method in the perceived madness of the former Soviet Union. As we neared the spectacular Chufut-Kale, where filming was to begin, we drove through the ancient Tatar capital of Bakhchisaray, central to the political and cultural life of the Crimean Tatars up until they were expelled by Stalin in 1944 for supposedly collaborating with the Nazis. Our arrival on the peninsula coincided with a mass return of the indigenous people with settlements springing up along the routes we took to work. Some very grand constructions could be seen as well as more humble dwellings. The one thing they had in common was the use of very distinctive-looking breeze blocks pocked with air holes which to the untutored eye looked like they were made from cattle dung. On a post-*Sharpe*, pre-Crimean annexation trip back to Yalta, I even noticed a mosque under construction; but, as with the fractious relationship the Tatars had with the murderous Stalin, the current

5

dictator, Vlad the Annexer, was pressuring his Crimean puppet regime to jail leaders in the Tatar community as they were the only group to protest the illegal annexation of Crimea in 2014.

Chufut-Kale is the ruin of a medieval city fortress abandoned since the nineteenth century, sitting high on a rocky outcrop with dwellings carved out of the rock. The name comes from the Tatar for Jewish fortress. It could easily have been the backdrop for one of those planets the cast of *Star Trek* land on, or a spaghetti western. The cameras were set up to shoot in what could only be described as a hovel deep within a dwelling. The scene, set in a barn, is the first time Sharpe encounters the Chosen Men, rudely waking them from their slumbers, resulting in the iconic Sharpe versus Harper fist fight. It's a scene steeped in violence and class-war angst: Sharpe, a working-class soldier promoted through acts of bravery, hated by superiors and inferiors alike, sent to take charge of soldiers perhaps equally as brave but not as lucky. It's a pivotal moment in the first episode and one of many scenes reshot four months later in Portugal; the Crimea version, shot at two locations in stultifying summer heat, was laboured, tense, and stunt doubles were used for much of the fight. The reshoot in the winter of 1992 was free-flowing, exciting and dripping with aggression; and without a stunt double in sight. This had a lot to do with Sean's approach but was also due to having top stunt coordinator Greg Powell, who arrived when Sean replaced Paul.

BETTER DEAD THAN RED

Filming abroad can be problematic at the best of times, so, when filming in a newly independent country formerly reliant on a larger more sophisticated neighbour, you would think the producers might have done due diligence in protecting the film unit during this turbulent and unpredictable time. In their minds they had achieved this through teaming up with the East-West Creative Association. Formed in 1989, the brainchild of special projects at Central Television, the East-West Creative Association specialised in facilitating British productions out in the former Soviet Union; they already had the Russian portion of Michael Palin's *Pole to Pole* under their belt even though that was a BBC production and Central is an ITV company. Here on the ground in Crimea, matters would be dealt with by Muscovite fixers Pavel Douvidson, Stefan Pojenan and the larger-than-life Igor Nossov. Nossov spoke English quite well and ran the military and government affairs – his grandfathers were generals in both the White and Red armies before the Russian Revolution so he was well connected. The Association, as we always referred to them, were essentially service providers responsible for hiring local crew and, like many organisations in positions of power in the kleptocratic Soviet Union, were committed to lining their own pockets as much as possible during production. Unfortunately, that reduced the Russian/Ukrainian crew to near serfdom as they were paid a fraction of the money the Association had told Central Television they would be paying.

Sharpe Film was a merger of two film companies, Celtic Film and Picture Palace, the former owned by Muir Sutherland, the man mainly responsible for getting *Sharpe* onto screen. In 1986, after a long and distinguished career at Thames Television as Director of Programming, Muir left to form his own company, Celtic Film. Andy Alan, Director of Programmes at Central TV, suggested Muir option the books as they were set in Spain; Muir had a Spanish wife, the delightful Mercedes. Alan promised Central could then later come onboard as a broadcaster and deficit financier after Muir fronted the development costs. Muir scoured Europe including the actual locations, Spain and Portugal; however, the budgets were way too high by British TV standards, so he had to look for another country to double for Spain. This took him to Hungary, Czech Republic and parts of former Yugoslavia such as Montenegro.

At this point, Muir's producer, Kenny McBain, tragically died of cancer. This is when Malcolm Craddock and his company, Picture Palace, stepped in; they had been friends for years and Muir had even helped at the start of Malcolm's career. Malcolm then offered to pay Muir 50 per cent of what he had spent up to then on development and false starts on pre-production (four years of costs). Muir agreed and they decided to form Sharpe Film, which would be a 50/50 venture; Muir would deal with ITV and all business matters, Malcolm would deal with day-to-day production issues, and all creative matters would be shared equally. This is when Richard Cressey of Central Television introduced Sharpe Film to the East-West Creative Association, who up till this point had only done documentaries.

What was clear was that Sharpe Film was woefully underprepared for taking a pampered western film unit into uncharted territory. Even if they'd been told what to expect by the East-West Creative Association, you could guarantee whatever they said was either an outright lie, or an over- or underexaggeration. Underexaggerate how long something would take and then overexaggerate the price. On-set tasks were handled with a large element of incompetence; the catalogue of blunders visited upon us down the years by the combined efforts of the English and Russian production offices was legendary.

Early on, we were blissfully unaware of the pitfalls we might face out here in the Wild East, but what became immediately apparent was a complete disruption of our intestinal tracts. There were many theories as to what ailed vast swathes of the British crew and where the lurgy originated. Some speculated that our tummy troubles could be traced back to our reliance on the Ukrainian (former Red) Army from Simferopol barracks. They took care of our every base camp need; they cleared obstacles, erected tents for every department and, crucially, provided the on-location water tank, with little or no effective sterilisation. Most put our stomach problems down to our delicate western guts having not yet acclimatised. We didn't have a British doctor and, after diagnosis, all the Crimean doctors had to offer were copious enemas. My money was on the Soviet army water bowser which suffered from the same inadequate sterilising regime as the kvass dispenser. Of course, it could also have been the food served up in the dining hall, which was neither tasty nor edible and left us underwhelmed; a lot of people went hungry, many became unwell fairly rapidly.

Interestingly, the Red Army's somewhat lax hygiene standards were in direct contrast to their entrepreneurial zeal, as very soon a rich and varied black market opened up to us, starting with belts, boots and badges soon escalating to full uniforms, night-vision goggles and a steady stream of Crimean marijuana. The fledgling capitalists quickly embraced free enterprise; their Colonel practically begged our producers to slap a ban on more purchases of army surplus. Except it wasn't surplus; the squaddies, in the race to unite us with as much military tat as possible, left the barrack stores empty. The squaddies weren't the only ones at it, the black-market economy thrived everywhere: unofficial cab rides, money changers, icons, caviar, all made available at very competitive prices.

Much like our digestive tracts, the work week rumbled on. The food got steadily worse: scrawny chicken portions, aubergine galore; endless piles of bulgar wheat and the ever-present *golubsti*, a classic Ukrainian dish consisting of cooked cabbage leaves wrapped around a variety of fillings. After a long day's slog on set, solace was to be found in the fifth-floor bar where a 100g of sliced cheese, some salted nuts and a beer proved a much better bet than mealtime in the dining hall. That's if you could stop Brian Cox snaffling your stash of nuts in between bouts of Tetris on his Game Boy.

On Saturdays, the front of the hotel thronged to the sound of wedding processions doing circuits of the roundabout while excitedly honking their car horns. Simferopol, what little we knew of it, was dusty, stale, lacking in attractions and simply awful, but gradually we would adapt to our strange surroundings, much as the riflemen of the 95th did back in the Iberian Peninsula. Yes, it was the 'Gateway to the Crimea', with our hotel an hour or so from some spectacular scenery. Production agreed it was an entertainment-free zone, but if we could just endure Simferopol for three weeks then we would be paid back in full, with a three-month stint on the Soviet Riviera, at Yalta.

A DAY THAT WILL LIVE ON IN INFAMY

Although the first work week was short, the days had been long, compounded by an almost three-hour round-trip commute to location; we desperately needed our first rest day. A trip to a beach on the west coast of Crimea was planned; in theory, an ideal excursion, but an event that took place on that day was to shape and leave an indelible mark on those present that year and set the rules for every successive series.

The weather was perfect for the beach as we stopped on the way to buy watermelon and grapes, absolute luxuries that overwhelmed our taste buds after the bland offerings served up at our hotel. Adjacent to the beach we found a piece of tarmac, a great place for a football match, I suggested, and we gathered for an innocent game of footie – no one could have predicted it would be otherwise. Considering myself a bit of an athlete, I proceeded with a pre-match stretching routine, prompting Paul McGann to remark, 'You're getting a bit serious, aren't you?' Fifteen minutes or so into the match, Paul stretched out his right leg to control a high, stray ball. As he made contact, his planted, left leg gave way, causing him to crumple to the ground in agony. Helping him to the side of the pitch, I will never forget the ashen look on Paul McGann's face as he sat down contemplating the damaged knee.

Initially, we all thought it was something he would shake off easily; the true extent of the injury wasn't immediately obvious, and the local medics were basically under orders to get Paul bandaged and back on set. We were one week into a sixteen-week shoot and we had a lame actor in the lead of an action picture. Working in the freshly broken up Soviet Union, everything proceeded in a fairly relaxed manner anyway, but Paul's injury sent everything into an unsettling limbo. We were all prey to selfish thoughts of how much overtime we would accrue as a result of the inevitable delays, though sympathy for Paul quickly took over. He had sustained a painful injury while in a foreign country, without English-speaking doctors to tell him the extent of the damage that would eventually lead to him being recast. A pall of doom hung over the unusually muted bus ride back to Simferopol; would Paul be able to continue shooting? Would this be the end of what I considered to be a dream job? To this day, I wonder whether, if Paul had joined me for a quick bit of toe-touching, would he have torn his cruciate?

Next morning on location we sheltered from the baking Crimean sun under Red Army canvas, awaiting Paul's delayed arrival on set, concerned for the future of the production. The treatment for his injury consisted of tightly wrapping his knee then discharging him back to the hotel. Making things even trickier, we were still shooting the Sharpe—Harper fight from 'Rifles'; there were stunt doubles, but they were only there to fling themselves across tables and out of windows. Paul could barely stand without propping himself up with his crutches. All his movements were slow and deliberate; creative camera angles had to be employed, with the action frequently stopping to insert the stunt doubles, it was torturous and director Jim Goddard wasn't best pleased.

The schedule moved us onto a fresh location for day and night shoots, where we would begin shooting 'Sharpe's Eagle', the second of the three novels we were bringing to life. It's logical to assume that when principal photography begins, you begin filming at page one of the screenplay, and then progress in sequence to the last page. That would require having every actor, every location and every set on standby, which is expensive and impractical. The first assistant director has the job of scheduling the scenes according to the availability of each of the above elements as well as taking into account reshoots. The following shooting location was closer to our Simferopol base than it was to Yalta – our next base of operations – and had been chosen for a scene from 'Eagle', necessitating a pause in shooting the 'Rifles' script. Of course, shooting out of sequence is something film actors are thoroughly accustomed to, and as long as you know your character trajectory, filming like this doesn't pose a problem. Plus, at that point in the first week of the first ever Sharpe shoot our characters were extremely lightly sketched with little to say or do.

A new episode would require fresh meat from the UK to join a food-deprived, discombobulated film unit, in chaos as a result of Paul's injury. The new location was a river that traversed fields in the middle of nowhere; called Kamishinka, its name is derived from the word 'kamushi', meaning reeds, which lined the banks of the waterway. Most of the action takes place on a wooden bridge beautifully constructed by local craftsmen with wood that had to be sourced from all over the Crimea. In the scene Colonel Simmerson, the hapless murdering officer, played by Michael Cochrane, exhorts his troops into a needless attack on a French scouting mission. His callow troops are easily overrun by battle-hardened French cavalry, ultimately resulting in the loss of the colours, a sin of the highest order. Sharpe and the Chosen are left with no choice but to destroy the bridge, rolling barrels of gunpowder into place, weaving fuses throughout the structure of the bridge: action that helped keep our minds off the chaos and doubt that still swirled around us once the cameras stopped rolling.

Although there was no fist fighting required of Sharpe, there was plenty of running around, kneeling to fire and marching scenes on the call sheet, which, as you could imagine, proved problematic with an injured knee. Paul's stunt double became increasingly pissed off at being required as a stand-in for long shots, a bit like asking an actor to be an extra. Eventually he kicked up a fuss and threatened to walk unless more money was forthcoming. Slowing down an already

13

slow-moving work schedule, Jim Goddard became frustrated with having a lame actor in the lead of his action picture. After a hard day on set, Jim drank his frustrations away in the bar; then, hungover in the searing heat of the following day, he would snap at cast and crew, being very cruel at times. When directing *Shanghai Surprise*, Jim encountered the thorny issue of what to call the Material Girl on set; telling her he wouldn't address her as Madonna, he settled on the name Daisy. If that's how he dealt with the notoriously headstrong queen of pop, what chance did we have of standing up to him? Fools wouldn't be suffered.

Compounding our troubles was Jim's inability to move easily between set-ups in the heat due to his huge physical stature. The editing department began to complain the rushes were giving them nothing to work with; scenes weren't being covered properly, so much so that they feared there wouldn't be an episode to broadcast. Confidence in those who were supposed to be in charge eroded and the atmosphere on set deteriorated significantly. Paul McGann's injury wasn't unique; Nolan Hemmings (Lieutenant Denny) lunged a little too hard with his sword, stabbing a stuntman in the armpit; some said the injury was a result of not having an English-speaking stunt coordinator and the recklessness of a disaffected director at the helm. Jim had started the project with a fit and healthy actor in the lead, now in Jim's mind the whole thing had been crippled by trying to film with a virtual invalid. The death, only four years earlier, of Roy Kinnear on *The Return of the Musketeers* wasn't far from our minds as we were being required to throw ourselves into battle with horses, bayonets and enthusiastic stuntmen flailing all around us. Kinnear had been shooting a big-budget movie in Spain when he fell off a horse, suffering severe pelvic injuries. If that could happen in a modern

European country like Spain, what chance would we have in a country like Ukraine, with no direct flights back to UK hospital care?

Anarchy reigned: some of the more militant actors plotted to get rid of the director; others urged Paul to pull the lead actor card and demand changes. The haphazard way in which production approached our health and safety left us feeling it was everyone for him- or herself; when I refer to 'production' I mean the on-line producer – top man out on location – his office staff and the exec producers, in short the decision makers. I distinctly remember retreating to my hotel room, thoroughly knackered, stomach rumbling, feeling scared and helpless, hoping for a little respite from the next shocking event that was surely in the pipeline. Of course, being a majority British film unit, we maintained a stoic outlook and tried to get on with the job without too much fuss, managing to create diversions from the predicament we faced. It would be disingenuous to suggest we didn't have a great laugh in between the chaos and uncertainty. Paul McGann had bought a shortwave radio for those of us missing football; at lunchtime we tuned in to the inaugural day of the English Premiership. There was the interesting distraction of two Russian actresses, Maya and Nataliya, arriving from Moscow to play maids in 'Eagle', and most of all there was the dangling carrot of our imminent move to the delights of the Soviet Riviera, Yalta, to keep our minds off our calamitous shoot.

During the final days in Simplyawful many of us were still coming to terms with the stomach ailments experienced by most of the cast and crew; I began noticing that as soon as I had finished eating, I felt the need to make haste to my room to evacuate, a very odd feeling for someone regular as clockwork. In the novels, Bernard Cornwell is fond of describing how the heat of battle induced bowel-loosening fear in soldiers under heavy fire; in this case we had our bowels loosened by the frightful cuisine on offer. Cast members were now routinely late for pick-up in the morning, due to extra time squatting above our green porcelain platform. Associate producer Neville Thompson waited in the hotel lobby calling our rooms to hurry us along if we hadn't arrived downstairs on time, handing us packs of Imodium as we boarded the minibus to prevent accidents during the day.

If you did require the conveniences while on set, a visit to the ironically named 'honey wagon' was in order; this was essentially a couple of hillbilly outhouses lashed onto the back of a truck accessed by rickety wooden stairs. Thankfully the outhouses had ample ventilation as the heat of a Crimean day made that area one to avoid. With business complete, the delightful honey-wagon lady would hand you soap, wait for you to lather up then pour water over your hands to rinse off; whereupon you were handed a wholly inadequate square of tissue paper on which to dry your hands. It was the Crimea in microcosm: well intentioned, pleasant people running things in antiquated, often illogical ways. Another example of this was the sterilising of the tea urn with a Dettol-like cleanser, tainting our morning cuppa with the taste of antiseptic for some time; a well-meaning attempt to save us from Simferopol stomach but with no thought of the consequences.

PROMISES OF A NEW SHANGRI-LA

August the 29th rolled around, departure from Simferopol day, destination Yalta, the Soviet Riviera and our main base for the next three months. Our Crimean honeymoon was well and truly over before we left Simferopol, so the move to the more picturesque Black Sea resort town was welcomed. In our sanctioned days off, we were determined to kick back and treat it as a holiday, especially as the powers had promised an upgrade in everything: entertainment, edible food and palatable drink. Paul would also be reunited with his family, who were arriving in Simferopol to join the trek down to Yalta.

Our Black Sea residence, the Rossiya sanatorium, was reportedly still controlled by the KGB, or FSB as it has since become. The splendid white stone building wasn't a hotel, but it had accommodation, treatment rooms, swimming pools and sun beds all set in stunning surroundings nestled on a cliff side overlooking the Black Sea. The transition between base camps allowed us a first few days in Yalta with no call sheets to obey, letting the unit indulge in what we'll euphemistically call bacchanalian excess; a reference to Harris's flippant response to Sharpe when they first meet: 'I'm a courtier to my lord Bacchus and an unremitting debtor.'

Film crews at the best of times like to let their hair down, but with the stresses and strains of existing in the newly independent Ukraine, a good party proved an especially effective stress buster. Paul McGann remarked that it would be the only occasion where people checking into a sanatorium would be coming out with deteriorating health. The Rossiya was, as promised, a significant upgrade on our Simferopol digs. Regular cast members had large rooms with spacious balconies replete with beds looking out over the Black Sea. Architecturally, it owed more to the style of an Italian villa with precious little to remind you of its Soviet origins, apart from the discreet hammer and sickle designed into the entrance arch. You got the full-on reminder of the great Soviet experiment after visiting the WC, using the toilet paper or getting between the rough bed sheets.

The sanatorium's grounds covered a wide area high on a hill on one side of Yalta's bay; at the top of one hill sat an impressive grand circular construction housing the dining hall which became sarcastically dubbed the Rotunda of Gastronomy. The building was a classic example of grand Soviet architecture from the sixties; its spherical shape reminded me of a Bond baddy's lair or even the UN debating chamber. Behind the main 'reception block' was a rectangular terrace with stairs that led down to a small building that became our common room/bar area. At the rear of the grounds was a precipitous drop to the sea with steep, winding tree-lined paths along which at intervals were placed scenic viewing gazebos, ideal for clandestine KGB meetings, I imagined. Eventually the path led, after a short ride in a lift, down to our sanatorium's private section of the beach.

In the centre of Yalta, a huge statue of Lenin was flanked by kiosks, each one selling the same beer, cigarettes and confectionery; to his right sat Yalta's post office, its interior dominated by a charming fresco depicting a figure of antiquity passing a scroll to a cosmonaut – probably Yuri Gagarin – with doves of peace fluttering all around, the sort of Soviet ephemera that really appealed to me. In downtown Yalta there were quite a few hard-currency shops, establishments like the 'Kodak Shop' and 'Bradleys of London' incongruously stocked with clothing, confectionery and strange American brands of beer such as 'Old Milwaukee'; places like this became a regular stop for unit members.

Rather disconcertingly on my first trip, I witnessed an ancient babushka dragging a large plastic bucket containing the remains of a cow's carcass replete with bloody rib cage poking out of the top – at least I hope it was a cow. Welcome to the Crimea, soft English lad!

Next to Bradleys was an open-air market or 'bazaar' with covered stalls selling everything under the sun; on the periphery of the stalls, unofficial salesmen, usually babushkas, perched their wares, dried fish, single cigarettes and vodka, on cardboard boxes. On our days off, the bazaar was a prime destination for killing time or picking up essential items; the other was the Yalta Hotel, which was an Intourist hotel, Intourist being a state-run tourist agency which guaranteed the hotel would be fit for foreigners. The huge hotel, rumoured to have been half owned by Richard Branson, was a place where you could spend the whole day getting lost in its bars, restaurants, hard-currency shops and ladies of the night. Best of all, the bars served draught beer, the only place that did in Yalta; the downside was the Yalta Hotel was a half-hour taxi ride from our sanatorium.

After several days off at the beach in the sunshine, it was beginning to feel like a Crimean holiday, and the discovery of a restaurant in town called Gourmand considerably eased our food woes. John Tams, Paul McGann and I ate there, enjoying a baked starter the locals call julienne, consisting of thin strips of mushroom baked with liberal amounts of cheese, followed by grilled sturgeon. Paul told us he had eaten there with Brian Cox, who was in taste-bud ecstasy after a simple slice of bread and butter; very strange as Brian was supposed to be on a macrobiotic diet.

However, all good things must come to an end and my Crimea vacation was interrupted by Harris's name on the call sheet; the point in 'Eagle' where Sharpe meets the dastardly Colonel Simmerson, serial flogger of troops, for the first time. The location was called Opolznevoye, particularly memorable for the terrain, a steep incline making it a real pain in the arse to stand, especially if your knee isn't 100 per cent fixed yet. The action takes place at Wellington's camp where Private Dobbs, a flogged soldier played by Paul Bigley, gets an excessive number of lashes for neglecting to wear a 'stock', a superfluous, tough leather neck brace. The lashes are gleefully watched by the sneering, contemptuous Lieutenant Berry, played by the impressive Daniel Craig, the epitome of manliness despite having to wear a dodgy brown wig. Off camera, when not in costume, Daniel reminded me of a young Steve McQueen, conducting himself with an air of supreme confidence, bordering on arrogance, all with a haughty look of condescension on his face. I found in him a kindred spirit, especially as I'm often accused of being an arrogant bastard! Though to this day Dan has fared rather better than me with it!

The entire 'Eagle' cast were all cool customers, arriving in-country to find an under-fire production; they took the chaos in their stride. Brash, British-based American Gavan O'Herlihy (Captain Leroy) was the first unit member to source a small toaster oven coupled with a hot plate which enabled the master chefs in the unit – mainly Portuguese hairdresser Sano De Perpessac – to whip up many simple but tasty dishes. This was the initial step towards self-sufficiency, allowing us to swerve the swill dished up at dinner at the Rossiya which looked just as underwhelming as the fare on offer at our Simferopol base. Billeted in a less grand section of the sanatorium, the 'Eagle' actors operated an open-door policy, with music – very often Van Morrison – wafting along the corridors and out through the windows; every night was party night as bacchanalian excess became the best way to escape the turmoil.

For one 'Eagle' cast member things started to get ugly. Jim Goddard, already stressed at having a 'lame actor' as the lead, began to psychologically flog Paul Bigley, shouting at him for little reason, cursing him loudly in front of the whole unit. It all came to a head when Paul, objecting to his treatment, was told by Jim to 'fuck off back to the hotel'; this didn't go unnoticed by an already aggrieved actors' 'union' already conspiring to find leverage to improve our situation. Obviously, the unrelenting abuse Paul Bigley received got out of hand; little wonder as Jim was under pressure to hit the shooting schedule while spanners were continually being chucked in the works. Jim's method of refuelling of an evening – like many of us – involved large amounts of hard alcohol leaving him hungover, bad-tempered and vengeful, taking it out on whoever happened to be near him the next day. Something had to give. Unfortunately, that something would be Paul McGann's knee. Again.

It had been a month since we left Heathrow, but it felt like we'd been away for years, creating a feeling of remoteness and detachment. When the proletariat – crew and actors on a lower pay grades like *moi* – wanted to call home, it required a trip to a room just off reception that housed a chair and table with a little orange telephone straight out of the seventies. With so many members of the film unit missing their loved ones, a queue often formed; even if the operator could understand you, there was no guarantee they could connect you. I think I called home once in our first six weeks in the Crimea. Much of our news from the outside world came via Daragh, who had his shortwave radio permanently tuned to BBC World Service; he would thoughtfully pin a handwritten summary of the news with added football results to a door by the exit of the building. This earned him one of the earliest nicknames on *Sharpe*: Paddy World News.

Production addressed this sense of not-so-splendid isolation by adding a video player and television to our common room/bar swiftly named by Paul Trussell 'the Goat and Balalaika'. If not killing time watching videos from home, getting wasted or attempting to engage with the actresses from Moscow, particularly Maya, there were other more high-octane post-glasnost opportunities to pass the time. Set designer Phil Elton, through his interpreter, organised flights over Yalta aboard an old army helicopter; as I watched the tandem rotors circling the sanatorium, I got an uneasy feeling in the pit of my stomach. In 1989 I had worked on *Memphis Belle*, shooting at RAF Binbrook in Lincolnshire, where they had seven of the fourteen remaining B-17 aircraft in existence standing by for take-offs and landings. After a while, cast members had been offered short rides to take photos and appreciate the majesty of these antique Second World War aircraft. That was until one of them crashed on landing, breaking the leg of an extra who had hitched a lift. If an accident like that could have happened in the UK, I dreaded what could happen in seat-of-your-pants, fly-by-night, post-perestroika Ukraine. Sensibly, any further helicopter excursions were strongly discouraged.

That said, I did wish we had a reliable, well-serviced helicopter to ferry us to our next location, Dimerdji, situated halfway up a peak in the Crimean Mountains. Known to locals as the Valley of Ghosts, it was hit by an earthquake in 1926 creating a massed jumble of boulders strewn among phallic weather-worn towers of volcanic rock, towers that swiftly earned the nickname 'Knob Mountain'. It was a spectacular, desolate landscape, awe-inspiring and frightening all at the same time. At our high altitude you could just about make out the Black Sea glistening in the far distance; below us on the lower slopes were peach orchards freshly stripped of their bounty.

The weather up on Dimerdji was slightly cooler than our Black Sea base where, despite it being late September, it was still fairly hot; the high temperatures combined with starvation rations led to many waistlines slimming down. Others with less fat to shed were beginning to look a bit gaunt. The daily commute up the mountain began to lose its allure and soon the schedule slipped into night shoots, tedious at the best of times. Rarely with dialogue, the Chosen are relegated to the background in most shots; we were beginning to feel a little like extras. Most evenings we were left to kick our heels back at the sanatorium while the unit toiled on. On such nights, the younger Chosen Men roamed the unpopulated Rossiya, looking for any distraction, more often than not ending up in reception sitting at a large round table in one corner.

One night as we sat telling disgusting jokes, Daragh entered the building with a look of extreme concern on his face, briefly stopping to inform us Paul McGann had reinjured his knee during a fight scene with Daniel Craig. Although it was more of a tweak not requiring him to redeploy his crutches, you could see the sense of frustration on Paul's face as he arrived 'home'; at least he had the support of his wife Annie and children awaiting him in his suite. Had the accident happened while filming in the UK, Paul would have had an operation on his knee while production was suspended or at least the schedule rejigged until the injury recovered. He may have needed to get his knee looked at properly, i.e. in the UK, but the original injury was sustained off set, on his own time, therefore absolving the production company of any responsibility or blame. Their choice was to soldier on, potentially putting the future health of Paul's knee in jeopardy.

SHARPE CONSPIRATORS

It was at this point that several heavyweight members of the cast, Brian Cox, Daragh and David Troughton, all now several pounds lighter from illness and undernourishment, took Paul aside to say it was time to pull the lead actor card, to demand improvements to our conditions. Daragh in particular had an acute knowledge of our rights as actors; he quickly assessed that production were taking liberties with our health and safety, painting as bleak a picture of the situation as possible. The pressure on Paul must have been immense; to save his knee he might put the whole production at risk of folding, but to carry on without addressing the injury could result in him walking with a limp for the rest of his days.

Stuart Sutherland maintains Sean Bean was the original choice to play Sharpe but he was unavailable on the required dates. Paul had arrived at the role after beating out most of the hot UK male acting talent, including his own brother Mark, Clive Owen, Iain Glenn, Steven Hartley and Rufus Sewell among others. Paul had played the title role in the 1990 film *The Monk*, which was produced by Muir Sutherland, and Paul recalls that was when he was first approached to play the role of Sharpe. Not being able to choose his own lead might at least have gone some way towards explaining the apparent lack of sympathy Jim Goddard displayed towards poor Paul.

At least this is how it seemed at the time as Jim made no allowances for the fragile state of Paul's knee, carrying on with risky action regardless of the consequences. Morale was at rock-bottom; we were almost starving and there absolutely no indication things would be getting better any time soon. In fact, they got worse. The final straw came when shooting a scene from 'Eagle' that required Sharpe and his men to stealthily traverse sloping terrain in pursuit of the flag-snatching French.

To reach the camera position from base camp, we were forced to climb a very steep incline. Not a problem for gung-ho Harris, but precisely the opposite of what a ruptured cruciate ligament needed to aid its recovery. We rallied to Paul's aid, firmly pushing his backside up the slope as he struggled with the climb. Arriving at the camera position, we were told the action involved us climbing even higher through a mass of thick, thorny bushes. It was ridiculous terrain to choose. Paul's knee was already taxed by the climb to this point, so it was no surprise that on the first take, without Chosen hands to prop him up, Paul's knee gave way for the third and final time. The writing was on the wall. Infuriatingly, it was later discovered that our vehicle could have taken us directly to the camera set-up, the driver just didn't know the way. Typical!

Returning to the Rossiya fully expecting more time off to party in the sun while Paul's knee recuperated once again, this time things were different. The following evening Paul convened a meeting of the Chosen Men in his suite to inform us he would be returning to England so that a proper examination of his knee could take place, with a view to resuming the shoot after a period of rest. We sat listening to Paul's best efforts to assure us the show would go on, but we weren't persuaded; we had our suspicions that this was curtains for *Sharpe*. At least production would have to honour the remainder of our contracts.

It was the last time we saw Paul in the Crimea.

The following day, executive producer Malcolm Craddock called the unit to gather in the Goat and Balalaika. Everyone thought they knew exactly what was coming; production would be shut down for a while then we'd be back shooting after a short break back home. Instead he announced that he was calling *force majeure* and the entire unit would pack their stuff, stand by and be ready for news from production. *Force majeure*, in the context of law, as defined by the *Concise Oxford Dictionary*, is 'an unforeseeable course of events excusing a person from fulfilment of contract'. This we didn't expect. Maybe we were going to have to fight for our money after all. Shortly afterwards, the producer, director and production office staff all hightailed it back to London, leaving behind a half-resigned, fully bemused film unit with no fixed date of departure and passports locked away somewhere in the production office. We were left in limbo, holed up in a sanatorium in which we were the sole occupants. The prospect of returning home filled us with joy, almost outweighing the possibility that this dream job could be over after only six weeks.

BACK TO LIFE, BACK TO REALITY

After a weekend of bacchanalian overkill, the film unit said goodbye to the collapsed Soviet Union, eventually departing for Moscow seven hours late at 2:30 a.m. and arriving at Sheremetyevo at six in the morning. We then headed to the Novotel to rest up for the afternoon British Airways flight back to normality. As our bus wound its way to the hotel, we were pulled over to the side of the road. A man in a long leather coat got on the bus, had a chat with the driver, took a look at the dishevelled mob on board and got off, slipping away into the dusky morning. Sometime later we were informed that our little stop was a mafia thug seeing if he could shake down the bus, but deciding against it as the risks of holding up a busload of foreigners far outweighed the rewards. This happened within the supposedly secure airport perimeter; it seemed as though glasnost-perestroika would be a boon for the Russian mafia, too.

Blissfully unaware of our brush with the new Russia, the unit checked into the hermetically sealed Novotel hotel. It was like entering the gates of heaven: everything was fresh, western and oasis-like, with a breakfast bar serving as close to a full English as you could wish for. Danish pastries, non-rancid butter and un-curdled milk, a joy after six weeks of deprivation; at least our final memory of Russia would be of gastronomic satisfaction.

Deep down, I hoped this wouldn't be curtains; having drunk deep of the *Sharpe* Kool-Aid, I couldn't see how a series with so much going for it could be abandoned to wither on the vine. Having by now ploughed through a few of the novels, I realised what an irresistibly cool show *Sharpe* could be; at that point I would have put money on us returning. But, just in case this was my last chance to check out Moscow, as the others crumpled into their beds I took the shuttle bus into town, passing anti-tank obstacles either side of the highway marking the extent of Hitler's advance into Russia in 1941. I did a whistle-stop tour of all the top tourist spots, Red Square, Lenin's Tomb, St Basil's, GUM department store... and McDonald's. Never was I so happy to wolf down a fish fillet, fries and Coke. On the shuttle back to the Novotel I consoled myself with the knowledge that if *Sharpe* was over then at least I would have seen the capital of the country I was seemingly destined to visit.

ALL CHANGE

The relief of coming home to the UK after a stretch in the former USSR was palpable; the joy was of course tempered by the uncertainty regarding our contracts; I might be about to lose the best, most highly paid job of my short career. Then, five days after leaving Russia, came the news we'd hoped for but not in the way we expected. Sharpe would rise again, not with Paul McGann, but in the form of an up-and-coming star from Sheffield called Sean Bean. It wasn't a shock appointment; from what I'd seen of him on screen, most recently in *Patriot Games*, he looked every inch the part. I was saddened at the callous discarding of Paul McGann, who was firmly established as our Sharpe, and angry that he'd been usurped without giving his knee the chance to recover.

However, alongside the heartfelt sympathy for Paul there was also the dawning realisation that the biggest, most lucrative job I'd ever been offered was still alive. I resolved that to preserve my sanity for the remainder of my fourteen-week tour I was going to pack my bags as if I was undertaking an expedition with the emphasis on maximum self-sufficiency. A gathering was called at my flat on Moscow Road: Brian Cox, Nolan Hemmings and the London-based Chosen Men, Paul Trussell and Michael Mears, met to commiserate with Paul. Seeing that the whole business was obviously weighing on his mind, we stuck to being cheery and supportive with banter and a little partying. I had thought of extending an invite to Sean, but none of us knew him well enough to call him direct; what a unique photo opportunity that would have made! Would the loss of the title role on *Sharpe* adversely affect Paul's career? We speculated as to whether Paul's misfortune and the way it was dealt with would be a blot on the future of the series. Little did we know that it was just the beginning of what we soon began to think of as the *Sharpe* jinx.

On 5 October, within thirteen days of fleeing the Crimea, we were back at Heathrow meeting our new Sharpe at, appropriately enough, a bar called Cloud Nine. It was a new beginning, with a new actor in the lead role and a different director at the helm. My first sight of Sean was of him standing by the bar with Daragh, drink and cigarette in hand. Based solely on what I had seen on screen I was expecting a brash, confident, big-headed braggart. The absolute opposite was true; he saved that stuff for when the cameras were rolling. We had been given a second chance to make this first series, nothing could faze us now. Our eyes were thoroughly fixed on the prize; we were aware of the pitfalls of filming out there, but, like the Chosen Men we were playing, we were going support our new Sharpe and make sure his time in the Crimea went smoothly.

For the past two months, the Chosen Men had been together as a unit; a full ten weeks as a team, seven of which had been spent in the Crimea filming, so we were already a pretty tight group. Aware of this, we made sure our arms were wide open in welcoming Sean into the fold, giving him every assurance that we would support him much in the way Sharpe would be protected by his men. Back at Moscow's Sheremetyevo, the dour, suspicious immigration officers painstakingly scrutinised our passports before we transferred onto an Aeroflot charter jet. Once aboard, Sean walked directly to the back of the plane, followed swiftly by the Chosen Men, his new gang of reprobates, where much merriment was had for the duration of the flight.

Other casualties left in the wake of *force majeure* were director Jim Goddard and the first Teresa, Diana Peñalver. To finance the re-cast, an insurance claim was made – the largest in British television history at the time; Jim Goddard was fired for supposedly putting actors in danger with his recklessness. I would argue that shooting in the freshly disintegrated Soviet Union to save a buck was chiefly responsible for putting the unit in danger.

The writing was on the wall for Jim when, shortly before *force majeure* was called, editor Robin Sayles, production designer Andrew Mollo and director of photography Ivan Strasburg had a secret meeting with Malcolm telling him the way Jim was shooting the action wasn't providing enough coverage to edit the scenes together, lack of different camera angles and takes that overlapped being the chief problem. Jim Goddard may have been particularly abusive to some members of the crew, creating an uncomfortable atmosphere on set, but he was the man who cast me as Rifleman Harris, created the look of the Chosen Men and, when not on set, was good with me and was a laugh to hang out with. Many thought this firing would be a blessed relief for Jim, as the conditions out in the Crimean heat were very hard on someone who was so substantially overweight, and perhaps he didn't fancy making three films out there, back-to-back.

Unfortunate Diana Peñalver lost her part in a TV legend as she was more of a match, in terms of physical stature, for Paul McGann, both of them being rather diminutive; the new Teresa, Assumpta Serna, was a far better match for Sean and her appearance fitted the description of the role to a tee. To guarantee our efforts reached the screen the following spring, the producers replaced Jim Goddard with Tom Clegg, veteran of countless TV series and feature films. I was a little taken aback to hear he'd been appointed as, shortly before *Sharpe*, I'd auditioned for *Between the Lines*, another cop show he was directing, and he was so impressed with my acting that he gave the role to someone else. So, I knew I wasn't his favourite actor, but I wasn't going to worry too much. After all, I was Chosen Man Harris.

Our union, British Actors' Equity, had received numerous complaints about Sharpe Film; those succumbing to illness made sure the union got a full rundown of the problems we had faced and where production had fallen short. A list of demands was presented to Malcolm and Muir that had to be met before we were allowed to step foot anywhere near the airport. Equity stipulated there must be an English-speaking UK nurse and stunt coordinator as part of the unit; there would have to be a vast improvement in the food and an all-round improvement in everything, the latter part being very general and fairly unverifiable. Of course, Equity couldn't reverse the path of the lurgy that had laid waste to the guts of many a unit member; laboratory analysis revealed the ailment to be microscopic pathogen, *Giardia lamblia*, a sort of amoebic dysentery. Major supplies of a drug called Flagyl were shipped out for those affected.

Having the enforced break back home had allowed us to stock up and ship out our favourite non-perishables as well as medicines, items of entertainment and anything else to set up a home away from home. Many 'cottage kitchens' sprung up in our rooms and on our balconies. Pot, pans and utensils were packed or nicked from the Rotunda. Sano, our Portuguese hairdresser, added a hot plate to her 'kitchen' and even after toiling six days at the coalface of Sean Bean, Daniel Craig and Assumpta Serna's hairstyles, Sunday would see her preparing delicious lunches eagerly devoured by an undernourished cast and crew.

Early on it became abundantly clear that individuals, certainly lifers – those in-country the entire tour – had to look out for themselves. Had the powers downplayed the difficulties of existing in the Crimea? Or had they just been insulated from it all, travelling in comfortable cars and eating in the best restaurants, content with the false assurances provided by our Russian co-producers regarding our health and safety, constantly blaming any problems on the disarray left in the wake the collapse of Soviet communism. There were times when we felt that the powers were powerless when dealing with anything other than getting the film in the can.

BACK IN THE SADDLE AGAIN

Arriving back at the Rossiya sanatorium was almost like a homecoming. We had received a stay of execution, the only casualty being the third and final episode; 'Sharpe's Gold' got dropped from the schedule as part of the insurance claim shuffle. *Force majeure* would deprive us of seeing Patrick Malahide and Bill Patterson, among others, in a faithful rendition of the novel. 'Rifles' and 'Eagle' remained on the schedule with scenes from 'Eagle' first up in the brave new Bean era. Sean wasn't going to be eased in gently; first order of business would be recreating the Battle of Talavera, filmed at a new location, Baidar Valley off the road to Sevastopol, not far from a place called Foros. It was there, only a year earlier, that President Gorbachev had been held under house arrest when hard-line communists attempted a coup, prompting Boris Yeltsin to jump onto a tank in front of the Russian White House to stop the coup, providing one of the most iconic images of the period. Hey, let's go *there* to make a TV series; looks perfect, someone must have thought.

Up in Baidar Valley we got our first taste of the changing weather, bitingly cold winds sweeping in from China, or so the locals told us. Horrible to work in, but, when recreating battles, it helps if conditions are a little grim. Our new director hit the ground running, moving through the scenes with the minimum of fuss, constantly roaming the entire set with cigarette in hand, contemplating the next shot. Tom was used to directing action, he knew exactly what he wanted and was possessed of tireless energy; the schedule was maintained, things flowed, and *Sharpe* was back in business. It quickly became apparent that Sean was perhaps closer than Paul to Bernard's description of our eponymous hero in the novels and seemed to really relish engaging in a bit of on-screen aggro.

Keeping actors safe on set would be the job of UK stunt coordinator Greg Powell; well-known in the stunt world, he had particular expertise with equine stunts. Chosen not only for his coordinating prowess, Greg had been tasked by British Actors' Equity to make sure that production maintained health and safety standards, which irked production very much. Our first assistant director, Marc Jenny, was particularly annoyed as he favoured pushing matters such as explosions and cavalry charges to their limits, with little regard for safety. Jenny, the rather forceful mouthpiece of the director, had a habit of disrespecting the extras and other locals in the film unit; I was amazed he had survived the insurance claim cull. Jenny had early on disabused us of any illusion that we were creating art on *Sharpe*, a watershed moment for the Chosen Men which added further to the malaise we were experiencing during the Goddard era. I remember, along with Michael Mears and Paul Trussell, pulling Marc aside back at the Rossiya – I don't recall the specific issue – where we were told we were more like factory workers than artists. This is probably why his services were retained; he was able to drive dispassionately through the schedule, completing all shots that day with minimum fuss.

Yet, despite the best intentions, injuries still occurred, luckily not to the star asset, though he did manage to clout a stuntman on the back of his head with his sword, thereby halting production and prompting our Ukrainian nurse, a dead ringer for Myra Hindley, into action. Our Russian-speaking stunt coordinator was a competent technician but spoke little English; the Soviet film industry seemed to encourage a more flamboyant style of stunt craft, doing stuff for real, relying less on camera angles and editing tricks. I'm not saying their brand of stunt work put us in danger, but you felt very safe when the hugely experienced Powell was on set, reducing fear levels somewhat; after all, this was an action picture, as Jim Goddard had been fond of saying!

After shooting the Battle of Talavera, there was no doubt that we were coming close to recreating what I had visualised when reading the *Sharpe* novels. I got a real frisson of excitement as we rose from the trench to repel the French attack and seeing Sean swat Napoleon's finest aside with his sword en route to snatching an imperial eagle; it was a shame we didn't have more bodies to beef up the French columns. Though I was impressed with the neat way the extras from Simferopol barracks were utilised; dressed as attacking British redcoats in the morning and changing into French uniforms after lunch. Recreating battle scenes where thousands perished on both sides can take it out of you and the Chosen Men were rewarded with several days off filming; fantastic, one might imagine think, but after checking out most of the best stuff Yalta has to offer you run out of original ways to kill the time.

As we were in a sanatorium, with the requisite slip of paper you were entitled to a full body massage, usually administered by a big, strong, white uniformed lady with at least one gold tooth. A more pleasurable pastime was exploring the limits of glasnost/perestroika with some heavy flirting with Maya, one of the actresses from Moscow. She spoke little English, my Russian was still limited, but we both had a smattering of Spanish. I even bought a Spanish/English dictionary to improve our conversation. I felt guilty about my girlfriend back home, but it was all pretty innocent: holding hands while walking Maya back to the Russian accommodation block or lingering at one of the gazebos overlooking the Black Sea. I knew it couldn't possibly go further. London seemed a long way away.

'THE NEEDLE'

Never had the arrival of an actor been met with so much anticipation as that of 'the Needle', aka Teresa, played by the impressive and charismatic Assumpta Serna recently arrived in-country. We were reliably informed by our hairdresser Sano that Assumpta had a reputation as a *femme fatale*.

Assumpta's first action was a reshoot of a scene originally filmed when McGann was Sharpe: a pivotal moment where Sharpe meets Teresa. The full cast of regulars were called; all eyes were on Assumpta for her debut action and she didn't disappoint, delivering her lines with the right amount of venom and steel; she was going to be a great match for Sean. A strong female character played by a cool, confident actress; as a fellow actor I was desperately sorry for Diana, our first Teresa, who, through no fault of her own, wound up out of a job. But as far as the image of a resolute rebel leader who'd been through hell and was intent on slaughtering as many French soldiers as possible, Assumpta fitted the bill perfectly.

A trick missed by our union Equity was failing to address the inadequacy of our ex-Red Army tented headquarters now regularly battered by cold winds. It was unrealistic to expect several

Winnebagos to be conjured up, though I'm sure somewhere it says the star of any television show or film should get a motor home. I contend that we spent more time in our ex-Red Army tents than in front of the camera – definitely the Chosen Men – so it would have helped to have a more salubrious place of relaxation. Certainly, pitching us all into one space with only fold-up camping furniture to repose on helped to bond us as a unit; many laughs were shared, plots hatched, disputes worked through, all within the rudimentary confines of our billowing canvas shelter.

Next on the schedule, we were returning to Simferopol to reshoot Simmerson losing the colours at Kamishinka, where hasty bridge repairs were taking place; thankfully it was only a fleeting visit. In Simferopol we would say goodbye to the remaining 'Eagle' cast, which, alas, included Maya, who had completed all her scenes as Josefina's maid. Returning to the Moscow Hotel, I greeted the hotel receptionist warmly, asking if I could change some dollars into coupons. Upon seeing my wad of local currency she accused me of being a *malinki* (little) capitalist. I took deep umbrage at this, as my wedge of the ever-diminishing currency was probably the equivalent of thirty dollars; though to the receptionist anyone from the other side of the Iron Curtain was a capitalist. More deserving of that description was our executive producer, Malcolm Craddock, recently in from London for the first time since Sean took over the role. That evening, the Chosen Men sat with him in the hotel's taste-free (in both decor and menu) Soviet-era restaurant where the change of Sharpe was the main topic of conversation. In between reluctant stabs at the inedible chow on our plates, Malcolm left us in no doubt that no actors were indispensable, no matter how big, all said with a slight grin and steely glint in his eye.

Back on set at Kamishinka, the bridge we blew up back in August was repaired and relaid with explosives and all scenes already completed before the hiatus were reshot. With the film safely in the can, we decamped back to the Moscow Hotel, where the only game in town was the fifth-floor bar, scene of extreme excess fuelled by the abundant, dirt-cheap vodka and champagne. I suppose the merriment looked particularly Hogarthian to me as I had kept straight as an arrow in anticipation of a meeting with Maya later that night. She had been obliged to go out for dinner with the Association's head honchos along with the actress playing Josefina's other maid. Eventually our rendezvous took place away from the bar in my room, where we seized our final hours together as, in the morning, we would part, never to see each other again.

Cupid's arrow had landed elsewhere in the unit. Assumpta had selected her chosen distraction in the form of Paul Trussell, Rifleman Tongue, my good friend and one of the boys. It was kind of like shooting fish in a barrel as Paul, briefed by Sano, had bravely volunteered himself to be man-eaten. Paul and I were not unique. Many of the unit were fraternising to varying degrees. In a four-month shoot, perhaps it was inevitable that a little romance would arise amid the quagmire of uncertainty in which we sometimes found ourselves.

IT'S A LONG, LONG ROAD

The pursuit of passion certainly smoothed out some of the less lovely aspects of our tour. Unfortunately, cases of Simferopol stomach continued to make it a rough ride for some. Production tackled this problem by unleashing the sanatorium medics to wield their Soviet-era enema pumps; this was the moment we really could have done with Florence Nightingale.

The situation was a far cry from early in the shoot when the descent into chaos left me feeling extremely bewildered and not a little spooked. After a crazy week of near-death experiences, disease, spirit-sapping catering and malnutrition, all you were good for was retiring to your room, slumping scrunched into a corner in a foetal ball, hoping that the merciful hand of death would claim you before morning; overly dramatic, yes, but at our lowest ebb that was how we felt. Those feelings hadn't entirely dissipated with the arrival of Sean; on set, Paul Trussell, debilitated by *Giardia lamblia*, remonstrated with Malcolm about the quality of the food. Our canvas home went awkwardly silent as Paul, blanket wrapped around his shoulders, tearfully ripped into Malcolm about the unsanitary conditions and the production's seeming lack of care; asserting that, as a result of the terrible unhygienic food being served to us, he was liable to fall ill and possibly die. Malcolm took on board the point Paul was making and dumped it on the already huge pile of Crimea-related problems.

BEAM ME UP, SCOTTY

On 3 November we were just over a month away from exiting the Crimea for a rosy Portuguese sojourn. As the date grew tantalisingly closer, the powers thought the promise of comparative paradise might pacify the unit and dampen our revolutionary fervour. The limits of our patience were tested once more with the move to our next location, a three-hour round trip necessitating brutally early wake-ups. Our route took us along the coast road in the direction of Sevastopol, through another vestige of former Soviet control: a checkpoint manned by a couple of naval personnel. I later learned the two cherubic-looking six-footers were Russian marines guarding the road down to Sevastopol and Balaclava, where the Russian Black Sea fleet was berthed. The two young marines looked over the contents of the minibus curiously, politely posing with me for a photo before waving us on our way. After driving endlessly through nondescript countryside, we reached what looked like a cattle farm. The 4 a.m. wake-up call, the interminable drive and the lack of a hot breakfast were all prices (almost) worth paying as we arrived to find another impressive location. A truly peculiar landscape that reminded me of natural backdrops used in the early *Planet of the Apes* films and not too dissimilar, but on a smaller scale than our first locations Chufut-Kale and the Baidar Valley. I later learned the two locations are part of the same geological formation.

At Eskikermen, we covered pivotal scenes from 'Rifles', chief among them the dramatic events surrounding Dunnett's massacre, including rescuing the mortally wounded Captain Murray and Perkins joining the gang. Harris is tasked with carrying the injured Murray up the slope to safety; Tim Bentinck playing Murray later remarked it was the only time he had been carried in his adult life. Good old Tim; meeting him at the read-through for *Sharpe* had sparked my real enthusiasm and appreciation for the *Sharpe* novels, while also piquing my curiosity about the Crimean War. On his death bed, Murray gives Sharpe his sword, thus emboldening Sharpe in his attempt to bring the ragtag Chosen Men to heel. The massacre is witnessed by Comandante Teresa from the opposite slope and she is impressed by Sharpe's decisive brutality when rescuing Murray from the French. We also shot one of my favourite Harper moments: against insurmountable odds, Harper takes out two French cavalrymen with only one musket ball and his ramrod, all scenes key to the development of the story and the evolution of Sharpe's relationship with the Chosen Men.

The Crimean countryside contributed greatly to the look and feel of *Sharpe*. Although we ended up there for reasons of economics above all else, the Crimean Peninsula is also the Hollywood of the Soviet film industry with two studios in Yalta. At Polikur studios, situated in the hills overlooking Yalta Bay, a Portuguese village had been superbly constructed by Phil Elton on their back lot. After the debilitating commute to Eskikermen, the brief drive to Polikur made the workday more agreeable; there was also the comfort of dressing rooms, hair and make-up rooms, all the stuff we were used to when working back home. Selfishly, I wished they could have shot the entire series at Polikur, but then we wouldn't have been treated to the amazing vistas we had enjoyed so far, nor could Polikur house large builds or accommodate dramatic cavalry charges.

Back at the sanatorium, we spent our evenings playing Risk and Scrabble, regaling the newly arrived *Rifles* cast with tales of Crimean hardships; Tim Bentinck, on board since day one, remarked at how much weight we had all lost. Our food supplies brought out when we returned to Yalta had dried up: now mealtimes were spent daydreaming about what sort of food we could have magically delivered from home. Sunday roast, pizza, Chinese food, steamed broccoli and fish and chips topped my fantasy menu. As if the ever-present food woes weren't enough, we were now beginning to experience power cuts, plunging the sanatorium into darkness for hours at a time, usually when we were at home in the evening. After a couple more blackouts, the production office distributed candles, engendering a real Blitz spirit, bringing back memories of the three-day week in Britain in the early seventies when lack of coal forced the country to shut down, the glow of candlelight and days off school almost making up for not being able to watch television.

Keeping British traditions alive out in the Crimea was essential. In November, this meant letting off some fireworks cheekily smuggled in from London. A small group of us felt it best to celebrate Guy Fawkes down on our private beach, which in darkness was reached with great difficulty down the steep winding path. Before we even got near to lighting the blue-touch paper, we heard shouting in Russian as a man popped up out of nowhere wildly gesticulating at us to get back to the sanatorium. Turned out he was one of our security team. Looking supremely hassled, he had stealthily ambushed us – hadn't we learned anything from Chosen Man school? He kept repeating the word 'granitza' which I later learned means 'border'; I guess he was just trying to keep us safe; or was it more the vestiges of the Soviet surveillance ethos too entrenched to shake off?

Our next location, Livadia Palace, hosted the summit that shaped post-war Europe, Yalta's main claim to fame. The Yalta Conference was where the Allied powers met to discuss ending the Second World War quickly and what the peace should look like afterwards. The Livadia estate had been a summer retreat of the Russian imperial family in the 1860s with the current version completed in 1911. Since then it had been a mental institution, a Nazi HQ and was now a thriving tourist attraction and museum. In one of its porticos we shot the final moments of *Rifles* where our eponymous hero is congratulated by Wellington's top brass: 'Well done, Pat,' Hogan blurts at Harper as he steps off the portico – an ad-lib, by the way. Not content with the abundant, witty and wonderful dialogue written for him by Eoghan Harris, Brian had to grab a scene stealer of a line right at the end. Seeing as Brian Cox was one of the best things in the first series, one had to bow to his expertise, especially in stealing a scene.

As the camera barely pointed towards the Chosen Men, I had ample time to explore the palace interior, and before long I stumbled upon the room where the actual conference was held, a high-ceilinged hall with a single round table and a large fireplace at one end. Around the table sat three large, padded chairs, evidently for Uncle Joe, Roosevelt and Churchill, with smaller chairs for their Chiefs of Staff; I noticed Stalin's delegation had one more chair than the Yanks or the Brits. Small desk flags indicated the seating positions of the respective leaders; I walked over to the table, pulled out Churchill's chair and plonked myself down. Within seconds, an irate babushka rushed out of nowhere – these locals were really good at that – shouting at me to presumably to get my disrespectful western arse the hell out of the chair. As I was dressed in full kit with rifle propped against the table, she did have a point.

It was now late November, less than two weeks from demob to Portugal, where all remaining scenes from both episodes would be completed; journey's end was enticingly close, but still not close enough. At first, it had been sort of exciting living by the seat of our pants; but being half starved and thoroughly hacked off with almost everything, a tad overexposed to all the potential dangers, both on and off set, the novelty began to wear off. The sense of remoteness brought on by our long Crimean secondment gave everything an air of detachment from normality, a kind of *Sharpe* Bubble developed; the outside world, including news from home, now barely registered.

From day one, I had faced all challenges with a hubristic, macho disregard for common sense, eager to prove I was as tough, resourceful and immovable as a real Chosen Man. Production benefited from this madness both on and off screen, in that they never had any need to look after my wellbeing in any way. Many a freshly arrived actor quickly became overwhelmed by the environment we had to work within. When it truly dawned on us that no one was really in full control or even knew what they were doing, that's when a degree of fear entered the equation. This resulted in lifers having to develop a thick skin, showing general contempt for the dangers and the chaos surrounding them, much like a soldier in the thick of warfare. This attitude, combined with our gaunt frames and hardened faces, gave us the genuine demeanour of combat-toughened foot soldiers on screen; an unintended positive consequence of the chaos – or was this part of an evil master plan dreamed up by the powers?

On the penultimate weekend of our Crimean tenure, a group night out was arranged by the unofficial *Sharpe* social club founded by lifers. First stop was the only decent restaurant we knew of in downtown Yalta, Gourmand, where many of us got our first taste of caviar; it was something I had never wanted to try, but quite liked after sampling. I thought I'd better have a taste before leaving as we might never return, though deep down I suspected *Sharpe* was going to be big. I was totally gripped by the characters, the historical background and the epic feel of the stories. Sean, by then, had an international profile and the camera absolutely loved his face; I could see us filming all the novels in the years to come and probably in cheap-as-chips Crimea. Daragh was fond of quoting betting odds on anything you could think of and he was pessimistic about there being a second series, so much so that he gave me odds of 15-1 on whether *Sharpe* would return next year. I placed a $100 bet.

Our group night out ended at downtown Yalta's main casino, the 777, where the elation of our last days in Yalta led me to drink away the last of my per diem money, which was only $20. This was one of the upsides of working out here: you could spend lavishly and still come home with change from twenty bucks. The next morning, I found out what a $20 beer and vodka hangover felt like, it was the mightiest headache I had ever experience so far on *Sharpe*; unfortunately, it was our day off and my last chance to go on Richard Moore's Crimean War tour. He had led trips to Inkerman, Balaclava and Sevastopol most weekends, but the following Saturday we would be off to Portugal. I boarded the minivan yearning for a cup of tea or a bottle of water, but the Rotunda wasn't open yet, nor were there any convenient rest stops along the highway to Sevastopol to ease the pain! Mercifully we pulled into a little roadside café on the outskirts of town, the sort of place I would normally avoid for fear of getting an upset stomach, but my fragile state left me no choice. Aside from the most welcome cup of tea I had drunk in all my months in-country, they served pilmeni, a stuffed, boiled dumpling which to me looked more like ravioli or tortellini. Traditionally they are stuffed with pork, and as the only flesh I ate was fish and chicken, I had to make do with some rather tough bread to go with my life-sustaining cup of tea; it seemed this part of the Crimea wasn't as developed as Yalta, possibly due to the fact there weren't any tourist attractions so close to a Russian submarine base.

The history lesson started at one end of the charge valley at Balaclava; my knowledge of the Crimean War was sketchy at best, but I had always assumed it was a victorious action. Richard Moore explained that, although it was heroic on the part of the Light

Brigade, high command's miscommunication had sent them on a suicide mission. The valley is now dominated by neat rows of peach trees as far as the eye can see; the redoubts are visible, but otherwise there is little to commemorate the battle bar a solitary obelisk stuck out in a field. We moved on to a purpose-built structure, housing dioramas of the Crimean War, as well one from the Great Patriotic War depicting the siege of Sevastopol. Richard's tours hadn't gone unnoticed by diorama staff, again consisting of a lone babushka who, according to our interpreter, took exception to Richard's tone when describing the exhibits. At least this babushka didn't sneak up on us, ninja-style, but she followed our every move, keeping a beady eye on Richard in particular. I can attest that he was telling a straight-down-the-middle account of the two dioramas, the Battle of Balaclava and the Siege of Sevastopol, no editorialising. Also, as she spoke no English it was hard to tell what her protestations were based on other than entrenched Soviet Cold War prejudice. Richard was responsible for teaching our Ukrainian squaddies how to march, load and act like British soldiers of the Napoleonic Wars; he hung out with them, stayed in their camp, treating them with the utmost respect and they loved him for it, so that babushka at the diorama was way off the mark.

The excursion's final stop took us to Balaclava with its deep-water harbour strewn with Soviet submarines in various states of disrepair. Up on the heights overlooking the harbour we snapped away with our cameras at the Black Sea fleet in our midst. It was quite surreal, seeing the warm-water port so coveted by the Soviets, let alone being allowed to take photos of Soviet submarines unmolested, an act for which I would surely have been shot or arrested before the fall of the Soviet Union. As our fascinating trip came to an end, the skies, already grey with rainclouds, darkened over Balaclava town; the muted colours of the surroundings and the descending darkness gave everything an atmosphere straight out of a Cold War spy film. What an amazing experience the whole day had been, something I'll never forget.

Thank God I hadn't let my colossal hangover prevent me from going.

HOME STRETCH

Our last week in the Crimea was spent at a wintery Dimerdji shooting the climax of 'Rifles'. Interior scenes from 'Eagle' would be filmed at another Yalta palace, Vorontsov, which happened to be Churchill's residence during the Yalta Conference. My final days in Ukraine became a blur of shopping, packing, recording the sights and any other delightful distractions. In early November when we reshot the bridge-blowing scene at Kamishinka, a new interpreter called Natasha had come on board, a Yalta native who spoke rather good English; a prerequisite of being an interpreter, I suppose. I first met her in the lobby of the Moscow Hotel as I was breezing past the huge line of local crew waiting for their room keys. She had already caught my eye on set, so I stopped for a chat; exasperated with the size of the queue, Natasha said, 'I wish I were a truck driver. I would have received my key by now,' which I found rather amusing. As Natasha is very beautiful, she didn't lack for attention and I had heard she was going out with a son of one of the Association's top men, so I figured her dance card was full. Still, that didn't stop her making an impression that stayed with me.

By early December Yalta got increasingly stormy, the Rossiya sanatorium regularly getting doused during tempestuous weather. At Dimerdji's elevated position the precipitation fell as snow, making our trek to set a treacherous one. Not the sort of weather for hanging out under canvas, so base camp was relocated to a village situated where the 'tarmac' road gives way to a steep, winding and rocky path to the summit. Here in the village's nursery school we would do costume, make-up and, after a protracted battle with the powers, have a hot breakfast prepared. From there a gigantic all-terrain military vehicle with its zillions of enormous tyres made light work of the precarious ascent, one of the benefits of having the Ukrainian army as part of our unit. As there was no base camp up on Dimerdji the transport doubled as our only shelter from the elements, so meals and short breaks were taken in there, too.

A hot cooked breakfast on set was one meal an early rising film crew really looked forward to. We had lobbied, protested and generally hectored the powers about the abysmal chow and the Stone Age methods of delivering hot food to set. We had met with the Association's top brass, Stefan Pojenan, who had promised to cure all food woes, but had failed dismally. One guarantee that came from the food summit was the promise of a hot cooked breakfast prepared at our base camp, so when we arrived at the Dimerdji nursery school we were looking forward to our first hot breakfast served on location. Much to our collective disappointment, no breakfast appeared. Blaming frozen gas lines and motor malfunctions didn't cut it: the time for drastic action had come. We had put up with so much shit during the last four months in-country and, much like Peter Finch in the movie Network, 'we were mad as hell and weren't going to take it anymore'. Led by Daragh, the Chosen Men's revolutionary spirit galvanised in the face of one more broken promise. Production had crossed a red line; we would have no choice but to go on strike.

On screen, Sharpe and the Chosen Men overcome insurmountable odds through their strength as a unit; now that resolve was being mirrored off camera. The multitude of troubles we had faced together since the beginning had forged a brotherhood of actors; we were mostly members of Equity, but their all-caring arms didn't really reach us out in the Crimea. Daragh had a good handle on Equity's law regarding shooting on location, pointing out all the production's lapses in duty of care, having had previous experience on another calamitous production filmed in the Canadian Arctic. Apparently on that shoot one careless actor even managed to get a local girl pregnant; what an irresponsible chap that actor must be. At the nursery school, Sean watched on in wonder as we told Sam Craddock, our beloved second assistant director and son of Malcolm, to get Tom on the walkie-talkie to tell him we would not be coming up to set. Sean didn't try to persuade us otherwise; perhaps he didn't feel that he could pull his weight at this early stage of his *Sharpe* tenure, yet he could see we were united fighting for a good cause that would benefit the whole unit.

Time ticked on as we waited for production's next move; news came down that Tom Clegg was pretty mad. Eventually Muir rolled up to see what all the fuss was about and in the elapsed time our resolve had hardened considerably. Muir had possibly spent less time in-country than Malcolm these past four months; we felt he might not have fully grasped the gravity of the situation. He reasoned that supplies were hard to get for a typical English breakfast such as bacon; with supreme timing and laser accuracy, a large, vacuum-sealed packet of bacon rashers – acquired at a Moscow hard-currency shop by an incoming actor – was perfectly lobbed, landing in the middle of the camp bed that separated us from Muir. The timing was exquisite; we were soon laughing uproariously, Muir perhaps less so. Once class had settled down, we made it clear that if there was no cooked breakfast the next day, we wouldn't hesitate in coming out on strike again. In truth we knew there was no hope of a proper full English breakfast being served up out here due to the dearth of supplies, but this broken promise was the straw that broke the camel's back so action had to be taken.

From that day on the whole unit, British and local crew, enjoyed a hot breakfast due to the action quickly becoming known as the 'Dimerdji Bacon Riot'. Our Muscovite wardrobe lady, Helen Khramova, christened Daragh and I Lenin and Felix Dzerzhinsky respectively; I had to research Mr Dzerzhinsky, who was head of the first two Soviet state security organisations, the feared Cheka and the OGPU. Needless to say, this liberal westerner wasn't thrilled with that comparison. Then again, Russians do admire their devious, murderous former spymasters, often elevating them to the top job, so maybe it was a compliment?

We returned to set after scorching half a day's shooting schedule to appreciative though clandestine nods from the crew; Tom seemed reconciled to the lost time and urged us to get on with the action. In all my time on *Sharpe* these were some of my very favourite scenes to work on; all the boys together saving the day and defeating the evil foe in the face of insurmountable odds. Kind of like securing a hot breakfast for the whole unit! Production designer Andrew Mollo and set designer Phil Elton, the team responsible for designing and building our amazingly convincing builds, had recreated a little piece of northern Spain halfway up a mountain in Ukraine, replete with pigs and chickens scrabbling in the dirt. I especially loved the surreal moment during a lull in the firing when a priest leads his choristers through the town square into the church we're defending. Classic stuff, exciting and satisfying to shoot; and to think I was getting paid to do this! We were also demob happy, delirious at the thought of liberation from the Crimea; the Chosen Men shot their last frames and our work here was done. We had a real sense of elation.

Another abiding memory of Dimerdji was a chat I had with Malcolm outside the nursery school. I sat with him to get his views on the recent industrial action, which he didn't seem unduly concerned about. Malcolm had anxieties on a grand scale in the aftermath of the McGann insurance claim; this show had to be a hit, or it would be his career taking the hit. I noticed that he had a copy of *Sharpe's Enemy*, which I'd recently read along with *Sharpe's Company* in my quest to see what adventures lay ahead of us, if indeed we were commissioned for a second series. Four years earlier, I had been in the West End doing a play with Pete Postlethwaite; naturally we spent a lot of time together and had stayed in touch since. Pointing to Malcolm's paperback copy of *Enemy*, I told him there was only one actor in the world who could play the role of Sergeant Hakeswill: Mr Peter Postlethwaite. I could see Malcolm took in the information, but his poker face showed no sign of acknowledging my recommendation.

Our last seventy-two hours were blissfully carefree; the mood was elevated enormously by the returning 'Eagle' cast; Mike Cochrane, Daniel Craig, Neil Dudgeon and Gavan O'Herlihy had suffered as much as anyone the slings and arrows of the turbulent early days. I got on especially well with Gavan due to my decade spent stateside; I was able speak to him in 'American' and enjoyed certain American sports. His patriotism extended to getting a room at the Yalta Hotel so that he could watch the '92 US Election as it unfolded on CNN. Above all, Gavan approached all the trials and tribulations the Crimea had to throw at us with a spirit of adventure, determined to make lemonade from the lemon grove Sharpe Film had dumped us into. Many of the day trippers had become overwhelmed by the daily tide of adversity we faced; David Troughton, terribly affected by *Giardia lamblia*, had already resolved never to return if *Sharpe* was shot in the Crimea, and he played a recurring character.

All cast members deserved a medal of valour for enduring our inaugural tour; in an indirect way I tried to make that happen. Just as in Simferopol, there was a network of free-market entrepreneurs who regularly visited the Rossiya to sell us Soviet military surplus, much to the annoyance of the sanatorium management. Using my room as a showroom, I sneaked in a couple of our local top salesmen so they could covertly flog their wares; Tim Bentinck purchased a set of night vision glasses, gleefully tested out on land outside the Rossiya's 'granitza'. Julian Fellowes christened me 'King Rat' after picking up a nice selection of medals, watches and leather map bags. The penultimate day was spent on a farewell tour of our favourite spots in town and dropping in to see the remaining scenes of 'Eagle' being shot at Vorontsov, another of the Romanovs' summer palaces. I sat having lunch while watching the contemptuous Berry, superbly played by Dan Craig, calling out Sharpe for a duel. The perpetual class war waged against Sharpe by chaps like Lieutenant Berry we thought sometimes mirrored the dealings between ITV and Sharpe Film, especially since Malcolm and Muir had been responsible for the largest insurance claim in British television history. From then on, Sharpe Film was treated contemptuously and had to labour under diminishing budgets. So, on *Sharpe*, money was always too tight to mention.

SUB-UKRAINIAN HOMESICK BLUES

After four months, we were a day away from departing the Crimea; after this long, an amazing bond had formed within the UK unit and in some cases was equally strong with local crew. We were happy to leave, but for them it was almost the end of the world as there hadn't been many western productions shot in Yalta. As demob approached, I found myself increasingly preoccupied with Natasha, the beautiful interpreter; smart and funny, she'd proved a real hit with everyone. Of course, I knew she was seeing someone, but so enamoured was I that I didn't see that as an obstacle. Especially as within twenty-four hours I would be brought brutally crashing back to reality in Lisbon, where many of our partners would be waiting at our hotel. I felt like I'd been held hostage in post-Soviet Ukraine and now, as if I was experiencing a form of Stockholm syndrome, I didn't want to return home to face harsh reality. Well, that was how I was feeling on the final night of our first Crimean campaign, in for a penny, in for a pound, as I knew Portugal was likely to be emotionally turbulent, to put it mildly, but I only had myself to blame.

Obviously my pursuit of Natasha wasn't that subtle, but to my surprise it had been noticed by one of the local crew who paid an unexpected visit to my room while I was packing. He was the only other natural redhead in the unit, a man I had never really talked to. I wondered if this chap, the assistant boom operator, was popping in to say how much he had admired my work these past few months, or possibly to usher me in to a Crimean redheads secret society. Instead he solemnly handed me a note then walked off down the corridor. Intrigued, I opened up the note which read, 'Stay away from her she will be trouble.' A mini shudder ran down my spine. I assumed he meant Natasha. Was I being warned off so that he could have a clear path? Did Natasha have connections to the local shell-suited mafia hard men so in evidence all around town? Or had Carrot Top been studying cockney rhyming slang, and was predicting one day Natasha would be my 'trouble and strife'? Highly unlikely, so I decided to keep half an eye over my shoulder until I got on the transport to the airport the next morning.

The party was held in the Rotunda of Gastronomy, now accessed by a tunnel directly underneath reception, recently reopened due to the almost hurricane-like weather crashing in off the Black Sea. I often wondered if this was a secret KGB escape route (seeing as the Rossiya was the security service's favourite seaside accommodation) or just a practical measure for staying dry on the way to dinner? Inside the Rotunda the dining tables were pushed to the side making the space look vast, allowing for a dance floor and an area for a live band. When the party hit full swing, several topless dancers began a cabaret act in front of the stage area. Crimean champagne flowed liberally, caviar and fresh salad festooned the tables; the grand reveal consisted of a whole roast hog ceremonially wheeled out; the Association really knew how to throw a party. I danced with Natasha, and even managed a stolen kiss as her current beau, son of Russian head honcho, failed to show at the party, choosing instead a night at the 777 casino. As we boogied on the dance floor, I kept an eye out over my shoulder in case any 'trouble' came my way; no more Crimean ambushes for this Chosen Man. I knew Natasha was only using me to take revenge on her boyfriend; but never was I so compliant in being used in this fashion as when we retired to my room.

CRIMEAN FAREWELL

As we gathered on the Rossiya forecourt on the morning of Saturday 5 December, it was with mixed emotions. We could see the sadness in the eyes of our Ukrainian friends as we exchanged hugs, addresses and any last-minute gifts; I remember warning Natasha off writing to me as my girlfriend was intensely jealous with methods of surveillance and evidence-gathering the KGB would be proud of. As our transport left the Rossiya driveway I was fairly safe in the knowledge that, barring a successful putsch by the communists or disastrous ratings, we would return to the Crimea for a second series. As we approached the airport my stomach knotted in trepidation at the prospect of reuniting with my girlfriend after three and a half months. Our relationship had been rocky for about two years. I sometimes felt we were only still together because we both lacked the courage to make a clean break. She was tempestuous by nature, to say the least, and never afraid to express her anger. So, I was all over the place mentally as each hour passed; checking the bags, clicking the seat belt and the aircraft doors closing for take-off all brought me closer to the cold, frightening light of reality. Even the heavily overloaded space cake secretly baked in the Rossiya kitchen couldn't help take my mind off the prickly predicament of my own making. The flight itself set records while breaking many rules of air travel all at the same time; starting with the fact that this was probably the first civilian flight from Simferopol, Ukraine, to Lisbon, Portugal, in history.

On board, the cabin was piled high with important flight cases that couldn't fit in the hold; seat belts were optional, and the smoke-filled cabin had the whiff of a rock star's 747. With no cabin crew to tell us off, Lyndon Davies and I decided we would take up a surfing stance in the aisle as the plane landed at Lisbon's Humberto Delgado Airport; absolutely idiotic but quite exhilarating. We sat on the tarmac for quite a while. I wasn't sure why at the time, but I was later told by Colin, the props man, that Aeroflot were so mistrusted that Lisbon airport officials came on to the plane demanding that the landing fees be paid in cash (several thousand dollars) before we were allowed to disembark. As we departed the aircraft in Lisbon it was discovered that the pilot had been served some of our space cake with his tea as we glided through European airspace; no wonder it was such a mellow ride. Border checks completed, we crossed into the land of fado, dried cod and port. A coach took us west of Lisbon to a town called Cascais. Almost a suburb of Lisbon, Cascais, the first town in Portugal to have electric lighting, sits looking out on the Atlantic Ocean. Once a fishing village it became a favourite haunt of Portuguese royalty, leading it to become a tourist destination.

By this point in the campaign, I was weary of body and mind; yes, there was the satisfaction of reaching the closing stages of a production fraught with problems, with the possibility we could be at the dawning of something epic, but all I wanted to do was sleep soundly for long periods while leading an abstemious life for the final three weeks of the shoot. Unfortunately, my girlfriend had no intention of indulging me in my wish for a peaceful existence. Our first night at the hotel was spent getting extremely intoxicated with Lyndon by my side protecting me from any probing questions directed at me. The bacchanalian excess continued in this vein right up to our first shooting day; foolishly, the night before I had finally got to bed at 6 a.m., missing my alarm call; I was awoken by an exasperated Colin phoning from reception telling me to get out of bed. Still severely disoriented, I scrambled downstairs to meet the minibus; mercifully for me, first action of the day was the Chosen Men being rudely awakened from their slumbers by an irate Sharpe. No acting would be required: Harris was genuinely asleep.

Fatigue proved no obstacle to us enthusiastically embracing the change in our culinary fortunes; compared with our post-Soviet cuisine, the Portuguese catering set-up was light years ahead in every way. Their mobile kitchen was gleaming, huge and overflowing with delicious treats. It was like stepping out of the Stone Age into a futuristic kitchen. There was no full English breakfast, but we didn't care. I particularly remember heartily devouring my first Pastel de Nata, Portuguese custard tarts, washed down with mugs of frothy, sweet, hot chocolate. We had experienced the famine; this was the feast. After a leisurely breakfast, we were able to retire to our Winnebagos, not a canvas tent, to await our call; luckily the kerfuffle inherent with our switching countries allowed us a very long morning nap. As Sir Ken Branagh once said, 'Never stand when you can sit, never sit when you can lie down,' an axiom we had added to on *Sharpe* with 'If you lie down, make sure you sleep.' Many hours past our call time we arrived on set, a long-abandoned complex of farmhouses perched on sloping ground; a spot just about as far west as you can go on the continent of Europe. We were again refilming scenes originally shot when Paul McGann was in the lead. I remember that was an unbearably hot August day up on Chufut-Kale; here in December by the Atlantic coast we were required to deploy our long underwear. The contrast was stark. However, they did manage to find an equally dank, dark, flea-bitten hovel for the Chosen Men to bed down in. At least we would have bales of hay to lie upon instead of the less comfy bunches of dried reeds used as mattresses the first time around.

As the Portuguese shoot progressed, word came from editor Robin Sayles about a several-minute deficit in the *Rifles* rough cut; to plug the gap, John Tams whipped up the Chosen Man identity parade scene where Harris delivers the line 'I can read, sir!' In retrospect, it dumbfounded me that the producers didn't think to include such a scene from the outset and, thanks only to the skills of Renaissance Man John Tams, the Chosen Men became a little less one-dimensional. Along with the awful cuisine in the Crimea, the underutilisation of the Chosen Men early on would become another major issue we had with the producers, but at that time, with the first series almost in the can after overcoming a sea of troubles, we were content with approaching wrap day, sanity and health intact – well, almost.

The day before the move to our new base in the Lisbon Hilton, while filming, some coarse black powder flew into Sean's eye when firing his rifle. The Chosen Men had undergone fairly rigorous basic training where the inherent dangers of shooting black powder were covered, including keeping your eye slightly back from the Baker's exhaust hole. Sean's introduction to the role necessitated a truncated course in black powder shooting, but nothing could legislate for the sudden change in wind direction as Sean got a good dose of grains in his eye. The producers freaked, filming was suspended for the day as Beano was stood down to rest; paranoia reigned in the production office. We were already up against it with the schedule and budget overruns. It was a minor injury which Sean didn't feel should impact on his post-shoot wind down, but he had to forgo his nightly trip to the bar for fear of being seen partying as usual instead of resting his injury. He got around this by joining the ongoing bacchanalian excess in my room; after partying into the wee hours, Lyndon and I did a secret-service-style sweep of the corridor and staircase, so

Sean could stumble to his suite unseen, one of the many occasions life imitated art on *Sharpe*.

By mid-December we had arrived at the Lisbon Hilton for the rest of the schedule. Our arrival in the Portuguese capital coincided with Bernard Cornwell's first visit to location which, as a newly minted fan of the novels, I was eagerly anticipating. Our first meeting with Bernard was at a restaurant in the famed Alfama district of Lisbon, specialising in fado, the national music of Portugal. All the heads of the departments were present, along with many of the cast and some with their partners. A great night was had by all as we soaked up the music and lashings of *vinho tinto*. When we'd had enough, the group gathered their things and requested the bill. By the time we were ready to leave, the bill, which was taking an inordinate amount of time to sort out, still hadn't arrived. Not that surprising due to the size of our party and the amount we'd imbibed. The bill finally arrived, and we understood quite quickly that the manager had seriously overegged it; that, or we were too drunk. However, we had some sober heads in the group, as well as some Portuguese speakers who, after negotiation, realised the manager was trying to pull a fast one on a bunch of English gringos. We outright refused to pay the inflated bill; instead, dumping a pile of escudos down on a table, more than sufficient in our minds, we motioned for our party to exit.

The restaurant was down in a cellar with the exit at the top of a steep staircase, which we could now see was being locked by a small, scared-looking waiter. This was like a red rag to a bull. Well-oiled and well-stuffed with pent-up anger after numerous rows with my girlfriend, I vaulted up the stairs, wrenched the waiter aside and unbolted the door. I defiantly yanked it open to find a more fearsome-looking dude standing in the street waiting for us armed with a small knife. Before I could raise even an eyebrow, let alone shout 'Chosen Men to me,' I felt a massive shove in my back, forcing me to the pavement, leaving me in the gutter staring at the moon over Lisbon. In a couple of seconds it was all over; our whole party was in the street unharmed, the chap sent to stop us, firmly dispatched. It turns out that Sean, in his haste to protect everyone, shoved me out of the way in order to have a clear run at the enemy; the sight of Sean Bean charging at him with intent made the knife-wielding thug run a mile.

I dusted myself off and noticed that Bernard Cornwell was grinning from ear to ear at witnessing life imitating his art; Sharpe and his men displaying the 'take charge nature' that was expected of the 95th Riflemen. Only later, when recounting the story, did the dangerousness of the incident dawn on me, how it could have possibly led to harm or a night in the cells. But we were fearless and were not going to let anything stand in our way. We had just done hard time in former Soviet Ukraine, in conditions that could make a grown man cry, so a cheating restaurant manager and two shortish chaps, no matter how ugly, weren't going to defeat us. Despite this being an exhilarating adrenaline-filled episode of our off-camera adventures, I began to wonder how much more aggro we would face on this first series. How many more hairy incidents with potentially harmful outcomes would have to be endured on *Sharpe*?

I'M A CHOSEN MAN, GET ME OUT OF HERE

It was a shame my relationship wars couldn't be dealt with as efficiently. I was deeply regretting suggesting my girlfriend join me out in Lisbon. The final humiliation came after a morning of arguments; I say humiliating, yet many onlookers found it absolutely hilarious. Extricating myself from the ongoing skirmish, I reported downstairs for my transport to work. Unfortunately the minivan taking us to location was parked directly under my room three floors above. I boarded the bus, relieved to escape the conflict, joking with those on board that I had just dodged a bullet; as I uttered my last syllable an item of clothing hit the pavement in front of our minivan. At first, I didn't realise where it came from until I recognised one of my T-shirts hitting the pavement; the entire bus looked up to see my girlfriend gleefully tossing my clothes out of the window onto the wet Lisbon street. I jumped out of the minivan to grab my clothing while begging the driver to leave immediately, but we were still waiting for one tardy actor to arrive before departing. The mortifyingly embarrassing moment seemed to last forever, but the actors on the bus were really tickled by it, particularly Brian Cox who sported an ear-to-ear grin and eyes that twinkled with delight.

The tardy actor finally arrived, I scooped up the remains of my wardrobe now covering the road and we made haste for the highway. Eventually, the on-board mickey-taking ceased and we settled down for the long trip south to a location across the Tagus River on the traffic-choked 25 de Abril suspension bridge. The morning's strife melted away as our location came into view, the beautiful church at Cabo Espichel, where all monastery exteriors from *Rifles* were to be shot. Once the Chosen Men had completed their fleeting appearance at the top of the scene, we took cover in our minivan, where Daragh informed me that overruns meant we weren't going to finish by Christmas, requiring a return after Boxing Day to wrap. Daragh hadn't earned the name Paddy World News for nothing.

Of course, the Portuguese leg of our first tour of duty wasn't all dark clouds and discord; in spite of the rough seas we'd faced, we never missed the opportunity to squeeze maximum fun out of whatever situation we might be in. I have wonderful memories of shooting scenes featuring the Chosen Men on their down time trading quips and banter, helping to further the development of our characters. Much of the action was shot in historic Lisbon with many scenes involving the Chosen Men in taverns. The memory of the incense-like smell of the pellets in the smoke machine has never left me – monastery herbs according to Daragh. With all the drinking, singing and fraternising with the locals – a bit like our day-to-day life in the Crimea – it's no wonder I look back warmly at parts of the Lisbon shoot.

Of course, this being *Sharpe*, there would be one more bump in the road before our Christmas Eve departure and I didn't mean metaphorically. On the drive to location somewhere in the countryside we encountered a chillingly unforgettable traffic accident. Sano, being a native of Lisbon, was able to drive herself to location from her house; this particular morning she had Assumpta in the passenger seat as she sped along the highway followed by the Chosen Man minivan. Suddenly, we noticed the traffic starting to thicken and eventually slow down to a trickle, prompting curses at whatever it was keeping us from our delicious on-set breakfast. Pretty soon we saw that the jam was the result of a road accident. As our transport inched past the wreck, we came upon the shocking sight of Sano's overturned car in a ditch by the side of the highway. It had been raining torrentially and, as she was late, I imagine Sano was driving pretty swiftly. Thankfully for all concerned, Assumpta came away with only minor injuries while Sano sustained a case of whiplash, requiring a neck brace, but nothing to keep her out of action for long. The shit would have hit the fan back in London had the leading lady been put out of action. As a result of this incident, actors were banned from driving independently to location due to insurance cover; first a ban on playing football, now this. Soon we'd be living in a nanny state!

At least the genuine accident put into perspective the car crash of my relationship, where very soon I wouldn't have the buffer of *Sharpe* to shield me. The time came for us to return to home for Christmas; my girlfriend and I were on a different flight from the rest of the crew, so I came down to the lobby to say my farewells to the unit. Possibly a good move as being confined on a plane with plenty of alcohol could have brought on another clothing defenestration-like incident; any chance to embarrass me in front of the unit would be gleefully grabbed.

FREE AT LAST, FREE AT LAST

Needless to say, Christmas in London wasn't particularly merry; apart from catching up on sleep, all I could think of was getting back on a Lisbon-bound plane to be reunited with my new-found family to complete the job started what seemed like years ago. Fortunately, that came on 27 December when we once again convened at Heathrow to complete principal photography on the first season of *Sharpe*. From our base in sunny Cascais, we would film the thrilling and ferocious Sharpe–Harper barn fight in an abandoned farmhouse a little way out of town. In a strange quirk of scheduling, this scene had been the first action tackled upon arrival in the Crimea back in the first week of August. A scene shot in two different countries with two different actors in the lead. Here, on a cool, sunny morning on the Iberian Peninsula all of us were comfortable in our *Sharpe* skins. We had overcome a never-ending litany of troubles, we now had an indefatigable director at the helm who genuinely loved the show; and, of course, we had Sean Bean. Comparing the two shooting days highlighted the progress we'd made these past four months, a sort of tale of two barn fights.

I could see Sean was in his element during fight scenes, not holding back with his grappling and thrown punches, getting stuck in with full-throttle aggression. This was in marked contrast to the way Daragh handled combat scenes, with more of a cautious, safety-first approach, preferring camera angles and fakery; no mad look in the eyes that I could see in Sean. In the episode, Sharpe has to fight Harper to prevent him leading a mutiny while also trying to impress upon the Chosen Men that he, Richard Sharpe, is the man they should follow. After filming that scene, I for one was certainly convinced.

For some reason, production was holding the wrap party at a top night spot with a day or two of filming still to complete. I felt we had marked so many farewells so far on this shoot; the Crimean wrap party at the Rotunda of Gastronomy had been enough for me, and this one felt a bit of an anticlimax. Lyndon and I left the club around midnight, walking through town to our hotel, where we went up to Sean's suite for a private wrap party, intending it to be a quickie as our call time was at eight the next morning. Time flew by as we chewed over what we had just gone through these past twenty-two weeks. Sean said he was going to insist there was a lot more interaction with the Chosen Men, if a second series got green-lit, as well as demand a general upgrade in our circumstances – especially the food situation if we ever landed back in the Crimea. We talked in circles all night, affirming the pride we had in our work and our desire to create a legend. At about 7 a.m., just after our bottle of Jim Beam ran dry, we thought it best to get ready to be in reception for our transport to work. As Lyndon and I were unsteadily exiting the suite, Sean started to rehearse, rewrite and refine the speech he gives to the Chosen Men after defeating Harper in the barn fight due to be shot that morning. I was full of admiration for his commitment to the cause.

And that's how my first *Sharpe* campaign concluded, a little later than anticipated and with a few more casualties then we would have wanted. We had wrapped in the relative comfort of Portugal, but had done hard time on the Crimean Peninsula making 1992 a bit of an *annus horribilis*; much as it had been for our dear Queen. We had completed principal photography on the first series in what was a true survival of the fittest; now it was time to wait till spring to find out if all the tumult had been worth it and if we were at the dawn of something rather large.

GREEN, GREEN GRASS

Of course, in early 1993 the success of *Sharpe* was far from a sure thing. There hadn't been a Napoleonic-era drama since the first original series of *Poldark* shot in the mid-1970s, certainly nothing set in the Napoleonic Wars. Our executive producers had been put firmly on the ITV naughty step on account of the record-breaking insurance claim, another fact that could have stood in the way of

Sharpe returning for a second series. Of course, if the ratings were high, none of that would matter. I was confident we had a hit on our hands. I even idly began compiling a mental list of what I would need for the next Crimean tour.

Sharpe's fame was still a little way off and the impact of the upheaval, bad food and perpetual peril over twenty-two weeks hit me like a ton of bricks. After one more argument with my girlfriend, I put an end to our turbulent relationship.

Tales of our exploits had become rife, with rumours galore swirling around the industry. At many castings I fielded questions about my *Sharpe* experiences: the McGann injury, the food, the weather, and the gangsters. Outside of work, life began to revolve around the *Sharpe* family; our shared experience of hardship and upheaval had served to bond us much like a regular army unit who'd seen heavy combat; or possibly more aptly, like convicts who'd shared a long stretch inside.

Fellow inmate, second assistant director Sam Craddock, kept us informed of any production developments. Early on, I gleaned that scripts for *Company*, *Enemy* and *Honour* had been commissioned; this didn't guarantee a second series would be green-lit, but it was a good indicator. Day-to-day life continued to be *Sharpe*-themed as I carried on immersing myself in the novels, eagerly devouring the stories charting the possible path our characters could take, not that Harris was originally written into the novels – that came with *Sharpe's Battle* in 1995 – but I could see the general direction of travel the Chosen Men might take and it wasn't pretty.

April the 22nd came around, a day I was looking forward to like a kid longs for Christmas; the day of the cast and crew screening, where we would see if all the blood, sweat, tears, faeces, vomit, gut-rot, enemas and general deprivation had been worth it. I was dying to see the general look of the show and how much Chosen Men action had escaped the cutting-room floor. We sat in the darkened screening room, the *Sharpe* theme boomed out and soon Private Sharpe had saved Wellington from being skewered by the French, deftly taking out three French cavalrymen one by one, and soon I was swept up in the story, completely forgetting I was watching something I appeared in.

After a recalibration of our alcohol intake and a time-killing drive around London eating McDonald's in a stretch limousine hired by Lyndon, we returned for an evening screening where the assembled members of the press viewed the fruits of our toil. After the screening a press conference was held; we were half anticipating and totally willing to field a question or two from the gentlemen of the press, but when we saw the top table only had chairs for Sean, Daragh, Tom, Malcolm and Muir we realised nobody really wanted to hear from us. We slunk despondently from the press conference to wait for Sean to finish up; doubts about how integral we were to the show began creeping back into my thinking. I was hoping *Sharpe* could be my big career break, catapulting me to another level; but sitting waiting for Sean, I realised that particular dream might be a bit overambitious. With interviews over, Sharpe and some of his Chosen Men took a stretch limo ride to my flat.

As we arrived, Paul Trussell started making his excuses to leave as he wasn't a fan of the type of hangover a Chosen night out could result in. As Paul trudged almost forlornly down the road to his nearby flat, I knew there was another reason he was separating himself from us: I was seeing the first casualty of the early dismantling of the Chosen Men. A second series wasn't a foregone conclusion, but the indications were that we were odds-on to go again. But before a second series actually got commissioned, Paul had been offered a part in a Mike Leigh play, a fantastic job with quite a long contract. You don't really turn down Mike Leigh when he comes knocking, even if you have the prospect of *Sharpe* on the horizon. Paul started leaning towards taking the theatre job despite me almost begging him not to, assuring him *Sharpe* could run and run; at least as long as Bernard's books lasted, or we were killed in the story. And although it was an honour to work with the great Mike Leigh, I knew *Sharpe* had quality written all over it and was destined for legendary status.

Paul wasn't convinced, and now I knew deep down from his premature exit that he had decided to take up the theatre offer, declining the chance of continuing on *Sharpe*. It wasn't all to do with Mike Leigh, though. Paul felt horribly let down by the management when dealing with the myriad difficulties faced out in the Crimea. Those in the know felt there was another, more emotionally driven reason for abandoning the *Sharpe* carnival: Assumpta Serna and the close of their relationship. This is probably the real reason Tongue didn't reappear for the second series, robbing us of a very distinctive Chosen Man. As the novels progressed Teresa gets bumped off; if Paul could have endured some temporary heartache, in return he might have had a good run on the show. I felt very sad. Paul was one of my main crew on year one; at least until Assumpta arrived on the scene.

IT WAS THE DAWNING OF A NEW ERA

At eight in the evening on Wednesday 5 May, *Sharpe's Rifles* aired, followed one week later by 'Eagle'; the secret was out, now the ratings and the man on the street would let us know if we had a hit on our hands. The viewing figures told the story; the average audience of the early shows was up to ten million and a 52 per cent share of the viewing audience. *Sharpe* was also cleverly scheduled in the Wednesday evening slot normally reserved for the Champions League, so much of the same audience was retained.

A few days later, I received a mysterious and slightly unnerving letter containing a newspaper article with a photo crudely hacked together almost in the manner of a ransom note. The photo showed a footballer scoring a goal with the headline '███████ IS FLEECED BY JASON'; a cut-out photo of Harris's head was stuck onto the footballer. Nothing handwritten, no return address, just the newspaper cut-out with the surname of the actual footballer, Wilcox, redacted, so the photo caption read 'WONDERFUL █████ – Jason █████ slots home for Blackburn's opening win ...'. The letter didn't arrive via my agent, but came straight to my home address, prompting worries that some deranged yet creative fan knew where I lived; it was a mystery that lingered for some time.

Although safe in the knowledge that another campaign was imminent with preparations for a second tour well under way, frustratingly none of the Chosen Men's agents had been called with a contract offer. An option to sign for a second series was never inserted into our contracts, as they tried to do with Brian Cox's, but he refused, either not wanting to be part of a long-running series or because he knew a lucrative stint in Hollywood lay just around the corner. Production probably felt sure that the Chosen Men wouldn't dare turn down a return to action, therefore we could be contracted at the very last minute.

At the time, I hadn't cottoned onto this, as I was wholly smitten with my little place in potential TV history, though the full force of this policy became apparent with subsequent contract negotiations. However, back then I was only concentrating on being the best Chosen Man on screen as well as the most adaptable survivor of life in post-Soviet Ukraine. Joining us on this year's tour was Pete Postlethwaite, who called to tell me he had been made an offer of two episodes as Obadiah Hakeswill and how much money should he ask for. I told him what the likes of Daragh and Assumpta were on, so he should tell his agent to use that as a guide. I was also very happy Malcolm had followed the advice offered that wintery day outside the Dimerdji nursery school. I had spent a fair amount of time with Pete five years earlier and I knew he was going to have a massive impact both on and off screen.

ON THE CAMPAIGN TRAIL

June rolled around and Sharpe Film finally contracted me at a 25 per cent pay rise, a welcome sign that my contribution was appreciated. Now virtual plans for a second tour could be put into effect with the first step being the purchase of a massive silver trunk, of the size you'd deploy for a world cruise on an ocean liner. The mistakes of the past would not be repeated; the lack of home comforts would not be the problem on the long Crimean tour ahead. Sadly, news on the grapevine told us of many first-campaign veterans who were not being asked back for a second tour. I knew it would be hard to assemble the exact same crew as the previous year as, unlike actors, members of the other departments are constantly busy with work. To me, it seemed wise to retain most of the battle-hardened crew from the previous tour capable of dealing with the extremes experienced on a Crimean tour; to say nothing of the camaraderie developed in overcoming that strife.

In mid-July, with almost a month till embarkation day, I made my first visit to Sean's house in Muswell Hill; Mel Hill, Sean's then wife, always made Chosen Men very welcome. Not only is she a talented, engaging actress, she's a warm, witty and intelligent woman to boot. I arrived a little early and Mel showed me down to what I would come to know as party central: the kitchen. We sat chatting while Sean was out at the shops. Mel told me she was overjoyed that the comradeship between Sharpe and his Chosen Men had spilled over to Civvy Street and valued the support we demonstrated for Sean when he first landed the part.

Beano got back from the high street looked rather pleased. I enquired, why? 'I've just paid off the mortgage!' he declared. Even though I wasn't a homeowner, I knew how wonderful that was. Sean didn't do a lot of unnecessary talking, a man of few words, never trying to dominate the conversation unlike many of the regulars on *Sharpe*. My pre-*Sharpe* impression of Sean came from viewing him in films such as *Stormy Monday* and *Patriot Games*; to me he was a cool, brash, blond hunk. The Sean I got to know was completely at odds with my ill-informed preconceptions. There was a hidden, sensitive side to Sean, a more artistic, creative side to his character that was fully revealed when he showed me up to his study. At one end of the room sat a sturdy antique desk, all walnut and green leather, next to an upright piano which Sean could play convincingly. What really debunked the clichéd view of hard-man Bean was an absolutely passable oil painting of a landscape set on an easel which – you guessed it – had been whipped up by Sean himself.

I soon moved onto full-scale preparation for another tour of

Sharpe, rising each morning with a huge smile on my face and a bounce in my step, in anticipation of turning more of Bernard's novels into television episodes. There was also the possibility of a reunion with Yalta native, Natasha the interpreter; so, lots to look forward to in the immediate future. Preparations officially kicked off with an appointment with the new costume designer, Robin Fraser Paye; more of a meet and greet than a fitting as my uniform was constituted from the same ensemble of rags I had worn in the previous series.

With costume sorted, I had an appointment with the Sharpe medic, Dr Gaynor, who jabbed me with all the inoculations I had endured in the run-up to *Sharpe* One. The final act of preparation for the second series was a visit to Sean's Muswell Hill local, the Heights, where Lyndon and I foolishly tried to keep up with the Yorkshire Lad, returning home just as the first chirps of birdsong erupted. Luckily there was a day of rest before we set off on our second *Sharpe* campaign.

2

BACK ON THE ROAD AGAIN

I n a classic case of tempting fate, production had chosen Friday 13 August as embarkation day for the second series. With a charter flight taking us directly onto the Crimean Peninsula, already an improvement on last year, things were looking up. In no time we were airside and sitting waiting while our luggage was taken onto the plane. At least that was the plan! We quickly learned our Ukrainian Airways charter hadn't even left Simferopol yet, meaning we would be waiting at least four hours before boarding. I shouldn't have been surprised; did I think the Crimea had miraculously got its shit together in the eight months we'd been away?

We had to endure nearly six hours of hanging around Stansted, a brand-new airport then, allowing plenty of time to acquaint ourselves with the new regulars like Michael Byrne – it was hard not to see him as the maniacal Nazi in *Raiders of the Lost Ark* – taking the role of exploring officer Nairn. Another debutante was Diana Perez playing Harper's girlfriend, Ramona; in the novels, she's called Isabella. Was the screenwriter properly briefed by the producers concerning the basic facts of the main characters? Apparently not.

Diana is a London-based, Colombian actress, full of energy and always on the go; physically, she slightly reminded me of the unfortunate Diana Peñalver, the McGann-era Teresa. Completing the new talent ascending the jetway was the terribly posh, highly inquisitive, real-life Baronet, Jeremy Child, who immediately took umbrage at us calling him Jezzer. Jezzer was playing Sir Augustus Farthingdale, so at least he would have the pleasure of playing Liz Hurley's husband in *Sharpe's Enemy*.

The flight was fairly sedate compared with previous charters, possibly down to waiting almost half a day to take off. Inside the cabin I got an early sensory blast of the smells of Ukraine; the plane's interior was grime-spattered and permeated by the smoke of cheap Soviet tobacco. The toilet looked like it had been transported unaltered from an Alphabet City crack house. Apparently, the airline charged production around twenty thousand dollars for the pleasure of delivering the unit to Simferopol. You would have thought they could have splashed out some of that on a new toilet seat. Air Ukraine had actually made a small stab at in-flight service with westernish-looking snacks washed down with unremarkable Crimean red wine. Arriving in Simferopol we could see sure signs of improvement in the form of a new terminal building under construction. We were met by our Association fixer, Igor Nossov, who made our transit to the bus swift and painless, no doubt facilitated by a backhander or two directed in the right places.

I didn't notice much improvement as we drove through the streets of the Crimean capital; it still looked pretty awful even in the bright summer sunshine. I suppose commencing the shoot in the armpit of the Crimea was a worst first scenario, designed so that we would be particularly grateful when decamping to Yalta. The real reason was the rates for Yalta's sanatoria were reduced on 1 September, so we had to reside in Simplyawful till then. Checking in at the Moscow Hotel again felt bizarrely like a homecoming; management had put their Sharpe dollars to good use with the addition of a casino and slot machines lining the lobby; the rest of the building was just as worn and neglected as it was when we'd arrived almost exactly a year ago.

I set about fitting out my room with the contents of my huge silver trunk, including a sound system, VHS and mobile kitchen. I was living by the Chosen Man code, adapt, improvise and overcome; whatever crap got thrown at me on the outside, I could take refuge in my home away from home. Positive reports were circulating about our new caterers, Set Meals, who had managed to dash out something edible; I also noticed a mobile kitchen parked in front of the hotel, meaning the elusive on-location cooked breakfast would be a reality. All hail the heroes of the Dimerdji Bacon Riot.

Our first Saturday in-country passed uneventfully as we were in recovery mode after the journey. The unrelenting heat was broken by a good old London-style downpour; I didn't remember it raining last time we were there in August. In the evening, veterans of the first tour gathered in Sean's suite for an inaugural bacchanalian session. Mightily fuelled up, we steamed on all night about what needed to be done to make this production a success, taking *Sharpe* to a revered status in the eyes of the public. I argued we were well on the way to achieving that. We debated ITV's decision to scrap the 'letter box' format on screen which allows the viewer to watch the picture in wide screen, framed exactly the way the director intended. Apparently, the sponsors complained that viewers couldn't concentrate on the commercials because of their eyes not adjusting to the full screen. There had also been letters from viewers complaining about the use of electric guitars in the episode's incidental music, especially when Los Pecos and the Needle take centre stage, claiming (I imagine) that electric guitars are anachronistic, but I thought they had really added to the coolness of the show. As witnessed a couple of decades later in the ultra-hip series *Peaky Blinders*.

The following day a group of us including Jeremy Childs, Assumpta and Mike Mears went on a tour of Simferopol led by a chap called Sacha, a journalist/lawyer who materialised at our hotel, possibly on the make, possibly KGB. We didn't know, but his English was very good, so we told him the places in town we wanted to visit, mainly shops. We took a trolley bus, the omnipresent mode of transport for the Soviet Union; built in the fifties with faded red and beige livery, you couldn't help but notice them. Unless of course you were waiting to board one; then they were like London buses, none for ages then three come along at once. Costing barely tuppence to ride, the trolley buses were very popular with Simferopudlians, making for a tightly packed, sweaty journey. Despite having one Crimean campaign under my belt, that was my first trolley-bus ride; at the time it felt like a suitably touristy activity, but from then on I always settled for the taxi option.

Our first stop took us to Bradley's of London, Simferopol branch, a hard-currency shop resembling a 1980s Housing Trust charity shop: drab and uninviting. Nevertheless, it sold many of the essentials westerners desired, like batteries, Kodak film, aspirin, cans of Coca-Cola and Snickers Bars; our teeth would take a pounding but at least we would have some home comforts. If you were a local, the favourite snack was salted unshelled sunflower seeds or *semichki*. I was astounded at the widespread love for *semichki*; it was the sort of stuff we used to feed hamsters in primary school. They were on sale everywhere, usually wrapped in a little cone of paper, often yesterday's newspaper, and incessantly munched by gold-toothed babushkas waiting at bus stops, market stalls or on the seafront.

The new spirit of free enterprise had been wholly embraced as we passed street vendors of varying levels of sophistication; I bought a set of kitchen knives from one chap though he seemed too proud or stupid to take my US currency. In among the street vendors roamed pairs of smart-looking western men dressed in dark blue suits. Could they be CIA field agents? No, too obvious. As I got a little closer, I could hear they were Americans spreading the Book of Mormon; things really were changing round here. Next stop, a black-market money changer where you generally got the best rates. We had to be careful this year as Phil Elton had already been arrested outside Yalta bazaar and held for a couple of hours after being caught illegally swapping his dollars for coupons. We accessed this currency exchange via an alley down the side of an Orthodox church. Once inside the building we discovered the money counter was at the back of a room showing porn on a TV screen. With that seedy episode out of the way, our new friend Sacha took us to a 'flourishing, free' bookstall which resembling a second-hand bookshop piled high with bargain-basement books.

Sacha highlighted one of the beautiful ironies so prevalent in the CIS (Commonwealth of Independent States); three years earlier, he had written articles denouncing the sleazy videotaped 'entertainment' featured at the 'bureau de change', even going as far as assisting the militia – that's what the police are called – in prosecuting the owner of this porno 'theatre' establishment. Now he was willingly delivering us to the self-same den of filth to do business with the porno kingpin. As Sacha saw us to the trolley-bus stop, he warned us in his impeccable English that the militia, although seemingly in charge of law and order, believed it to be the solemn duty of the criminal fraternity, who they are in cahoots with, to rip off westerners at every opportunity. On that cheery note we jumped on the No. 2 trolley bus back to the Moscow Hotel. Maybe Sacha was in with the criminals, maybe he was an ex-KGB spy; whatever he was, as a savvy Londoner I'm not easily played by a con.

RETURN OF THE PACK

We arrived at a location called Belogorsk to tackle the first day of principal photography on series two with the opening scene of *Enemy*. It was a bummer that we were entering our second tour minus crucial members from the first campaign; most keenly felt by me was the absence of Rifleman Tongue, founder member of the Chosen Men, a very small club and now 20 per cent lighter. An equally devastating loss was the refusal of Brian Cox to sign up. Brian, along with David Troughton, had expressed determination never to be anywhere near *Sharpe* in the Crimea again. A great shame as Cox and Troughton were a powerful duo, acting practically everyone else off the screen. We may have lost talented stalwarts from the first campaign, but in year two they'd secured some great new, very well-known talent including Pete Postlethwaite, Alice Krige and the aforementioned Mike Byrne, playing Nairn.

Three episodes were scheduled this time, 'Company', 'Enemy' and 'Honour', stories I'd committed to memory and was keenly looking forward to. So, within eight months of us wrapping on the first series, we were back in the sweltering armpit of the Crimea, Simferopol, a little older but also a little wiser about surviving *Sharpe* in the Ukraine, with the man playing our eponymous hero taking it all in his stride. It was evident Sean was much more comfortable in his 'Sharpe skin'. This time he was nobody's replacement, had a series under his belt and had received the approval of the viewing public there could be no mistaking: Sean Bean *was* Richard Sharpe. Beano also began to flex his star muscle, with production giving him a personal driver and his own personal assistant, Guy Pugh, a Cambridge graduate, fluent in Russian. Guy worked really hard, was great to have around and, as Sean still shared an ex-Red Army canvas tent with us, it meant Guy was on hand to help the Chosen Men with the odd translation or two.

Back on set it felt like I'd never been away, with everything so familiar and, dare I say it, normal: strapping Ukrainian squaddies lounging around location, neat rows of little white tents, our Muscovite costume lady, Helen Khramova, talking fifty to the dozen at me in Russian and the fierce heat of the Crimean sun. I couldn't help noticing that filming began exactly a year to the day since the ill-fated game of football. Belogorsk, our new location, had echoes of previous *Sharpe* backdrops, like Chufut-Kale and Eskikermen, cliffs hewn from jutting outcrops of chalky rock. Belogorsk, or 'White Mountain', looked as if the white cliffs of Dover had abruptly sprung up in relatively flat terrain. On a clifftop sat our base camp, located on a wide plateau bereft of any trees, leaving us no natural shade from the oppressive heat. This year the actors could relax in modern, French-made nylon tents that wouldn't have been out of place on a campsite in the Dordogne; we weren't sure if they'd stand up to the worst the Crimean weather threw at them, but at least aesthetically they were more appealing than our Red Army canvas tents, which were still utilised for wardrobe, make-up and the dining 'hall'.

The first action saw Sir Augustus Farthingdale's arrival at camp to find Sharpe engaging in a game of rugby with his Chosen Men, much to Sir Augustus's disgust; a scene reminiscent of Major Dunnett interrupting the Sharpe–Harper barn fight in *Rifles*. If a scene works once, why not try it again, eh? The opening days of this tour ran very smoothly; the local camera crew were much more efficient, as was the costume department. There were new appointees, an English camera crew led by Arthur Wooster, veteran director of photography, and stunt coordinator Dinny Powell, uncle of Greg from the previous campaign. The sound department remained unchanged with Chris Wrangler in charge, assisted by his Israeli boom operator, David Lis. The props were still being attended to by *Sharpe* veteran Colin Thurston. It was all change in the make-up department; much to our chagrin our lovely lassies from Lisbon, Sano and Margarida Miranda, had been dropped. Newly appointed Penny Smith, renowned in her field, had worked on *Lady Chatterley's Lover* with Sean, and her assistant, Charmaine Gruhn, really weren't fully prepared for what was about to hit them.

A tearful confrontation in my room with Charmaine brought it all to a head. Just days into the shoot and already we had dramas. A make-up department appointee I heartily approved of was their choice of interpreter, the lovely Natasha Lakhmaniuk, making the early-morning arrival to the make-up chair just that little bit sweeter. Also joining the make-up team was Tom Clegg's daughter Fiona; they weren't afraid of a little nepotism on *Sharpe*, but from past experience the offspring of the powers were some of the hardest working on the unit.

The inaugural working week ended with our first night shoot; a pleasurable evening's work making for a relaxed time on set and giving new regular Diana Perez, playing Ramona, her first run out. More 'Enemy' cast arrived in-country, including Phil Whitchurch, cast as Frederickson, a regular in the novels, and the man I only knew as Young Sherlock Holmes, Nicholas Rowe, here to play Rocket Man, Captain Gilliard. I knew Frederickson, or Sweet William, was a serious character central to *Sharpe*, almost as close a friend to Sharpe as Harper. I never for one moment saw him as a slapstick comedy character, which seemed to be production's vision; adorning Frederickson with a ridiculous comedy wig, eye patch and false teeth. More 'Pirates of the Crimea' than Sharpe in the peninsula.

The shoot whizzed by and we were back at the hotel by midnight. At that hour, the sensible move would have been to hit the hay, especially as I was day-tripping to Yalta later that morning. However, we were pretty euphoric at being reunited so a gathering on the fourth-floor lounge ensued. An hour later Sean, trailed by Daragh, joined the party, quickly followed by Assumpta, Diana, Jezzer, Guy and the camera boys. At 3 a.m. a triumvirate of swarthy Russians, each dressed in a leather jacket and garish shell-suit ensemble, took a shine to our get-together. Fortunately, we had Sean's PA Guy on hand, who sacrificed himself by going off to their suite for a friendly, Russian-style greeting drink. Poor Guy, I didn't see him again that night; he really took one for the team. I called it a night just before dawn thoroughly scrambled on duty-free whisky.

I rose with comparative ease considering the previous night's fun, raring to revisit Yalta, the Soviet Riviera and our home for the majority of this shoot. The next morning Lyndon, Mike Mears and I loaded into a minibus with Jeremy Childs to show him around Yalta and check out our new accommodation, the Chernomore (Black Sea) sanatorium. Our erstwhile home, the Rossiya sanatorium, weren't overly impressed by some of our habits during our tenancy, resulting in their management prohibitively hiking the rates this time around. After checking our new digs, we trawled through all the old shopping haunts, even discovering a new German hard-currency supermarket selling boxes of Kellogg's Frosties for ten bucks a pop. Yalta was positively buzzing, jammed like Oxford Street at Christmas; then again, it was a seaside resort in mid-August. With business concluded, we stopped at the Yalta Hotel, where we supped some well-earned draught beer before heading up the main highway to hell, or Simferopol as the locals knew it.

RUMBLES OF DISCONTENT

By 24 August, we were experiencing some of the warmest weather we'd encountered during our time in the Crimea and some of the old bugbears began to raise their ugly heads. On location we were shooting the scenes involving the deployment of Congreve rockets, action that saw the Chosen Men rendered mute in the background, which began to grate as temperatures hit 33° Celsius. We were called for 8:30 with which we duly complied; as we stood on set gently broiling in the heat, we noticed the horses which were needed in shot were slowly ambling towards the camera. When I realised second assistant Marc Jenny had called us to set even before the horses, I flipped out. It seemed the pen-pushing schedule-makers saw us as minor in importance, slightly lower in rank than the equine cast.

It wasn't a new phenomenon, it was a familiar gripe; the Chosen

81

Men were seen not as individuals but as an entity, a thing to position and shuffle around like a piece of scenery or a cannon. Last year our primary concern had been with survival, both physical and mental; as well as concerns for our place in the *Sharpe* pecking order. After the success of year one, particularly the positive feedback the Chosen Men received, we thought we were due a little respect from production. The Bacon Riot hackles began to rise within me; I made my displeasure known to Tom and Marc, which I thought would calm me down, but it just served to rile me even more. Eventually we were stood down to our tent, which told me we hadn't really needed to be on set at that time. Maybe it was stupid of me to think the job we'd done on the last tour would have bought us a little credit with the powers; but production minimised our importance. We weren't feeling the dividend of success, in terms of either involvement or respect, and only slightly financially. I was well and truly hacked off, writing in the diary: '... so, I'm saying this in print! No *Sharpe* Three for me, unless of course they throw dosh galore at me. Which of course they won't.'

We remembered all too well how last year we were used as background dressing with precious few lines of dialogue, barely reacting when a Chosen reaction was absolutely required. Mike Mears began to call us the Chosen Flock, partly because of the fact that we were grouped together like a bunch of sheep, but also because we were often used as wallpaper to adorn the rear of the frame. Proud though we were to be part of our closely bonded Chosen group, we were also adamant we were a team made up of four distinctive parts capable of operating as individuals, but strongest as a team; this had been played out both in front of and off camera.

With all-out revolution postponed, we kicked back at the hotel, turning the fourth-floor corridor into a chill-out zone. From the far end of the corridor a female form could be seen approaching. It was Liz Hurley, looking like a normal woman, not the on-screen goddess image I had of her, but nevertheless lovely, gravitating effortlessly to her rightful place, at the centre of a group of adoring males. She arrived looking rather disconcerted; not that surprising as your first taste of Simplyawful could be more than a little unsettling. But it wasn't the thought of having to exist out here in the Crimea that left her distraught; preying on her mind was the fact she felt Sean Bean was immune to her charms.

Before we had the pleasure of Liz's presence, Daragh told me of a little walk he took with her where he told her the lads were positively salivating at the prospect of her arrival. I guess she might have assumed Sean was one of those lads. The inhabitants of the fourth-floor corridor, chiefly me, feigned no such lack of interest, placing her in a position of near-adoration within our 'club'. I assured Liz that Sean wasn't very outgoing – unless he'd had a few bevvies – in fact he was almost shy. He never sought female company, preferring a bar full of the lads; never once did I see him take advantage of his heart-throb status, and anyway he was married. And like you, Liz, you don't really need to fancy anyone when everyone fancies you; this last bit I didn't have the courage to say to her face. To our glee, Liz was an Olympic Champion Flirt, a sport at which we all became happily proficient. Of course, her concerns were purely professional, as in the story her character, Lady Farthingdale, spends a night of passion with Sharpe. Never had I wanted to be Sharpe more than now.

As delightful as it was having Liz on the team, it soon came time to shoot the emotionally draining funeral scene of a major show regular: Teresa Moreno. Teresa's burial site at Belogorsk was truly spectacular; high on a chalky cliff overlooking a lush valley dotted with farmhouses. Arranged in file on the cliff were the 60th Rifles flanked by the Chosen Men and Los Pecos, Teresa's guerrillas, and a battery of Congreve rockets all primed and ready. Perhaps a little too primed. In the story of 'Enemy' the army top brass didn't at first embrace the rockets, as it was felt they were too unpredictable; the same was proving true with our rockets created by our pyrotechnicians, Gobi and Dima. The day before, an errant missile had landed on the roof of a set, rapidly setting fire to it; fortunately, only a camera dolly – used to roll a camera down a track – was housed inside, saved heroically by a hulking Ukrainian chap. Today, a wayward rocket had glided off course, setting fire to a patch of grass across the gorge perilously close to our lunch tent; in the end football fields of dry brush were scorched. Fears of the *Sharpe* jinx inevitably lurked in all our minds. Ironically, the same erratic targeting of the rockets mirrored what happened in the 'Enemy' script when several projectiles missed their targets, one almost taking out Sharpe and Harper.

As the schedule trundled on, there was a changing of the guard in the acting department. We bade a temporary farewell to the naturally charming Nick Rowe who had fitted in splendidly to Camp Sharpe, embracing all the fun on offer while doing the business on camera every time. Next inmate due was Helena Michell, and flying in with Helena was my casting recommendation for Obadiah Hakeswill. A party was laid on for the outgoing cast, with a decent amount of grog, but not enough to put on a Sharpe-style buzz. I was wasted enough to acquire a cherry-tomato-sized blister on my nose after horsing around with Mike Byrne who I'd noticed possessed a penchant for mischief. While play-fighting I got Mike in a headlock; to extricate himself he pinched my nose a little too excessively, leaving me with a throbbing schnozzle which he seemed quite proud of. I tried to shake the smirk off his face, telling him he'd better go down to production to explain how a regular cast member had been disfigured. After detecting a tiny flicker of worry, I laughingly assuring him that production wouldn't care if a Chosen Man lost an eye as long as he could show up to decorate the back of a shot with the horses.

I rose early on Sunday morning to ride in the car sent to get Pete Postlethwaite and Helena from the airport. Pete walked into the humming terminal building looking none the worse for wear since we last laid eyes on each other, which had been on a ward in King's College Hospital in the spring of 1989 where he was recovering from testicular cancer. Helena, playing Sarah Dubreton, was pleasantly surprised at this unexpected welcome; on the ride back to our hotel I briefed them on what they could expect from a stretch on *Sharpe*. Once they'd settled in and met the rest of the unit we were joined by Liz Hurley and 'baby boy' – Liz's name for Lyndon – for cups of tea and tuna melts on my balcony capped off with a bottle of red wine; that was as soft an arrival in the Crimea as you could ask for. A welcome provided by campaign veterans who recognised the challenges of a long stint in the Crimea and, though Liz and Helena weren't staying long, Pete would be with us out on location for almost ten weeks.

FORLORN HOPE

Pete's arrival coincided with a light work week for the Chosen, allowing us to show him the ropes. This mostly consisted of chilling out with Lyndon in my room while listening to Dylan, Floyd and Led Zep: a bit like university really. On the schedule we were combining episodes with scenes from 'Company' and 'Honour' on the call sheet; this meant the imminent arrival of our new Wellington, Hugh Fraser, joined by other 'Company' cast members. I had been looking forward to the challenge of recreating the Siege of Badajoz; that's until I saw the script, not written this time by Eoghan Harris, a writer who had established the informal, often humorous way Sharpe, Harper and the Chosen interacted. Eoghan's scripts gave life to the Chosen Men, made them more three-dimensional, freeing them up from clichéd costume drama speech. 'Company' script was diametrically opposite; the Chosen Men are almost mute or uttering strange broken sentences which didn't fit clever-clogs Harris. Trouble was, the script has been penned by respected screen writer Charles Wood, veteran of stage, television and silver screen with credits including the Beatles film *Help!*, *The Charge of the Light Brigade* and *Tumbledown*; so, because of the last two, he knew his way around stories with a military theme. For Charles Wood, foot soldiers in the Napoleonic Wars weren't well spoken and nor did they converse on equal terms with their superior officers. This problem was compounded by Tom Clegg's reverence for Wood, treating his script like a sacred text; it was going to be tough times ahead for this Chosen Man. At least I had the comfort of my burgeoning relationship with Natasha to ward off the negatives of life on tour in the Crimea.

On 2 September we arrived at the spectacular Chufut-Kale with a change of episode on the call sheet from 'Enemy' to 'Company'; I could see they were pulling out all the stops for 'Company': multiple wagons, horses and every extra they could muster. Very Cecil B.

DeMille! The action saw Wellington and his staff followed by a whole baggage train rumbling across the countryside; the scope of the scene was impressively epic, very much like a proper feature film. At lunch, our new caterers, Set Meals, whipped up three epic courses, making filming on location with *Sharpe* so much more palatable. However, I was starting to get the first grumbles of the intestinal strife that had beset my digestive system the year before. Oh well: only three and a half more months to go.

As we'd used up all the locations Simferopol had to offer, this would be our penultimate weekend before moving down to Yalta. My newly acquired friend, journalist, possibly KGB and ex-lawyer Sacha arranged for us to get access to the Centre for Physical Culture adjacent to the Meteor stadium for a sports day. It was a significant bonding exercise for the whole unit; even Beano couldn't resist the urge for a kickabout as an illicit game of football broke out. Sean made as if to take the field but was stopped in his tracks by Muir, who quietly yet firmly dissuaded him, but not us, from playing. No surprise, really, in light of the McGann episode; that said, having played footie with Sean between tours it would have been the opposition at risk of injury from Sean's gung-ho, uncompromising style of play. Precisely the attributes we so love in Sharpe!

The following morning was spent having tea with Pete and Daragh on my balcony; as I was equipped with a mini kitchen, my room was a regular stop for lifers. I travelled to location with Mike Byrne, who I now strenuously avoided play-fighting with. At Chufut-Kale they had again emptied the contents of the toy box to capture this evening's huge set-up, picking up the scene we had started the previous week, with Wellington's top brass perched atop their steeds, weaving among campfires at Ciudad Rodrigo. The Chosen Men find themselves camped by the roadside counting the booty swiped in the aftermath of the battle, one of the precious few Chosen Man scenes in 'Company'. Nairn passes, throwing a few words our way before Hugh Fraser, looking every inch the depiction of Wellington on the reverse of the five-pound note, leads his officers past us. With that scene in the can, the unit prepared for night shooting, allowing Sharpe, Harper and the Chosen to repair to our canvas green room for what we knew could be a long wait. Then the heavens opened.

I DIDN'T CHOOSE YOU

We returned the following night to complete the previous evening's washed-out action; unfortunately, we waited seven hours before getting on camera. We passed the time with a game of throwing hangers at a clothes rail, getting points if the hanger hooked the rail, which soon graduated to placing bets in head-to-head competition. All great fun, but there was no disguising the fact that we had been called way too early, treating the Chosen Men as one blob to be wheeled out like a prop. The trouble was, Chosen Men were victims of their own survival success; we had done it all before, we could hack it, the powers needn't worry about us therefore we were forgotten. We were left to our own devices, as there were more sensitive souls to be coddled arriving at regular intervals. With that section of 'Company' complete, we switched back to shooting 'Enemy' at a new location on the Belbek River, a significant location during the Crimean War at the Battle of Alma.

We settled into the Belbek Community Centre, its walls adorned with huge paintings in the Soviet realism style, still majorly miffed at the huge waiting times we had endured lately. Daragh opened a book on how many hours would pass between our allotted call time and when we are actually called to set, a chance for Big D to win a little money back after the clothes hanger game. Our wait was only four hours, which was bad enough, but the discontent was deflected by shooting a lovely Chosen Man vignette set by the dried-up riverbed where we discuss stealing lambs and soldier etiquette. It was the most dialogue Harris had uttered to date; thank you to my favourite *Sharpe* screenwriter Eoghan Harris, responsible for the 'Enemy' script. After lunch, we were shunted off into the background like a Chosen chorus line; waiting in a line, perchance to be seen.

Next up, the Chosen flock were standing in the background of Sharpe and Teresa's final scene before our hero sends his wife on a mission that would result in her death. They kiss, they look sad and Teresa disappears into the mountains, only to reappear as a corpse. After a couple of takes, Assumpta asked Tom if she shouldn't look at us, gesture to us or even say something to the Chosen Men? Tom said 'Nah!' scrunching his face in disgust at the suggestion. For me, the subtext read: the Chosen are just an entity who stand mute in the back of the frame, certainly never interacting with anyone important. Why would she bid farewell to men she'd fought beside over the hills and far away before going off on a dangerous mission?

I was fuming as our transport rattled back down the highway home, but it was nothing a little partying on our floor wouldn't help. I ended up in Lyndon's new bar ironing out the bumps of the day. As I was supping cans of cheap German lager, Sean sidled up to me: 'Did you get that thing I sent?' he said. You what? I thought. To my genuine amazement, Sean had been the creator of the doctored newspaper article from the sports page featuring Harris's face glued onto a footballer scoring a goal. Sean was full of these little surprises. I loved him for it and it certainly made for a positive end to the day.

The following morning, I had a visit to my room from producer Simon, who had learned about the aggravation at Belbek the previous day from Assumpta and Pete, who had listened to me venting. So I was forewarned about his appearance. I knew it was just part of a box-ticking exercise, that nothing would change, but I wanted to lay out all of our gripes for the record. I stated that despite being present during the darkest days of the last campaign, keeping people amused, entertained, properly fed, deflecting the malaise that could take hold on Sharpe in the Crimea, we were still treated as an afterthought. We were led to believe that the Chosen Men would become a little more three-dimensional in the second series. Tom Clegg and the executive producers were supposed to be the guardians of this promise; instead we'd accrued zero credit accommodation-wise or transport-wise, with precious little respect paid to the Chosen Men's importance to the story, which I felt was all highlighted the day before in the farewell to Teresa scene.

Riding to Belbek the next day I related this to the boys, Daragh listening with particular interest; by journey's end the chief revolutionaries were galvanised in their attitude to not take shit from the powers, be it Tom, Simon or his deputy Clive. We approached the camera position ready for combat, determined to defend our right to be respected by production; reaching the riverbank, we realised our call had preceded that of the extras playing the 60th Rifles, who were nowhere to be seen. Not a good start to proceedings, though one we were discouragingly familiar with. Before long, Clive Hedges, Simon's right-hand man, ambled over to chummy up to us; the collective desire to tell him to fuck off was overwhelming. Instead we ripped into him on every non-artistic aspect of the production we felt was deficient. The hotel phones, charging Phil Whitchurch to send a fax home, the massive waiting times, the broken tea breaks, the transport; you name it, we let go with all seven barrels. A skirmish not unnoticed by the film unit.

Clive retreated, tail between his legs, just as the tea and sandwiches arrived, not a moment too soon. With the tea tantalisingly within reach, Sam called us to set, which we politely rebuffed, stating, 'Not before we have a cuppa' during the union-sanctioned tea break. Tom, overhearing this, steamed over to us telling us to 'get your fucking gear on. No time for tea.' Daragh rose angrily, loudly saying, 'How dare you talk to us like that? We're here waiting forty-five minutes and you call us just as the tea arrives. Fuck that!' Tom got the point. The real seeds of discontent with Tom dated back to a party at my London flat between campaigns, where, tongues loosened by drink, Tom admitted he probably wouldn't have cast us as the Chosen Men – I'm sure he didn't mean John Tams as it was only Paul (Isaiah Tongue), Lyndon and myself in attendance. I didn't hear him say the words, but it was reliably reported back to me. It was a devastating blow to our pride and, frankly, for me, an almost heartbreaking realisation that, had Tom been in charge from the beginning, I would never have been cast as Harris. Unfortunately, this felt like a barrier between Tom and me. Talk about 'I didn't choose you' – Sharpe's line to the Chosen Men in episode one of the series. The mood was eased somewhat by a spectacular sunset splashing the sky with a beautiful array of reds and yellows. Tom came to the community centre at dinner break to apologise; detente prevailed.

DASVIDANIYA SIMPLYAWFUL

At last our Simferopol sentence was at an end, with no time off for good behaviour. It was rest day at the Moscow Hotel and the unit was positively buzzing at our imminent exit from Simplyawful. As we were upping sticks to a new base, executive produce Malcolm Craddock had flown in via Frankfurt. I spoke to him in the dining hall applauding the first-rate casting decision to give Pete the role of Hakeswill as per our conversation last year. Malcolm looked at me blankly, claiming to have no recollection of that conversation and my recommendation to cast Pete. There wasn't even a hint of a cheeky smile; he really meant it. After dinner we set up my television in the fourth-floor lounge, and the unit gathered to watch a recording of the previous night's broadcast of *Match of the Day*; a day-old video of English football was like gold and kept the homesickness at bay.

Production had combined moving day with a shoot at our old chum Dimerdji, conveniently situated on the highway down to Yalta, where we would cover the over-the-hills-and-far-away shot as well as Isabella's visit to Teresa's sister to see Sharpe's child, Antonia. It must have made for some awkward conversation: 'Hi, I'm the hussy who shagged your brother-in-law the night before your sister was killed.' Once La Hurley had wrapped, she returned to the UK for a little break; she had barely been here but had oozed her way into our affections with her outrageous flirting and gleeful mining of gossip; particularly the gripes we Chosen Men had with the powers. It was fun to have her in the gang, frequenting our corridor in Hugh Grant's pyjamas, granting us little pecks on the cheek as we dutifully lined up to bid her good night; why couldn't she play a regular character?

We got through the call sheet quickly, allowing time for some hard-currency shopping and a pint of lager at the Yalta Hotel before settling in at the Chernomore sanatorium, our home for the next quarter of the year. It was hard not to be underwhelmed by our new Black Sea base when compared to the architectural splendour of the Rossiya, last year's sanatorium. The Chernomore was a gnarly concrete barracks, more akin to hotels from the 1960s Costa Blanca. To the side of the sanatorium entrance stood an entire unfinished wing, abandoned years earlier and replete with rusty scaffolding and mouldy concrete, resembling a sort of Costa Del Sol interruptus. One imagines they simply ran out of money for finishing off construction. Luckily, I could take control of the interior, creating my own lair, which I set about lethargically, hindered slightly by Diana Perez bouncing around between our rooms. This lady was a real live wire, with space cadet tendencies making for a hilarious evening. With our arrival on the Soviet Riviera a slew of 'Enemy' cast joined us, including Tony Haygarth, lead French baddie Féodor Atkine, here to play the dastardly Colonel Ducos, François Guétary, the suave French officer Dubreton, and Morgan Jones, playing the deserter Kelly.

The long-range schedule had given the Chosen Men six clear days off filming which begged the question, why not let us take a break back in the UK to recharge the batteries? I guess it was cheaper to hold us on location where there was little chance of absconding. At this point I had almost everything I needed with me here on the Black Sea, although I knew that complacency could get tested on a long stretch at HMP Crimea. After a couple of days of beach fun, bacchanalian excess and general time-wasting in downtown Yalta, Lyndon, Nick Rowe and I went to visit the set conveniently housed at Polikur, a short ride through town traffic or a quicker one if you drove along the motorway skirting the rising ground of the Crimean

Mountains. That got you across the bay far faster. Normally you wouldn't pop into work when not required, but boredom had driven us to it; there was also the added incentive of a good lunch prepared by our new caterers. Exploring the set, I discovered a card school with Féodor, Helena, Liz, Penny Smith, head of make-up, and Mike Mears. Don't think it was poker, I didn't see any money changing hands, but Liz did remark to me that Mike was unpleasantly competitive; that's the Mike I know and love, along with Sean one of the few males immune to Liz's charms.

As we arrived, they were shooting Sharpe's arrival at the deserters' headquarters within the convent where the negotiation for hostages begins. Sharpe is accompanied by French officer Dubreton, whose wife is held hostage along with Farthingdale's wife, played by Helena and Liz respectively. As was the custom on *Sharpe*, the eponymous hero must have a sword fight with any officer in French uniform; during the final take, Sean lunged a little too enthusiastically, causing his sword to glance off Dubreton's defensive parry, and jabbed the point into François' cheek millimetres beneath his right eye. I guess François wasn't ready for Sean's robust approach to all forms of combat; this was an action picture after all, but that was another really close call. Sean was visibly shaken by events, probably recalling the time he almost lost an eye to a hooked spear wielded by Harrison Ford during a fight scene in *Patriot Games*. Death to the French and all that; one wondered if this was the *Sharpe* jinx in action?

Leaving Polikur, I sought out Natasha in make-up; now we were based back in Yalta she had been staying at home. As I hadn't been on the call sheet lately, our paths weren't crossing. This made Natasha very cross and I got a telling-off for not paying enough attention to her; I responded by saying it wasn't good to spend too much time together. I didn't hear the end of that for a couple of decades. After work up on the thespians' floor of the Chernomore, Féodor had brought from Paris a suitcase stuffed with chunks of pungent cheese accompanied by eight bottles of very decent French plonk. He had set everything up in our lounge for all to enjoy, including the entire production office, who were hopefully learning a thing or two about alleviating some of the privations of Yalta.

September the 20th brought an abrupt end to my extended sunshine break; I was stiff as hell after a game of football with the security boys which turned out to be more like war with a football as they felt it necessary to bring in a couple of ringers. The ride to work was a pleasure as we were still shooting at the Polikur, the Hollywood of the Crimea, or Poliwood as I had recently nicknamed it. All week we were shooting the assault on the deserters' hideout in the town chapel with lots of gunfire, throwing 'grenades' and hand-to-hand combat, the stuff of dreams for a young actor. Before a frame could be shot, we had to deal with an invasion of a different sort: an entire battalion of wasps had decided to park itself in the entrance to the chapel. Props man Colin came to the rescue, managing to herd most of them away; some things even Sharpe and the Chosen Men couldn't handle.

With the swarm suppressed, it was time for stuntman Harris to tackle a few pesky deserters by leaping over a table and taking one of them out; I was happy Tom had chosen me for this stunt, although I was beginning to rue the previous day's crunching football match. Tom warned me to be careful. I didn't heed his advice and on the second take I promptly turned my ankle, already weakened from footie. When the shot was complete, I left to wrap up my ankle while chilling with a cup of tea on standby for the next action. This came after lunch with one of Hakeswill's deputies, Smithers, who to me looked like a Muscovite Pete Postlethwaite, but larger. Stunt coordinator Dinny Powell took us through preparations for the fight, managing to kick the shit out of me in the process; yesterday's footballing war was looking increasingly ill-advised. With the deserters dispatched, the Chosen Men freed the damsels in distress locked within the building, not before Sharpe got to 'debrief' Isabella overnight in her prison cell. Maybe the Chosen Men would get the girl one day!

I awoke the next morning with the beginnings of a cold, which could have been the result of bacchanalian excess, but partying too hard was the default setting on *Sharpe* so I self-diagnosed a cold, hoping it wasn't something worse. After work I was invited to dinner in Assumpta's suite with a couple of French baddies, Féodor and François, as well as well-known actor Patrick Bauchau, Assumpta's lover in LA. He looked slightly ill at ease at being out of his comfort zone and in a place where he was merely a 'camp follower'. Féodor was a bit of a nutty professor, entertaining to the end; François and I had done an episode of *Bergerac* together, so we had plenty to talk about. The conversation was punctuated by two phone calls from Scott Cleverdon in the UK; they had tried to keep it under cover, but Scott had, unsurprisingly, become gradually ensnared by Assumpta's charms. I assumed Assumpta would field Scott's call swiftly and discreetly seeing as her current live-in lover of some years' standing was in the room. No such nicety was observed. Assumpta talked at length, not hiding her delight or the fact that she was conversing with a lover. I'm sure Patrick didn't have a leg to stand on as he was still officially married to Brigitte Bardot's sister, Mijanou. He must have been fully clued up and surely accustomed to it by now; he knew that in the end, when she'd had her fun, she would return home to him, as in the case of Paul Trussell. That was one interesting, if somewhat uncomfortable evening.

The final sections of 'Enemy' were covered while having to deal with some sort of Ukrainian lurgy; I arrived at make-up feeling sorry for myself only to find one of the Muscovite actresses seated in the chair crying her eyes out. I imagined some personal tragedy had befallen her; I didn't want to ask. I found out later that the Russian rouble had been devalued by almost half, hitting her current wages, not to mention anything stashed away for a rainy day. Real-life tragedy did touch the unit. Our Israeli boom operator David Lis's father had died, necessitating an immediate exit from location to be at the funeral. It looked as if they would have to replace him with another boom swinger from the UK.

To while away the vast waiting times on a night shoot I brought my copy of *Sharpe's Waterloo*, a great book though with little Chosen Man action; reading the novels I came to realise we were more of a confection cooked up for the television incarnation of *Sharpe*. I was saddened to read on page 342 that Hagman takes a musket ball to the chest, blowing his lungs out in the process, something I warned John Tams about. Hopefully the producers would have learned by then to cherish the Chosen Men, letting all four of us roll off into the sunset over the hills and far away. Yeah, right!

After wrap I went to the Yalta Hotel with Sean and Daragh for a pint, where we watched an old, clumsily dubbed episode of *The Sweeney* showing on the main Russian channel, an episode directed by Tom Clegg! How funny; what next, *Sharpe* on Russian telly? The rapid intake of four pints of draught lager amplified my flu bug, causing me to shiver uncontrollably. Beano's driver whisked us back to the Chernomore, where I jumped into bed fully clothed, still shivering and sweating profusely. This was the legendary Russian flu that was often mentioned when I was a kid in England. Natasha came by to comfort me; we watched a video of Tom Cruise and Nicole Kidman in *Far and Away*, which lulled me nicely to sleep. I could deny it no longer: interpreter Natasha was fast becoming girlfriend Natasha. I had everything – a little slice of home away from the sometimes toxic on-set hinterland and a beautiful girl by my side.

THERE MAY BE TROUBLE AHEAD

Mercifully, there was only one more shooting day before adjusting from night to day shoots with a three-day furlough giving me a chance to recover. To celebrate wrapping 'Enemy', a modest shindig had been arranged where production promised to screen a very rough cut, but, like many assurances from production, it never materialised. With 'Enemy' in the can, we had to bid farewell to François, Helena, Morgan, Nick Rowe and, last but not least, Liz Hurley. The following day, members of the 'Company' cast took up residence. Lyndon and I greeted them in the dining hall dressed in Ukrainian/Russian folk shirts to give the impression we'd gone native. In truth, I was kind of heading that way.

October was upon us, the valley's foliage resembled fall in New England, but the weather high in the Crimean Mountains was getting wintery. It was cold, miserable, wet and muddy when we arrived at base camp to find our nylon camping tents had vanished, replaced by our less-than-salubrious, flapping in the wind, Red Army canvas tent. Gloomy, dirty and sodden; the weather was perfect for the trench-digging scenes we were covering. Our UK nurse decided my cold would require a slug of Day Nurse; unfortunately, it made me feel even worse as I spent the entire day wet to the bone and smeared with mud. The glamour of film-making!

Day two was no different, more trench warfare in the mud, though it seemed intestinal warfare had broken out in the camera team. Neil Brown, our clapper loader, had had his last meal on *Sharpe* due to a flare-up of our old nemesis *Giardia lamblia*. Apparently, he had succumbed to the dreaded Simferopol stomach after drinking kvass, the 'brew' made from fermented bread, sold from large-wheeled vessels which were possibly never properly cleaned. Many of us didn't have the option of returning home; John Tams had been suffering dreadfully from a dodgy tummy since the first tour but had never been offered home rest. Production knew full well our delicate western stomachs were the weakest link out in the Crimea; perhaps they should have warned the unit to stay clear of curiosities like kvass. A replacement would now be flown out; coming the other way was outgoing boom operator David Lis's replacement, St. Clair Davis, a six-foot lad from Stoke Newington with short dreadlocks who could seriously vie with me on the hairstyle front.

On set we were continuing the daylight assault on Badajoz's great wall; Sharpe emerges from the trenches to fight hand-to-hand with spades, pickaxe handles and whatever tool comes to hand. Despite the inclement conditions, I loved shooting scenes like this; all the boys together facing danger and overcoming a numerically superior force. Everything given a veneer of reality by the magnificent re-creation of a breached section of the fortification surrounding Badajoz; regrettably I got slightly carried away attempting to leap heroically from a trench, pulling a muscle in my lower back. Russian flu, now this; on *Sharpe*, when it rains, it pours and when it pours you get wet. I soldiered on as best I could, comforted by the knowledge the work week was almost done, and I would be ably cared for by Nurse Natasha, who had invited me to dinner along with the rest of the make-up team at her parents' place on our day off. Yikes, I was getting in deep; hadn't bargained for that. Make-up artist Charmaine confidently predicted I'd refuse the invite, so I made it a point to accept with all the implications it entailed.

The work week ended with a change of location within the valley where Wellington's camp has been set up for the Harper flogging scene and the surrendering of our green jackets to the dastardly Hakeswill. We wrapped early, arriving back at the sanatorium to find care packages from the UK had landed. After listening to the BBC's World Service sports report, we had dinner and adjourned to the bar where, among other conversations, producer Simon delivered some tragic news. On a trip to Dimerdji to check on the set construction, he was met by the work crew ascending the mountain in a minibus with the local head of construction, Cassian, dead from a heart attack inside. *Sharpe*'s first death, an incident casting into insignificance the supposed struggles we faced. In our crude western way, we had a whip-round at the bar for his widow; crude, but what else could the unit do? The news hit Natasha hard; she was naturally very upset. I was definitely beginning to believe in the Sharpe jinx.

Blessed Sunday arrived, still with back pain, though less fluey, permitting me actually to fully taste my food. Natasha went off to town to help make-up head Penny do her shopping; after eating I headed to town to meet them in front of Bradley's of London. When I got to the rendezvous, Natasha looked pleasantly surprised, having believed Charmaine when she said that I would be a no-show. I must say I did get a little nervous as our minibus drove toward Natasha's block of flats. Why should I be nervous? It wasn't as if I was going to ask Natasha's parents for her hand in marriage?

Interestingly, her dad wasn't in attendance as he was the manager of an Italian restaurant in a building called the Swallow's Nest, a famous Crimean landmark made even more so after Liz Hurley dined there. I had met Natasha's mum, Valentina, briefly at Polikur; she seemed a pleasant, serene sort of woman, very pretty with a lovely smile to boot. Natasha's sister, Lyosya, spoke very good English, if with a slight American accent having been on a student exchange trip to Exeter, New Hampshire, a programme Natasha had also participated in. It was clear brains and beauty ran through the women in the family. This was my first taste of a real 'Soviet' household; though in truth it was very like a modest European two-room apartment, tastefully decorated with a fair number of antiques adorning the shelves. The food was delicious, exploding the myth that nice food couldn't be cooked in the Crimea. Obviously, production's scrimping on the catering budget was to blame; they must have hoped people would blame the old cliché of bad Russian cooking.

We took a few photos and said our goodbyes before heading back home where I took maximum ribbing from crew members assembled at the bar. I was also getting maximum gyp from my back injury; stunt coordinator Dinny volunteered to administer an old-school back massage, possibly the type a boxer in a sweaty gym might receive. Paraffin and best brown paper would probably have been as effective; the massage didn't alleviate the muscle pain, but I was really relieved when he was done; all the while Natasha looked on with concern. Of more concern was news crackling over the shortwave of an attempted coup in Moscow. President Yeltsin tried to dissolve the Supreme Soviet, resulting in street fighting and protestors talking over the iconic Ostankino Tower, home of Russia's number one television station. Yeltsin ordered in the army to take back the tower killing hundreds in the process; the most deaths in the street since the Russian Revolution of 1917. Pretty worrying stuff, but at least the communist coup-plotters lost out in the end, averting the possible reconstruction of the Evil Empire and any attempts to take back Ukraine. In other news, Michael Jordan had retired from basketball to pursue a career in Major League baseball; the world really was in turmoil!

The new work week began with a succession of unkind five-in-the-morning calls made all the more pleasant by a persistent cold drizzle. When Lyndon and I arrived to do our bit at Wellington's camp, it appeared we were again there before even the extras were called to set; then we noticed our starting position was miles away from camera, which only fuelled our anger. We registered our dissatisfaction with Tom and Marc before steaming back to the tent in time to save it from being blown away in a sudden violent gust of wind, originating (once again) from China if the locals were to be believed.

We sat stewing during the lunch break, returning to set a couple of hours later only to stand waiting while they completed twenty-three shots without us, all the while the watery October sun steadily dipping towards the horizon. Racing against the fading light, a shot with Lyndon and I was hastily assembled; just as we were ready to turn over the camera, director of photography Arthur Wooster declared there wasn't enough light to film the scene. Lyndon and I were incandescent with rage and left the set kicking our shakos along the ground in a petulant display of disgust. Compounding the misery John Tams told me to 'shut up, 'cos I can't stand to see you like this'. Yes, Lyndon and I were overtly stroppy in making our complaints, but this was a break in the unity that won the day during the Bacon Riot at the end of the first series. It suddenly made me feel bad for standing up for something I thought I was due. A little respect!

At home I showered and made dinner in my room with Natasha, staying in the comfortable cocoon of my own space, not wanting to see anyone bar Lyndon or Pete. The replacement boom operator, St. Clair Davis, dropped in to report the word 'on the street'; seeing as he was new to Camp Sharpe we were more than interested in what he had to say. Of course, he was on our side but told us some of the crew were muttering that we had no reason to moan as we hardly ever worked. A fair enough assessment, but that was a dagger to my heart, only adding to my sense of abject desolation, seeing as the argument wasn't about having to be on set. We were fighting for respect, trying to realise promises that were made last year. I wanted to tell Saint to inform the crew they could bloody well kiss our arses next time they were eating a hot bacon butty halfway up Dimerdji above the snow line.

Soon Lyndon joined us for dinner, followed by Sean and Pete a bit later, which, after an ultra-quick appraisal of the situation, did not feel like it was merely a social call, feeling more like a visit from two prefects – less so Pete – to upbraid the naughty lower-class men. Possibly after a report from John Tams, Sean duly attempted to discuss the day's skirmish, saying we needed to keep things harmonious while in-country and that expressing our anger like that – kicking shakos – made for disharmony. We had signed up for a second series, therefore there was nothing to complain about at this stage. He concluded by saying we couldn't walk onto another show asking all that we were expecting. I was so pissed off, it was the closest I had come to getting angry with Beano; I kept my cool, however, countering, lawyer-like, all the issues Sean had raised; mainly pointing out that our gripes dated back to our first Crimean campaign, where we were continuously disrespected.

Worse for me was Tom treating the Chosen contribution as unimportant or peripheral in terms of shot selection and not shooting stage directions that concerned us. We weren't asking to be the stars of the show; we just wanted our skills to be utilised fully and if we weren't going to get fat wages then at least treat us with a little dignity. Also, we wouldn't dream of walking onto another show and moaning or expecting anything. But we *hadn't* just walked onto this show; we were thirty weeks into this franchise with the ring of vague, post-season-one promises still ringing in our ears. Then, pausing for effect, I reminded Sean that Lyndon and I had been putting up with the powers and the world of shit they volunteered us for a full six weeks before he arrived. We left it there, my last statement hitting home with Beano. Pete lightened the atmosphere by saying, 'Forget the ruck, chaps, go straight to the hats,' referring to the 'Dimerdji Bacon Riot' baseball caps we had made up after the first tour.

Clearing the air like that was a relief; I just wished John Tams had been there, too. Pete then related an incident that took place when he was filming *Cutthroat Island* with Geena Davies, where production treated the posh characters with respect, leaving the actors playing pirate characters to their own devices. After a long, hot day of shooting Pete arrived in his hotel room still in full pirate kit to await the appropriate departments, make-up and wardrobe, to come and get him out of his costume and clean him up. They never arrived.

Pete staged a one-man sit-in, calmly drinking beer and smoking ciggies in his room till daybreak when production came frantically searching for the absent pirate. It was a story told to illustrate that this kind of shit went on all the time and that basically we should fight on. That's how I interpreted it anyway. With the conference out of the way, we sat watching telly; Beano hadn't seen last year's episodes all the way through, so we watched 'Rifles' and 'Eagle' back to back, commenting and joining in like an audience at a late-night screening of *The Rocky Horror Picture Show*.

Tuesday 5 October – a year since the dawning of the Bean era. Marc Jenny argued that the date should be earlier, when he signed on the dotted line. I countered, telling him Sharpe ain't Sharpe until he's met his Chosen Men and that was a year ago today over breakfast drinks at Heathrow. Everything on set was sweetness and light, smiles and politeness with barely any waiting around. The scene was shot as per the script with Chosen stage directions shot as I imagined; maybe somebody up there didn't think we were prima donnas and was heeding our gripes. A peaceful, uneventful workday, followed by a calm evening; all quiet on the eastern front.

STUCK IN THE MIDDLE WITH YOU

As we moved towards the halfway stage of the shoot, it felt like we'd been at the immensely versatile Baidar Valley forever. I had decided there was no real point in complaining about the way we were used in front of the camera while shooting 'Company'. The script had rendered the Chosen Men inarticulate blobs, with no bearing on the narrative, popping up occasionally only as a counterbalance to an episode chock full of toffs. Our transport departed into the pre-dawn darkness; pulling in at base camp, make-up head Penny Smith made a beeline for Daragh as we exited the van. Thinking nothing of it, the rest of us dispersed to do the pre-shoot ritual: costume, make-up, hair followed by breakfast and an interminably long wait.

Routine complete, I checked in on Pete ahead of popping up to set; suddenly, the distinct and scary sound of Daragh's angry voice boomed out through the green canvas partition. It transpired that Penny had accosted Daragh to plead with him to 'bear with us, the make-up budget is gone and I have to spend my own money', which to me really beggared belief. Penny's Russian make-up assistant proceeded to apply a low-budget version of previous products used, causing irritation to Daragh's skin. He erupted, a bit like his face, chucking things and shouting as he stormed out of the tent, almost hitting Natasha with a colour palate, or so I'm reliably informed. Poor Daragh, he hadn't been present at the previous day's ruck and subsequent 'kiss and make up' session, so he still had steam to vent. Hopefully the imminent arrival of Mrs O'Malley would keep him chilled out. The crux of so many quarrels on *Sharpe* was the continual squeeze on the budget which seemed to be having an impact on all departments.

At the Chernomore, the following morning was spent with Natasha having an idyllic Sunday morning breakfast and video-watching session; this was beginning to exceed the parameters of a location romance as clever-clogs Harris might surmise. Later in the day a new intake of actors arrived, bringing post and care packages. The week ahead was to be another slow one for me with the change of location from Baidar back to Dimerdji for the Forlorn Hope's breaching of the wall and the ensuing skirmishes.

Dimerdji housed another magnificently constructed set, the reverse side of Badajoz's fortifications, the view townsfolk would have had as they were invaded by blood-lusting soldiers, intent on violent revenge after seeing so many comrades die in the long siege. It was another brilliantly realistic build by Phil Elton adapted from the old 'Torrecastro' set utilised on *Rifles*, Phil told me when he first arrived at Dimerdji to see how the set had fared after being abandoned for ten months. He found the little village squatted in by travellers who had built campfires and had washing hanging out on a line. Production had to pay local villagers to help clear them out.

Now we were back on nights, the day began with 'breakfast' at 4:30 in the afternoon as the sun dipped behind the horizon delivering in a mind-blowing sunset over Dimerdji. The night was notable as Assumpta and Scott appeared in public as a couple for the first time, never leaving each other's side and gazing into each other's eyes lovingly at every opportunity; I couldn't help but feel a pang of empathetic heartbreak for Paul Trussell.

On 13 October it was two months since we'd left Stansted and, bar any tragedy befalling us, less than two months till wrapping the whole shoot. On our first tour, two months was the longest period we'd spent banged up inside HMP Crimea; this year we were doing the full four-month stretch. So we were now in uncharted territory; how loopy would it get from here on in? The midway milestone happened to coincide with a visit from my old mate Sacha, journalist and ex-lawyer, who had been attending a Black Sea conference. Natasha and her best friend Igor managed to persuade our security detail, some of whom were from Moldova, that Sacha was my dad visiting from London, much to their amusement as in the former Soviet Union they made fun of Moldovans for being stupid. It was fairly hard to not recognise Sacha as a local with his Soviet-era clothing, his battered leather briefcase and the fact that he spoke fluent Russian; the clincher was the liberal sprinkling of gold in his dentition, as sure a sign as any that you grew up in 'Russia'.

The weekend rolled in with a double birthday – Tom Clegg's and third unit manager Christian Abomnes'. A celebration dinner at an Armenian restaurant was arranged, where the food was very edible, the drink flowed and slurry, slushy speeches were made, including one by an almost tearful Tom and a very merry Pete, who thanked all those who had been on the show last year while looking at current producer Simon and ended by toasting the *Sharpe* campaign veterans who made it more tolerable for those who followed. A song was performed by a new addition, a chirpy cockney called Eddie, here to help with the lighting during the two-week night shoot. Potentially an awkward moment for a newcomer fresh off the shuttle, but the song, about friendship (I think) was sung in a really touching, heartfelt manner. Possibly because he was from outside the bubble it affected us, though possibly it was the haze of alcohol; but, whatever it was, it served as a bonding moment for the whole unit.

The following day I got a close-up view of more love in the Crimea when I invited Scott and Assumpta over for brunch. Assumpta and Scott had tried to keep their union on the down-low. Possibly Assumpta didn't want to rub the relationship in the faces of the unit who might be unhappy for Paul, although that liaison now seemed a long time ago. It transpired these guys were truly getting serious. Assumpta told me she was packing up in LA and moving back to Europe, starting with a stay in London. They seemed incredibly compatible. I was very happy for them now, more than I was sad for Paul.

HEADING INTO THE BACK STRAIGHT

The next week we were back at Polikur, where our much-used town square set saw our heroes fulfilling some essential soldierly duties. Harris made busy fixing the company's boots in a nod to the factual Harris of the *Recollections of Rifleman Harris* book, who was the company cobbler. The same square or plaza was the location of the Sharpe—Hakeswill reunion scene; Daragh had been dropped from the scene due to the rash on his face having puffed up pretty badly, acute enough for the schedule to be altered. Simon intoned gravely that they would have a Learjet standing by to whisk Big D back to Gatwick and then on to a Harley Street dermatologist to fix the problem, if you can believe that. Critical though it was, the gallows humour set in and Daragh had another nickname: Learjet. We always take the mick out of those we love the most.

Day two of Polikur and a sad moment we knew was coming: the Needle's last stand and Assumpta's final day on *Sharpe*. Again, we were stepping out of the chronology and switching episodes to shoot one of 'Enemy' final scenes. She almost didn't make it to set as there was still something unsettled in her contract causing her to stage a sit-in, refusing to leave her dressing room until the issue was resolved, much to the displeasure of the crew left standing by in limbo. On her last slate the customary farewell salute was a little more muted than usual, signalling the end of the Serna era. With Teresa's scenes in the can, it was time for the Chosen to finish their action on this episode with a speaking scene for yours truly; Tom gave the scene a lot of attention, getting really close, kneeling next to me explaining in great detail how the scene should progress, even down to the inflection at the end of my line. It was odd to be directed so intensely by Tom, but encouraging, nonetheless, to be treated like a proper actor instead of one of the extras.

Wrapping early, we rattled home in our luxury transport anticipating two social events held in a recreation room one floor up from the bar. With curious scheduling, Richard Moore was holding a Sharpe quiz at the same time as Assumpta's leaving party, rendering the soirée a bit of a damp squib. I did win the quiz, though, earning three Crimean War uniform buttons dug up by Rifleman Moore at Balaclava. Triumphant at victory, Lyndon, Sean and I slipped away from the party to drink vodka shots with all the inevitable, destructive results. Natasha was staying at home as it was closer to Polikur, allowing me to indulge in my status as a courtier to my lord Bacchus; behaving 'outrageously' according to Lyndon. Next morning, I woke up with the lights on and my socks still firmly on my feet, so he may have had a point; the perils of vodka drinking with Sean and Lyndon.

As the days got shorter, we entered almost two weeks' worth of dreaded night shoots to cover the night assault on the walls of Badajoz, imposing an upside-down schedule on the unit. Two weeks of staying up all night, waiting for your dinner at two in the morning, can leave you with no idea whether you're coming or going. In general, Crimean weather is very mild well into the autumn; up there at Baidar we were a little closer to the heavens and more susceptible to the elements. The night air was now seriously frigid with winds that cut brutally through you. Naturally, this schedule impacted the crew far more than the actors, who weren't required on every call sheet; as we were the only inhabitants at the sanatorium, all services went onto the upside-down schedule with the bar opening at 4 a.m. in time for the returning unit to get their requisite alcohol allowance.

At ten in the morning the bar closed so that the crew could get a good day's sleep before travelling to set again at four in the afternoon. Actors whose bodies had adapted to the reverse schedule and weren't on the call sheet faced a sanatorium resembling a landlocked *Mary Celeste*, abandoned and bereft of human souls.

On set it was a world of darkness, lit solely by noisy generators that often needed to be shut down for the take; base camp had to be located behind the massive Badajoz set construction so as not to limit any wide shots. The ground where we erected our tent had more rocks than grass, useless for keeping your balance in a game of hangers, but perfectly adequate for distractions such as Scrabble, Risk and chess to while away the extended waiting times. The crew didn't have a green room in which to shelter from the elements, but they sure knew how to dress for it, many of them resembling mountaineers at Everest base camp minus the crampons and oxygen. The action undertaken was some of the most exciting, epic battle scenes we had filmed to date with large explosions, gunfire and stuntmen flying every which way as we recreated truly brutal combat, compensating somewhat for the lack of Chosen Man dialogue. There's nothing more exhilarating than charging full throttle with your comrades, large explosions going off everywhere, behind your maniacal leader exhorting you on to probable death. This was what I had signed up for! Some time later, I was told the army Colonel thanked Igor Nossov as his soldiers playing extras got a little taste of simulated battle, which was invaluable training.

However, Charles Wood's 'Company' featured some nice scenes for Sharpe's supremo, Lord Wellington; another role, like Sharpe, where comparisons will forever be made, sparking a debate as to who's better, Troughton or Fraser. Troughton was a physically larger, more imposing figure possessed of a power and authority that exploded on the screen, almost a pugilist Wellington. Fraser, on the other hand, was far more cerebral, understated and less flashy, like a chess master, yet with equivalent gravitas; they were very different interpretations but equally compelling. I had got to know Hugh a lot better than David, who hung out more with the 'Eagle' cast on the first *Sharpe*. Plus there was the time Troughton's wife, who was visiting the location, wandered down to the Chosen Man floor, had a great time, but was found to be experiencing the effects of bacchanalian excess.

When Hugh arrived in the Crimea, he hung out with the Chosen Men a bit more. He empathised with our plight, saying he also sometimes felt marginalised, plopped in the background and given sparse dialogue in his role as Hastings in *Poirot*. It seemed Hugh's talents weren't just in the acting department. I later discovered he wrote the theme tune to *Rainbow*, an iconic children's television programme back in the late seventies and early eighties, so he wasn't just a pretty nose (which was prosthetic anyway). Hugh was also my near neighbour back in London, so we hit it off straight away.

The week of darkness was up for the Chosen, leaving the valiant crew to bang off the remaining scenes on the breached wall where flailing stuntmen and soft actors came away from the fray dodging serious misfortune. Alas, the same couldn't be said for one of our newest arrivals, Saint the boom operator, who in the darkness at the foot of the breach tripped, dislocating his shoulder and ruling him out of the rest of the shoot, lending more credence to the notion of a *Sharpe* jinx. It was a huge blow to the social scene; he was now an integral part of the gang.

The disjointed schedule meant I had only seen Natasha on set as she was staying at home, putting further strain on the closeness we had been nurturing. John Tams began to ride to work in Sean's car, claiming he didn't feel safe in our vehicles. This caused a certain amount of division among the Chosen Men, which in turn prompted concern from Beano. It had been an expensive week for the unit, disrupting the cosy normality we had fostered and relied on as a buffer against the aggravation of a long Crimean tour.

It was early November and the Chosen contribution to 'Company' was at a close, which heralded the commencement of the final episode of this campaign, 'Sharpe's Honour'. There were still some outstanding Hakeswill scenes from 'Company' to shoot, giving Pete that extra week in the Crimea, much to the joy of the unit. With spare time on his hands, Pete decided to take a round trip to Simferopol on a trolley bus accompanied by half a crate of beer; an excellent way to interface with the local populace according to Pete. The episode change had brought Muir Sutherland in from the UK with a posse including Bernard Cornwell, his agent Toby Eady and a friend of Bernard's from the US; arriving into the peninsula with them were members of the 'Honour' cast, including Edward Atterton, playing the dashing D'Alembord. Bernard very kindly took selected unit members to dinner at the Yalta Hotel; Bernard is always great company and it was wonderful to see him still beaming at witnessing his creation brought to life with such success.

ALL DOWNHILL FROM HERE

Our first action in 'Honour' was one to remember: the Chosen Men delivering the Harpers' first child. Unusually, it was shot inside a tent erected in the foyer of Polikur studios. They had about four blow heaters on the go, so it felt very hospital-like. All four Chosen Men and Ramona crammed in a two-man tent reminded me of a scene from the Marx Brothers film, *A Night at the Opera*, where they try to cram an unfeasibly large number of people into a ship's cabin with all the hilarious consequences that entails, arses in faces, etc. Production had managed to persuade a mother to lend her recently born baby for the scene filmed in this unorthodox shooting location. Straight afterwards, we shot Pete's last scene from 'Company', thus completing the fourth entry to the *Sharpe* oeuvre; after seeing rough edits of Pete's stuff, the producers were already ruing the decision to kill off Hakeswill. Perhaps that would stop them bumping off popular *Sharpe* characters in the future. Pete was seen off with a suitably extreme bout of bacchanalian excess that carried on well into the following morning as our body clocks were still in nocturnal mode. Pete would be sorely missed; he had spent ten weeks at Camp Sharpe, seamlessly integrating himself into the family. His portrayal of Hakeswill, surely Sharpe's fiercest foe, expertly trod the line between eliciting pathos and inspiring hatred. To affirm his legendary status in the business, while on *Sharpe* it was announced he had been nominated for an Oscar as Best Supporting Actor for *In the Name of the Father*.

With Pete released back to civilisation, more 'Honour' cast arrived: Nickolas Grace, Alice Krige, and Matthew Scurfield playing the fearsome El Matarife. Their first action took us back up into the frigid air of Baidar Valley; daylight would now be at a premium, as the clocks turned back at the end of October. With an hour chipped off daylight, our calls became even earlier, requiring us to set out into the almost pitch-black morning. We had long grumbled about our transport, mainly because they were all basically jalopies that had been on the road for eons. Many were uncomfortable and rickety with little ventilation in the summer and often ineffective heating come wintertime. At this point of the shoot, we had inherited what we thought was the most decent minivan in the fleet, with an impeccable, comfortable interior driven by a handsome older chap called Valentine.

However, one chilly morning it appeared Valentine's scrupulous maintenance of the van's interior hadn't extended to the engine as we broke down soon after hitting the highway. Well aware this was the Crimea, where every conceivable curve ball had been hurled our way, we waited and, fairly quickly by Crimean standards, Valentine got us back under way. From base to Baidar it took an hour, and during that time we lost power four more times. The good-natured banter and gallows humour ran out as real fear began to take a grip. The coastal highway hugs the undulating curves at the base of the Crimean Mountains sometimes with precious little hard shoulder for breakdowns; the problem is exacerbated if it's on a bend in the road, which happened on the final two engine failures. We were so freaked out that John and I stood on the unlit road at either end of the vehicle holding aloft lighters vainly trying to warn any oncoming vehicles. Traffic was admittedly sparse at that time in the morning, but it was the main highway to Sevastopol, so huge trucks barrelling down the road could be expected at any time.

An inattentive or drunk trucker could have taken out Harper and all the Chosen Men in one fell swoop. We eventually arrived at location, picked up piecemeal by other passing *Sharpe* vehicles; once the fear had subsided, the anger set in. Daragh, already an uneasy passenger in Crimean vehicles, ripped into production. A summit meeting between producer Simon and Daragh, our most resolute negotiator, not to mention the scariest, was held inside one of the minivans at base camp. Daragh emerged triumphant from the meeting declaring peace in our time with no need for a strike; we would be driven to set in cars from now on. The minivan era was officially at an end. Just as another strike was averted, the snow began to fall.

I'M BEGINNING TO GET A BAD FEEELING ABOUT THIS

The week ended with a three-day hiatus from set, even for Beano, which was unusual for him as production normally flogged him to death. Only four more Crimean Saturdays remained; Lyndon had lately been setting up a disco in the reception area in front of the bar. At this point, partying had been taken to new extremes, usually pumped along by DJ Lyndon's choice of dance tunes. Not everyone was a fan of heavy dance music, but they generally let Lyndon get on with it; on this particular occasion Daragh loomed up to the DJ console demanding that the CD he was brandishing in his hand be played. Normally not an untoward request; trouble was Lyndon didn't feel that Buddy Holly was suitable for a playlist at a rave even though, interestingly enough, Mr Holly had written a song called 'Rave On'. Lyndon rather contemptuously shouted across his console, 'Play Buddy Holly? That'll be the day.' At three in the morning, Big D, like everyone in the room, was a little worse for wear and didn't see the funny side, throwing the CD at Lyndon while shoving over the DJ console at the same time, scattering beer and CDs everywhere and putting a temporary halt to the raving. From that point on the confrontation was known as the 'Buddy Holly Incident', causing much mirth when it was mentioned. But never in front of Daragh. A few days later, when things had died down, Daragh was heard to say: 'Ah, Lyndon. All the qualities of a dog, except the loyalty,' one of Big D's many humorous sayings, delivered with maximum fondness, of course.

Thank God we had all of Sunday to recover from the merriment; our next action was recreating a Sunday sermon delivered by the camp vicar in the early part of 'Honour', where Sharpe is arrested for duelling and therefore murder. We drove to Baidar in two cars, two Chosen Men per vehicle; on the face of it a victory, we thought, but the powers had the last laugh, supplying us with clapped-out Ladas, not the more 'luxurious' four-door Volgas that transported those on a higher pay grade. At least the ride to work was a lot quicker and the car actually had seat belts, though in all likelihood were no safer than the worst of the minivans. Moving through the week we revisited another part of the vast Baidar Valley to shoot Sharpe's vicious fight with El Matarife, or the Slaughterman; a rock-strewn bowl where in 'Eagle' Sharpe illustrates the hell of battle to the assembled South Essex. By the close of the work week, heavy snow had begun to fall up on the valley which I thought would bring a halt to filming, as it might be hard to maintain continuity with previous scenes shot in dry, fine weather. But we soldiered on, Tom claiming falling snow wouldn't register on camera; more tricks from the mendacious art called film-making.

Of course, the decision to plough on was based mainly on financial concerns (Daragh's facial flare-up had already put us behind schedule), not on the health and safety of the unit. On the morning of 18 November, the snow lay deep and crisp and even, resembling a winter wonderland; okay not so deep, but still treacherous underfoot and requiring the first use of a Taurus, the all-terrain military vehicle that proved so useful in the snow of Dimerdji. Here at Baidar we had already seen a jeep sliding into a Volga, causing more than minor damage. Uncomfortable though the freezing conditions and snow might be, the valley did look beautiful. When lunch was called, some of the crew decided to return from location to base camp on horseback, not uncommon as there were many proficient horse riders in the unit. However, when a member of the camera crew, Phil Jones, decided to mount up, riding a horse was fairly new to him. It was a decision that would change his life forever. The horses broke into a semi-gallop on the treacherous, rocky, snow-covered ground; Phil's horse slipped or reared, throwing him from the saddle, his head striking a boulder as he hit the ground. It was a sickening, life-threatening injury that would eventually require a private air ambulance to fly Phil back to the UK for surgery.

Needless to say, a cloud descended over the whole unit in the aftermath of this incident, harking back to the dark days of the McGann injury, except that Paul was able to hobble along with his work while Phil would be left fighting for his life. The parallels, of course, being their accidents didn't happen while filming. My *Sharpe* jinx theory was gathering unwelcome corroboration. This being Sharpe Film, we battled on with the schedule, filming scenes from 'Honour' set at a British encampment by the side of a frozen pond. As well as looking visually stunning, soldiers in uniform were scattered around the pond's edge chopping wood and building fires, a picture made all the more magical by the light dusting of snow on the ground. The scenes were memorable and pleasurable to shoot, especially Harper revealing that Sharpe hadn't been executed after all and then leading us off to liberate him from Colonel Ducos's jail. Plus, we were quite close to demob, which helped to enhance my mood.

It had been a taxing week, but we were so tantalisingly close to wrap that we should have been floating blissfully on air. Setbacks came thick and fast on *Sharpe*, and we should have been thoroughly used to it by now, but Phil was a well-liked member of the crew and we were still uncertain of his prognosis. Due to the severity of his injury he was admitted into a naval hospital in Sevastopol, from where he was flown from a military base in Belbek for the flight to the UK as part of *Sharpe*'s international medical insurance policy. Malcolm had flown in to replace Simon Lewis, who had accompanied the air ambulance; a crew dinner was held at the Oreanda Hotel, the grandest establishment in Yalta. It was a lot smaller than the immense Yalta Hotel and should probably have been where the unit was housed had they not tried to do *Sharpe* on a skin-tight budget. Dinner that evening was a lot more subdued than normal; the new intake of 'Honour' actors must have thought we were a very abstemious, boring crew. I got to bed before midnight, surely a record for a Saturday night on *Sharpe*. There were other reasons for keeping a clear head: the following day I was going for Sunday lunch at Natasha's parents' place. This time I would meet her father. Though I was gradually falling in love with the prettiest girl in Yalta, nay, the entire Crimea, I wasn't asking for her hand in marriage, so I wasn't feeling nervous. Much. I needn't have been, as the afternoon passed in a relaxed manner with Natasha assuring me that her unsmiling dad wasn't disapproving of me. It was just the way he was. Yeah, living under Soviet communism would do that to you; then again, her mum, Valentina, was constantly smiling, so I wasn't sure what to think.

My penultimate week on this marathon Crimean tour of attrition was relatively light, affording me time to start thinking about our demob from the peninsula and the aftermath vis-à-vis Natasha. Getting back to Yalta would mean taking on the laborious task of securing a visa at the Russian Embassy in London. Equally problematic would be getting her a visa to visit London without me attending the visa interview; however, that bridge would have to be crossed, possibly several times, in the near future. Half the week swished by with trips to town, drinks with Malcolm, swims in the newly discovered vast, indoor, saltwater swimming pool and saunas.

The remainder of the week was spent at snow-covered Dimerdji, filming the Chosen's liberation of their leader from French custody, laying waste to their ammunition dump for good measure. Again, memorable scenes to shoot, especially as I scorched the skin off my right hand setting alight a fuse with the flintlock of my Baker. I hoped it would look really cool in the finished episode. I took quite a kicking filming the rest of the sequence, too, particularly when entering Sharpe's cell; our hero, unaware it's his own men dressed as French Voltigeurs liberating him, attacks us. Not one to hold back, Sean went to take me out, slamming me up against the cell wall and almost crushing my larynx in the process as he held fast to my collar. So when you see Harris in the scene pleading for a cessation of hostilities, that's genuine concern for my own wellbeing; it's an example of why Beano is such a good Sharpe. He's totally in touch with his inner psycho.

I ended the week battered, burned and bruised, yet content at having completed filming some of the more exhilarating scenes of Chosen derring-do. Dimerdji had got quite a dusting of snow during the week but it hadn't stopped us filming; what did halt the shoot was a heavy layer of mist causing us to relocate to Polikur only minutes after we had departed make-up, now situated in the cosy Dimerdji nursery school. Our scenes required Dimerdji, so the Chosen Men were stood down, to learn the not entirely unexpected news that our tour would be extended by two days. Unfortunately, as the unit vehicles descended the treacherously slippery and winding path, the truck with the honey wagon strapped to it turned over on one of the bends with the buckets used to collect the sewage spilling everywhere. I shall not describe the mess left for the unit manager to deal with.

After dinner many of the unit gathered in the actors' lounge to party; I brought out my VHS player to watch a movie, unwisely leaving it out in the lounge overnight. Next morning, as I blearily exited my room, the VHS player, which had been left on top of the TV, was gone from our supposedly secure sanatorium interior. It had the stench of an inside job; probably one of the guards, knowing we were soon off home, took it upon himself to acquire a farewell gift. I didn't even bother to report the theft; I had watched most of my stash of videos and would have to make do with MTV, NBC Super channel and Russian television in the final ten days of this campaign. On the plus side, William O'Hill had paid out my account which was a handsome four hundred quid after betting there would be a second series of *Sharpe*, as well as my wins at the hanger throwing game.

TAKE ME HOME, COUNTRY ROADS

Finally, the home stretch of our longest Crimean stint ever had arrived. Soon all would be over. I was feeling extremely conflicted, though; I yearned to be back home in London but that meant leaving Natasha behind; I didn't think I'd be facing this particular dilemma when setting out from England almost four months ago. At Dimerdji the liberation of Sharpe continued; it was rather nice wearing smart French uniforms for a change; by comparison, our Chosen Men costumes had become rags. Nearly as ragged as some of the crew's spirits; we arrived one morning to the sight of Penny, wrapped in a foil blanket to ward off the cold, being escorted from the mountain slope back to base camp. Penny's cry for help, if slightly dramatic, was a reaction that campaign veterans would recognise, but I suppose no more dramatic than going on strike to demand a hot breakfast. Continually having to wade through a river of shit, the indifference or impotence of production to shield us from stresses and, in Penny's case, strife over an inter-departmental power struggle – Penny's second-in-command had started to go above her head – all had taken their toll, and we were only eight days from demob.

With the light clearly visible at the end of the tunnel, more 'day trippers' arrived for the closing scenes of 'Honour', notably Ron Cook, playing Napoleon, who had worked with Lyndon on *The Singing Detective*. He remarked on how Lyndon had transformed from a cherubic, innocent little boy into a raving late teen; two tours on *Sharpe* could have that effect. Their arrival coincided with the official announcement of our departure day: Wednesday 8 December, just five days short of four months.

My last visit to Dimerdji that year saw Sharpe and his Chosen ascending a snowy slope to take out a French cannon emplacement under heavy fire, in a re-creation of the decisive action in the Vittoria campaign. As there were no more battle scenes to shoot, the pyrotechnic boys unloaded the remains of their gunpowder stash into the charges. The combination of huge explosions, a demob-happy crew and the exhilaration of battle could only have one outcome on *Sharpe*: near disaster! Rifleman Moore was making his debut in front of camera acting as a super-extra attached to the Chosen Men for the assault. Before action was called, Marc Jenny plotted a safe path through the 'minefield' that kept us within frame. As Richard Moore wasn't a lily-livered actor, he probably wasn't paying proper attention; in his mind he really was at Vittoria steeling himself for the push up the hill; Konstantin Stanislavski, inventor of method acting, would have been proud. Action was called, we set off remembering to keep our mouths open to protect our ears from the compression of the blasts; fluorescent ear plugs would have been visible on camera, not to mention looking very un-macho for a Chosen Man. Inevitably Richard's path took him next to a particularly colossal blast spraying stones and scraps of the charge into the right side of his face causing lots of blood flow. It looked awful and a little too close to his eye. Had it been Sean or Daragh there would have been hell to pay; mutilation of extras like Rifleman Moore or a Chosen Man, not so much. However, some might say that, as military adviser, Richard's importance to *Sharpe* might have outweighed that of a bit-part actor like myself.

End-of-term fever now ruled with parties popping up all around the Chernomore in the lead-up to the official wrap party. One evening I noticed Sean hitting the bar with a vengeance. He didn't show it, but he was under enormous pressure, was worked really hard and was required on set in almost every shot; production's way of getting their money's worth from Sean, I guess. So it was more an outpouring of relief that made Beano get so mashed, and let's face it getting mashed on *Sharpe* was a form of escape for all of us. Of course, Sean had absolutely nothing to prove with his approach to the role; he embodied Sharpe, effortlessly ticking all the boxes demanded of a true action hero and the camera loved his face.

On 8 December 1993, two coaches pulled out of the Chernomore sanatorium bound for Simferopol airport, thus ending the second *Sharpe* campaign. As the bus trundled along the motorway I sat staring forlornly out of the window; there was none of the elation of last year's departure. I should have been on top of the world; I was part of a potential television legend, every penny earned in four months had piled up, barely touched in my bank account, and I was returning home. Home to a choice of edible food on demand, to see family, friends and go to Chelsea games. For all that, I felt hollow and slightly discombobulated. Noting my melancholy, Charmaine sat beside me to enquire why. Rather dramatically, surprising even myself, I declared that I was leaving behind the girl I was going to marry, despite having previously disavowed any notion of tying the knot.

Our plane landed back at Stansted after an uneventful flight. Waiting for the carousel to spit out our bags, I noticed the arrivals terminal seemed intensely bright, loud and overwhelming; it was a jarring welcome back to the capitalist world. Still not sated after four months of non-stop partying, a final soirée was arranged on the bus trip back to London. Upon arriving home, a group of those without family commitments repaired to my flat for one last blowout. The final actions of a long, hard campaign, it was almost as if we didn't want it to end, didn't want to face up to reality.

INTERBELLUM II

I suppose one more night as a courtier to my lord Bacchus wasn't the best way to slip back into 'normal' life and jumping back on the London treadmill would soon have to be faced. My first mission was a trip to Bromley Place, asking whether Sharpe Film could assist me in getting a Russian visa to visit Natasha. Applying independently at the embassy would have been a real hassle in terms of paperwork, not to mention the cost, so I was grateful to Cindy Winter at the production office for her help. Once my visa was granted, Natasha and I arranged to meet up in Moscow, saving me from the ordeal of two flights to get to Yalta.

On 21 December, Lyndon and I were invited to Sean's for Xmas drinks, with all the attendant damage to the system that entailed. Just before New Year I received an unexpected call from Liz Hurley; turned out Hugh Grant's football team, Penguin Books, needed an extra man and I duly obliged, playing in goal against a team from the V&A. As the match entered its closing stages, Hugh dropped back towards goal, tackling a V&A forward in the box; the man from the museum made a meal of the challenge, resulting in a soft penalty. I gave Hugh the 'don't worry about it, my son' hand gesture, adjusted my goalie gloves and puffed myself up while shooting mind-distracting vibes at the penalty taker. The kick came, I went the right way, getting a little piece of the ball with my right hand, which, for a split second, I thought was a save, only to look back to see the ball nestling in the back of the net. The game ended in a draw. Had I not spent four months getting wasted in the Crimea, I would have stopped that shot and gone down in Penguin Books football team folklore. Alas, it wasn't to be, but Hugh was still impressed and thankful that I had showed up. We repaired to Hugh's place in Fulham for a post-match cup of tea with Liz, still in her favoured outfit of Hugh's pyjama top. Banished forever from my mind was the media-fed image of Hugh as an effete, stuttering, gawky, fop; Hugh was a cool, funny, totally normal chap, apart from the red-hot film career and one of the world's most desirable women on his arm. The bastard!

By mid-January, post-production on 'Company', 'Enemy' and 'Honour' was entering the final stages and the Chosen Men were called for a voice syncing session. ADR, or voice syncing, is a chance to smooth out any sound drop-outs and muffled lines as well as adding the shouts, screams and groans of battle. The Chosen, not blessed with an abundance of lines, especially in 'Company', always performed their lines perfectly, so we weren't there to correct fluffed dialogue. Our job that day was to record any incidental shouts, particularly in 'Honour', where we dressed as Voltigeurs to rescue Sharpe, shouting 'cholera, cholera' to ward off any close scrutiny from Ducos's guards. The session allowed for a mini Sharpe reunion in the lounge of the Coach and Horses where the Chosen Men, Sean, Daragh and Tom Clegg were joined by Nick Rowe and cameraman Martin Hume. Martin came with an update on Phil Jones the grip, who was still in very bad shape after his fall from a horse at Baidar Valley; an absolutely horrific situation for Phil and his family.

MARCHING ON MOSCOW

I collected my Russian visa, allowing me to book flights for a reunion with Natasha. Actually, it was *Sharpe* secretary Cindy who booked my tickets, so it seemed the powers endorsed our *Sharpe*-generated romance. Shame I had chosen the middle of a Russian winter for my trip. Ever attuned to news from the East, I read in the newspaper that Clinton and Yeltsin had signed the Kremlin accords which stopped the policy of pre-programmed targeting of each other's countries. The treaty also provided for the dismantling of Ukraine's entire nuclear arsenal with a promise that the West would guarantee their safety in the event of an attack; comforting to know, seeing as calamitous outcomes were never far away in the former Soviet Union. Natasha had repeatedly expressed fears that the communists could return, thrusting Ukraine back into the 'good old days', to which I always replied that ex-Soviets had bitten too deeply on the sweet apple of capitalism to return to communism. It seemed inconceivable that any aggression could come from former big brother up north in the Kremlin, so it appeared Ukraine was safe!

On 1 February I touched down in Moscow, though not totally realising it at the time, to begin a new chapter in my life. Having experienced nine Massachusetts winters, I felt fairly confident of my ability to deal with whatever ravages a Moscow winter had to offer. Two days in, and the mercury dropped to minus 27° Celsius; taking into account the wind chill factor the temperature was more like minus 40° Celsius. The plan was to spend a couple of nights in a hotel then find an apartment to rent for the rest of our stay. Applying for a Russian tourist visa required you first to pay for a hotel voucher, which was only available from a narrow range of Intourist hotels. As my visa was booked through Sharpe Film, I circumvented the cost of a hotel voucher, which I was feeling pretty smug about; any feelings of self-satisfaction quickly waned as I discovered hotel after hotel fully booked or charging several hundred dollars per night. Now,

I had come armed with a fistful of dollars and a credit card, but I refused to pay sky-high hotel prices in the capital of the former Evil Empire. Maybe Muscovites were drunk on capitalism or it was simple case of supply and demand with plane loads of western businessmen flocking to the Wild East for a fast rouble and driving up the rates.

Eventually we found a place at the Sovincentre where we spent an idyllic few days, lazing around in our room. When we did venture out into the cold, past the clock in reception that on the hour boomed out the opening bars of Rimsky-Korsakov's *Scheherazade*, it was purely for sightseeing or the hunt for decent food, a far easier task in Moscow than down on the peninsula. To my cost, I discovered my leather jacket and Crombie combo proved unfit for purpose in the scything winds that whipped across Red Square. Once we'd done the tourist bit, the hunt for an apartment began, pumping all our connections with former Russian crew members. Secretly I was also hitting my old mate Sacha Puttnam, who was studying in Moscow, for any contacts he had at the British Embassy, hoping to quickly get a visa for Natasha so she could return with me to the UK. I was counting on consular officials having some awareness of a mainly British film unit transiting through Moscow these past two years. An interview was booked, the application was successful and a visa was granted, which we collected the very next day. There would be no teary goodbyes this time around.

Our flat hunt came up trumps with Julia, an interpreter from our second tour, finding us a neat apartment at a very reasonable rate in the outer reaches of Moscow. The trek into Moscow on the metro took forty-five minutes to reach Red Square from our stop, Schelkovskaya, at the very end of the line. That round trip meant we often spent a couple of hours on the subway almost every day; it was a great chance to get to know the city by watching its inhabitants commute. The hopeful, optimistic faces of young Muscovites and the hard-bitten, older generation, worn-down by communism. I can't imagine what they all thought of my appearance; nevertheless, I became pretty adept at getting about on the subway at a time when there was absolutely no signage in English. The downside was that it proved an effective way to catch Russian flu.

Thanks to an old friend of Natasha's, an actor in the Russian movie industry, Irina Schmeleva, we got a heavy dose of culture with an invitation to a performance of *The Marriage of Figaro* at the Lenkom Theatre and got to hang out with actors in the green room in the Taganka Theatre. However, the bit of culture that made me sit bolt upright in my seat was a film festival screening held at the prestigious Dom Kino, or 'house of film'. The movie was a pretty unremarkable tale about a sultan and his harem set in a Central Asian kingdom several centuries ago. Much of the film I barely understood, but my attention was suddenly riveted by the members of the harem, one of whom was Maya, object of my affections from the first year of *Sharpe*. My liaison with Maya pre-dated Natasha's arrival, plus she really liked Maya, so a potentially awkward moment passed without any dramas.

NO TURNING BACK

On 19 February I boarded a flight back to London with my love from the Crimea by my side; happy to have fled the sub-zero temperatures, the shell-suited, leather-jacketed, queue-jumping mafia goons and the monumental subway commutes. Having said that, we had a lovely time living together as a proper couple in our cosy, snow-bound apartment; now it was time to be together in the 'real world'. Natasha was no stranger to the West, having visited the US on that student exchange programme as well as visiting Russia's neighbour Finland, so hitting London wasn't as overwhelming as it might have been. Plus, there was a whole extended family there to greet her: the Sharpe family.

Natasha's appearance heralded the Sharpe social whirl going into overdrive with visits from all points of the Sharpe compass; cast and crew from both campaigns popped over to my flat. Drinks with Nick Rowe, tea with Tim Bentinck, lunch with the Sutherlands and watching the Oscars with Paul Trussell, and dinner at Sean and Mel's. A close-knit family born out of the chaos, hardship and deprivation of the Crimean *Sharpes*; Lyndon drove us down to Shropshire to visit Pete and his wife Jaqs. Beautiful scenery, quaint old pubs and trying not to get too hungover; it was lovely spending time with the Postlethwaites, but it was scary trying to keep up with Pete.

Before making the Moscow trip, I had booked tickets to visit my parents in Massachusetts. As there was little chance of getting a US visa for Natasha quickly, and with over a month left on her British visa, she decided she would stay in London while I flew off to America for a couple of weeks. My trip encompassed a swing through LA to visit an old schoolfriend, Jordan Stone, working in the film industry, and a visit to the O'Malleys in their West Hollywood apartment. While getting soused at one of Big D's new favoured watering holes, I gleaned information about the next series we would be filming 'Sword', 'Gold' and a brand-new story, 'Sharpe's Battle'. I wondered if they would be filming the 'Gold' script as it was originally written with the same cast.

While in LA, my mate Jordan got us an invite to actor Billy Zane's birthday party at a house up in the Hollywood Hills. As I had hung out with Billy a fair bit while working on *Memphis Belle* five years earlier, I didn't feel awkward showing up at the party. Arriving at an amazing residence overlooking LA's shiny lights, I thought, damn, I know Billy works a lot, but this place is fairly spectacular. Pretty soon I bumped into Billy saying a very quick hello as he made his way around the spacious home; I found out the house was on loan from an actor friend for the night. My next encounter was with the homeowner himself; as he walked across the room our eyes met with some sort of vague recognition. As he got closer, the penny dropped for both of us: it was Patrick Bauchau, Assumpta's former lover of some years who I had last seen in Ms Serna's suite in Yalta. I tried tactfully to recap where we had met, but the look on his face was one of a man freshly reminded of bad times; our chat was brief, and I didn't stay long at the party after that.

Sharpe's reach had extended across an ocean, a continent and 6,700 miles, but now it was time to return to my love from the Crimea waiting for me in London, stopping on the East Coast to say goodbye to my parents in Amherst. At the local multiplex I caught the newly released *Four Weddings and a Funeral*, Hugh Grant's latest film. I was told Liz caused a stir at the opening, upstaging everyone by wearing a flesh-revealing Versace number held together with a bunch of safety pins; that wouldn't hurt the ratings when 'Sharpe's Enemy' aired at the end of May.

Back in the UK I bade farewell to Natasha feeling fairly certain we'd be reunited in a few months. On 7 May 1994, Sheffield United visited Stamford Bridge to play Chelsea in the season finale, having to avoid defeat to escape relegation. At half-time, I checked to see if

I could find Beano among the massed ranks of Blades fans. He must have had the same idea and we met at the foot of the stairs leading to the away fans; he was looking happy with himself, as well you might if you were Sean Bean, but this was true happiness. Sheffield were winning 1-0 at half-time and therefore on course to avoid relegation. He intimated the third series was 99 per cent confirmed with just a few details to straighten out; very reassuring as it was directly from the horse's mouth. Of course, my agent wouldn't get the call with details of my deal for a while. We kept our meeting short as I felt the eyes of all the Blades fans in the stand were upon us, so we took our seats on either side of the divide for the second half of the game. Chelsea equalised then scored a last-minute winner, a result that relegated Beano's beloved Blades. I didn't try to find Sean to say goodbye after the match.

Beano's news about a third series helped dispel any doubt in Natasha's mind, promising to make our impending separation a brief one. Natasha's last evening was spent at the Groucho Club as Malcolm Craddock's guest; chief interpreter Irina Meldris was also in attendance. I knew Irina was high up in the East-West Creative Association and the organisation had a London office, she could be seen on screen interpreting for Michael Palin in his series *Pole to Pole* as he passed through the Soviet Union. I took her presence as more evidence of the Sharpe machine mobilising for a third campaign. Not that Malcolm was in any way forthcoming about verifying the rumours, maintaining his best poker face, claiming nothing had been confirmed yet or even if they were planning to have Harris ride again. He did manage to let slip that he and Muir would be taking a two-thirds cut in their respective fees; my heart bled, just a little. Malcolm highlighting his struggles with ITV, to deflect from divulging any secrets, was par for the course, so I wasn't unduly concerned about what lay over those faraway hills.

On 7 July, my agent called with details of my third series contract. It was long expected, yet I was delighted to be taking the first steps towards signing up for campaign number three; that joy was short-lived when I was told there was no money in the acting budget to give me an increase in pay. I was hardly expecting a massive raise, but I lived in possibly forlorn hope. The powers claimed ITV was demanding *Sharpe* be made for less money and Sean's contract when replacing Paul McGann was one that escalated steeply each year, forcing cutbacks in other areas of the cast, namely the Chosen Men. After instructing my agent to play a little hard ball with the negotiations, the casting director, on production's instructions, fired off a threat to hurry up or they would find someone else to play the role.

That may have been some of the more palatable news that first week of July; calls were put in to the other Chosen Men to find out if they had been met with the same hard line. Michael Mears was only offered a one-episode appearance though it transpired this was a mutual decision. Mike said he had an offer to do an Alan Ayckbourn play that would almost certainly transfer to the West End. It had echoes of when Paul Trussell chose other work rather than sign for another series, complicated in his case, of course, by affairs of the heart. As Paul wasn't invited back for the third tour, the 'Isaiah Law' stated that if you declined *Sharpe* once you'd never be asked back again.

The nuclear bombshell dropped after a phone call to Lyndon, who was distraught and angry, not only about being left out of the final episode of this upcoming series, but effectively saying goodbye

133

to *Sharpe* forever with the death of Perkins written into 'Sharpe's Battle'. It seemed we had become expendable. Need to save money? Let's reduce one of the elements of the show that fans really love. At the conclusion of *Sharpe* Two with four Chosen Men left standing, you couldn't help but think that all the producers saw was a target-rich environment. They could tug on the heartstrings of the audience while saving several thousand pounds with one stroke of the pen. Double, bubble as they say! The old *Sharpe* angst was back, even before we had boarded the plane; yet I was in two minds. I had the prospect of a reunion with Natasha, not to mention the sixteen weeks' employment, the resort location and the non-stop party with your mates. And, in truth, by now I had become almost institutionalised, thoroughly used to incarceration within the *Sharpe* cycle. I wasn't going to quit halfway to the summit of television legend, I wouldn't buck the status quo; such was my love for the project I would almost have done *Sharpe* for free, a fact I, of course, kept quiet from the producers.

3

THE YEAR OF
LIVING DANGEROUSLY

O n Friday 5 August 1994, the Sharpe caravan headed one more time towards Stansted airport. New associate producer Ray Frift fancied he could get cargo loaded and unit embarked with no more than ninety minutes' delay. Anxious to prove his point, Ray chivvied the stragglers like a sheep dog, herding them towards the gate, causing a bit of friction between the production office and veterans of past campaigns. Around 1:30 in the afternoon, dangerously close to ninety minutes late, we were all aboard waiting to depart, only to discover they still hadn't loaded a consignment of four thousand sausages into the hold.

I couldn't help harking wistfully back to the Dimerdji Bacon Riot where our rebellion guaranteed people's right to a hot breakfast on location and how the delay for sausages was a direct result of that and therefore our fault. No good deed goes unpunished. There was also admonishment from the new regime after Jeremy 'Jezzer' Childs (Colonel Augustus Farthingdale), blabbed in *Tatler* about how much we liked a party on *Sharpe*; and I quote: 'they were the biggest partyers I had ever worked with, they smoked and drank with a fervour unwitnessed and this was all before we left Stansted'. His comments prompted the new management to warn us that our style of post-shoot relaxing would not be tolerated under the new regime. I thought to myself, fat chance of putting a curb on our excesses; after a little spell in the Crimea they too would be longing to get out of their heads. Interesting times were ahead!

As Sharpe charter flights went, this was one of the smoothest, calmest trips so far; the plane's interior didn't reek, the cabin's decor wasn't knackered and they even served a fairly decent meal, a radical departure from previous departures. As the plane landed on Simferopol's ridiculously long runway, I could see parched terrain on either side of the landing strip. With the plane stationary on the tarmac, the cabin door opened, letting the blazing late afternoon heat envelope us. I knew a Crimea summer could be toasty, but this was a new level of heat. Relieved to get under cover of the terminal for the customary checks, I noticed our coach pulling up outside. Moments later out spilled Igor Dymetriev, top Yalta interpreter and his best mate, Natasha; first sighting of my love from the Crimea for three months. So, as counter-intuitive as it seemed, to all intents and purposes I had actually arrived 'home'.

This year we were bypassing the Moscow Hotel in favour of a stay at the Tavria Hotel; a lot smaller than the Moscow and even more basic, if that was possible. The hotel bar's furnishings were clad in red leather and it was a favourite of the local mafia or racketeers, we were told; apparently, only the other week a mobster had been 'rubbed out' on the premises. Nice one Sharpe Film! Chucking us into the firing line yet again; in truth, this was the new norm in the ex-Soviet Union. With little protection from the law, the new mafia went about doing as they pleased with impunity. I can only imagine that we were protected because the Association were a kind of mafia in themselves, capable of putting the frighteners on anyone messing with the foreigners. Funnily enough, our new associate producer Ray reminded us of a 1960s East End gangster, sporting shades and talking like one of the Kray gang. The image was further reinforced in his commandeering of the largest banqueting table in the bar, for his 'mob': new line producer Chris Burt and Tom Clegg, all long-time associates, holding court like grizzled wise guys.

THREE'S A CHARM

The first day of principal photography soon arrived and so began on our third trip to the rodeo. The charm, the allure, the intrigue of being out in the former Soviet Union had all but vanished, certainly for two-tour veterans. The opening salvos would be fired at stalwart *Sharpe* location, Eskikermen. Daragh had been logging the time we had done on *Sharpe*, reliably informing me that this was week forty-one. Waking for the 6 a.m. call was the hardest it had ever been, the two-day acclimatisation period having been spent blatantly disregarding the powers' warnings to curb our bacchanalian excesses. This, combined with the three-hour time difference, the debilitating heat and a sleep-disturbing duet of mosquitos and barking dog, meant that I had about ninety minutes' sleep before my first trip to location.

At this early hour, the eerily beautiful base camp was mercifully cool. Less attractive was our base camp itself, set up by our mates from Simferopol barracks, consisting of the familiar knackered canvas tents housing the various departments, set up adjacent to a small reservoir, its bank ringed with tide marks showing the evidence of ongoing evaporation. Again, they had put us in camping-style nylon tents, perfectly adequate when the weather was benign at the front end of the shoot, but as soon as the winds from China got going we'd be back under army canvas in no time.

Veterans were overjoyed to have Sano, chief architect of Harris's hairstyle, back in the fold, though she was now subordinate to make-up chief Jacquetta Levon. Jacquetta, in an attempt to run things efficiently for a change, called me before leaving the UK to tell Natasha to read the script before we started shooting. I didn't bother telling her I hadn't received my script at that point, so I doubted there was one doing the rounds in Yalta for her to familiarise herself with. There were other *Sharpe* debutants on the crew; first assistant director Marc Jenny had made way for Michael Mallinson and it was all change in the camera department, too, most notably Chris Abomnes, a two-tour veteran promoted from the ranks to become a focus puller. Perhaps the worst reverse was losing Set Meals, their cooks Giles and Rachel had become an integral part of the Sharpe social circle and, going by the fleeting pass I made of the cafeteria, the standards of the new caterers were as barrel-scrapingly low as that of our chefs from year one.

First up this tour was 'Sharpe's Gold', not the story reverentially following Bernard's novel, but a bastardised, non-typical *Sharpe* yarn bearing absolutely no relation to any of the previous five episodes. If they wanted to shoot the original 'Gold' script with the same cast, production would have had to honour the original contract as well as pay out for a new one. In this parsimonious climate, paying actors twice for doing one job was anathema to production; instead we were left with Sharpe battling a bunch of Aztec-worshipping, skin-flaying psychos led by a baddie prone to making cat noises. It seemed ITV was still smarting from their insurance premium going up, so were now reluctant to grant Malcolm and Muir the budget lavished on episodes like 'Company' and were now demanding every episode be brought in more quickly and for less money. After three series, *Sharpe* had become just another product on the shelves of ITV, with any pretence that we were creating art thrown out of the window.

Two hours past our scheduled on-set arrival time, we were called to line up for the camera. Once the Chosen were shown their starting positions it quickly became apparent that we were yet again extreme background dressing; barely half a day had elapsed, the honeymoon was already over and we got an early reminder of our position in the lower echelons of the Sharpe food chain. However, literally and figuratively, we knew where we stood and so we dutifully waited to film Bess and Ellie Nugent gallop into camp, dismounting at Wellington's tent. All captured on a wide shot with a camera positioned on a crane, very cinematic. With all elements for the shot in place, it transpired that at her audition, Jayne Ashbourne, playing Ellie Nugent, had perhaps been a little economical with the truth when describing her equestrian skills. The shot was delayed for an hour while they kitted out stuntwoman Zuliya in Jayne's costume for the scene.

It had been one hell of a first morning: the delays, the dust, the unbearable heat, lack of water and confirmation of our lower than a snake's belly status in the scene; surely it couldn't get any worse? Of course it could; lunch was called and we got affirmation of how inept our new caterers were, with a disappointing, limited and underwhelming spread. Why was I surprised? No longer would I waste words slagging off the standard of on-set cuisine. But developments like the reduction of the Chosen contribution, the pay freeze, the barely perceptible improvements in circumstances and the attempt at nanny-state control had made conditions ripe for revolution; and it was only the first day of shooting. Thankfully we were stood down and whisked back to the Tavria after lunch.

AUTUMN OF DISCONTENT

As the first week wore on, more 'Gold' cast were dropped into the fray via Istanbul, the new preferred route – I imagine because it was more cost effective – including Provost Marshal Philip McGough and a couple of actors playing deserters, Jake Abrahams and Peter Hugo Daley. Jake I had met some years earlier in Liverpool with Paul McGann, enjoying an after-hours shindig at Jake's dad's pub. We got on well and he would slot perfectly into the *Sharpe* gang. Mr Hugo Daley appeared to be absolutely bonkers, especially after a couple of beers and a smoke, so he would also fit in splendidly. To ease their way into life at Camp Sharpe, they naturally gravitated to the rooms Lyndon and I occupied as we represented the unofficial welcoming committee. Someone guaranteed a warm welcome was the man playing our eponymous hero, Sean Mark Bean, flying in six days after the main unit.

Sean was eased into the shoot with the trademark end-of-episode shot of us walking over the hills. Beano looked great: tanned, fit and appearing much the better for having given up cigarettes. This year he had the newly acquired perk of a motorhome with its very own driver, Gary Fiddler, who had looked after the motorhomes on a drama I had shot the year before. After a mercifully short shooting day, we repaired to the heat of the Tavria where we initiated Sean into the now burgeoning Boules Society. Games were played on a purpose-built court above the outdoor bar thus initiating a new time-killing pursuit; soon money was changing hands in head-to-head matches. This time, instead of just laying the odds, Daragh was competing in the games, taking a hundred dollars off me before I clawed back fifty bucks in a tense match.

Anything to take our minds off the heat, which far exceeded the previous two campaigns, so much so that the Crimea was now officially in drought, resulting in water cut-offs at the Tavria. Only one week into the production, we arrived at the hotel having just shot in some of the hottest, sweatiest conditions hitherto experienced. A shower and a cold beer were the only things we craved; but we returned to find that washing in any shape or form was impossible due to the water being cut off; you couldn't even flush the toilet. Among the tidal wave of papers sent to us in the run-up to embarkation was a promise to make sure the unit had water at least twice a day, which meant production knew all about the water problems. Worse than being unable to wash was that if you used the toilet during a shutdown your unflushed leavings sat there for at least ten hours. Now, water cut-offs were nothing new on *Sharpe*, but in the past they were limited and were over within a couple of hours; possibly after someone had received the appropriate bribe. This latest cut-off lasted most of the Friday and into the Saturday, breaching the 'water twice a day' promise made by production.

Sunrise on 15 August was magnificent; the drive to Eskikermen took us through flat, rolling farmland, stopping at a level crossing as locomotives still adorned with the Soviet star passed through. That was probably as good as the day got; on set it was another scorcher and we gently broiled in the fierce Crimean heat while shooting a scene with the Nugents. Rosie Linehan playing Bess Nugent, a distant relative of Wellington, was an interesting character off camera; back at the Tavria, Rosie summoned Lyndon, Mike Mears and me into her room for a chat. We listened politely as she began telling us 'this show was slowly turning her mad'. She continued, 'I've sorted out more insurance cover for myself because of the horses, the water situation and the kids on the fourth floor getting wasted, coming home from partying and starting fires.' I didn't like it that she kept her eyes firmly fixed on mine throughout the whole monologue.

Later I found out she had committed her fears to paper which she had absent-mindedly left by the communal phone; Lyndon found the list, made multiple photocopies and hung them around the hotel as a prank. So, though Rosie's meeting was an attempt to pre-empt any aggro that inevitably would have come her way, the damage was done. As soon as production got wind of it, they would identify the main culprits as 'the wasted kids on the fourth floor', not the wild horses or lack of water. I supposed we could expect more 'nanny state' declarations from the production secretary. Lyndon's prank may have misfired, but it was good Rosie's concerns were aired, especially the water shut-offs which were now an annoyingly regular occurrence. The very next evening, production accountant Pat came looking for Daragh. Lyndon replied we hadn't seen him for some time, but, eager to glean the inside dirt on the unfolding situation, could we give him a message? Duly divulging, she had overheard Daragh talking to his agent in LA, complaining that production were in breach of contract regarding the water situation; Pat fully expected Daragh to down tools and not show up for work the next day.

Morning came with full anticipation of industrial action on the horizon; production was taking the piss, metaphorically, of course, as the piss remained in our toilets for hours at a time. The Bacon Riot spirit began to rise within us. No words needed to be exchanged: we knew that if this continued we would have to take action. Quite a busy morning already without so much as an inch of film put through the 'gate'; we were shooting the preposterous Richard Sharpe versus Ellie Nugent shooting match, a bit like Bob Hope going up against Calamity Jane in *The Paleface*. As was the custom the Chosen were mostly lashed together in the background for most of the scene. The construction of the scene took forty or more shots to put together, each shot seemingly taking forever, as if nobody really knew what they were doing. Maybe it was the heat, the dehydration or the fact that we couldn't flush the loo after number ones, let alone a number two; either way this was Sharpe in the Crimea, there was always something niggling away at your patience, sanity and resolve to carry on.

A water crisis meeting was called to order in the bar on the evening of 16 August, exactly two years to the day since Paul McGann had sustained his initial knee injury sending the production into chaos. On the face of it, lack of water was a less serious occurrence; nevertheless, it had all the potential to cause disorder further down the line. The meeting was short and pointless as all the powers could offer was 'It's not our fault, bear with us as we try to fix it.' Before Chris Burt could finish his last sentence, Daragh steamed in, accusatory tone in his voice, enquiring if 'he [Chris] considered the company to be in breach of contract' with regard to the lack of water. Heads shook in denial. Daragh followed up asking if they would be briefing new arrivals about the water deficiency, slightly flummoxing

Chris, but he replied in the affirmative. Tom made a feeble attempt at backing up his old-school British TV mafia chums, claiming locals were undergoing the same problems. I countered that we were out here under Equity rules with contractually agreed standards, and in light of our previous two Crimean campaigns, maintenance of the unit's health and safety should be paramount.

Moments after the meeting adjourned, Sean could be heard berating Tom about not standing up for us – 'I'm sick of you taking their side all the time' – before steaming out of the bar followed by the remaining Chosen. Stopping on the dirt path a few yards from the bar entrance, the heavy thrum of cicadas filling the air, Sean turned to us and growled, 'Right, lads, if this carries on in Yalta, we know what to do.' 'Sir, yes sir!' was going off in my head, but we already knew what time it was: time to summon up the Dimerdji Bacon Riot spirit. Chris Burt had probably been warned what a handful Daragh and some of the Chosen Men could be; troublemakers who would disrupt the shoot and were the source of all evil known to man. We considered it fighting for justice and fairness against those who dared take liberties with us and the powers were doing precisely that with their handling of the water crisis. However, unlike the Bacon Riot, now the top man was angry about the situation. Moments later, we realised we'd have to re-enter the bar as, being a little off the beaten track with no taxis or trams in sight, there was nowhere else close enough to get a drink.

THERE'S A HOLE IN MY BUCKET

Production started issuing daily 'water reports' restating the promise to guarantee water for an hour, twice a day. In addition, we were issued covered green metal buckets to fill up when the water was on, guaranteeing at least one face wash, a rinse after brushing teeth and possibly one and a half toilet flushes. A giant water bowser now arrived daily at the Tavria, so we could fill our buckets in the hours when the water was off. One morning, the water ran out after only thirty minutes, forcing a grovelling apology on the following day's water report. Things were complicated further as we moved into night shoots necessitating inconvenient washing times for those not required on the call sheet. It began to dawn on me that if they could be so sure the water would come on at the allotted times, they must have some sort of control of the supply. Possibly the budget cuts had left us unable to afford a constant supply of water. That, or a bribe hadn't landed in the appropriate pocket.

The first night shoot had to be cancelled as Hugh Ross, playing Monroe, had stiffness in his back as well as a nasty rash that had spread from his back around to his chest; a new one added to the list of Sharpe ailments. Hugh was ready to roll the following night for our first encounter with the mysterious El Casco, played by Spanish actor Abel Folk. Though he was charming and excellent in the role, I saw it as a part for Antonio Banderas. Dream on! In the scene we were required for more Chosen flock action; the trick was to not be directly on Sean's shoulder in the master shot. If you were directly behind Sean in a static shot, you'd be stuck there for Sean's close-ups – which were many – so a blurry part of your body can be seen behind Beano. As it happened, I was placed just behind Sean, obliging me to be standing by to be a blur in the background.

The next night, we shot a scene containing the most lines Harris had uttered on *Sharpe* to date, where the learned Rifleman tipsily extols the virtues of a future baby Harper. The 'actor' playing the recent Harper offspring wasn't getting a lot of shuteye due to being on constant standby. By three in the morning he was at his grisliest, just as we had to film my dialogue, letting rip with all his tiny lung power, making it very hard to deliver my lines properly. I noticed the baby only seemed to wail when Ramona and Harper were passing the child to each other. Chosen Men didn't get many takes to do their stuff, partly because Tom knew we usually nailed it at the first time of asking, so I had to try and shout above the baby, not ideal. Daragh and Ramona were going to have to learn some baby-handling skills if we were to have more scenes of domestic bliss chez Harper. That or recast the baby!

As our third week rolled on, more 'Gold' cast arrived in-country, including a reappearance of Philip McGough and a cheeky nineteen-year-old scouser called Phil Dowd, a first-timer here to play Private Skillycorn. An archetypal scally, he quickly made an impact partying in the Red Bar and chatting up two local girls who we feared could be mafia arm candy. In the short time he had been there, Philip McGough, an intrepid actor, had stepped far out of the Sharpe Bubble to places even I would fear to tread. Somehow, he met up with a group of Tatars, Crimea's indigenous people, who invited him to a wedding party where live sheep were slaughtered and naturally the vodka flowed like water. Philip did his level best to keep up, resulting in him last seen being carried semi-conscious to his bed, making our bacchanalian excess look like kindergarten stuff. Unsurprisingly, Philip looked a little bleary-eyed on location next day for a fairly large set-up involving Skillycorn marching to the gallows. Off camera we were hoping Phil Dowd didn't face the same fate as the scouse Romeo continued to dice with death by persistently hounding the local girls in the Red Bar. Visions of his corpse rolled in a carpet and dumped on the Tavria boules court danced through our minds; forgetting, of course, that we were probably protected by even heavier villains in the employ of the East-West Creative Association.

'GOLD' RUSH

There was one conundrum that couldn't be solved with a couple of well-directed heavies, that being the problem of transport, a challenge we thought had been solved at the tail end of last year. This year so far, we had had multiple vehicles; we were even shunted into a rickety minivan on one occasion. The transport was supposed to be exclusively for us (Lyndon and me) with other cast members having to lump it in a minivan, but so far on this tour production persisted in using our car as spare transport for other actors; something, of course, they didn't impose on those higher up the food chain. One morning Ian Shaw (Provost Ayres) rode in our car to work, giving us an outside opinion on the dire state of our transport. On this occasion the steering seemed to work independently of the wheels, producing a couple of hairy swerves while speeding to location; we even had to jolt the driver awake after he appeared to be in the first stages of nodding off at the wheel. Lyndon and I were almost inured to the constant peril; Ian, on the other hand, was horrified that production was playing so fast and loose with our safety.

Once on location, we let Ian lodge the complaint to the production office as they weren't prone to heeding Chosen concerns. That day's set-up was at the end of the valley floor in a wooded area directly beneath impressive, towering rock formations, some shaped like skulls, quite appropriate as the kooky 'Gold' script was more *Tales of the Unexpected* than *Sharpe*. First up, the Chosen were employed as horse handlers. I ended up next to a horse's head in the background of a shot trying desperately to stop the horse stealing the scene. The afternoon was a purely Chosen affair, as Sharpe assembled his men for a raid on a French camp, the sort of action that made the death-defying drive seem worth it. In the attack, we discovered El Casco had already paid a visit with twisted and cruel results, one of the many bizarre deviations from Bernard's original story. I learned the choice of screenwriter, Nigel Kneale, came from out of left field. Primarily known for *The Quatermass Experiment* and its sequels, he also penned *Halloween III: Season of the Witch*, though later having his name removed; so he was primarily a science fiction/horror writer. Undoubtedly, Mr Kneale was accomplished and venerated within the industry, but it was weird inserting Aztec-worshipping Spanish guerrillas into *Sharpe*. Kneale's screenplay was mainly faithful to the first two chapters of the novel, recreated almost scene for scene with Provost Ayres nabbing Private Batten for looting; strange how the name Ayres was retained, yet Skillicorn was thought an improvement on Batten.

In the original story, Hogan orders Sharpe to guard the Spanish junta's gold; this morphed into the hunt for Wellington's strayed relations, the Nugents. The attack on Almeida's defensive fortifications was reduced to an assault on Barbier's chocolate soldiers, and the fearsome El Catolico mutated into the meowing El Casco; and those were just some of the departures from the novel. Other novels underwent adaptation, but it seems 'Gold' had made the journey twice over, resulting in an outlandish fantasy tale with barely any connection to the history of war on the Iberian Peninsula.

With a squint of the mind's eye, it didn't take much to see ourselves in a cowboy flick; a sort of borscht western. If this downright peculiar reworking of 'Gold' passed without anyone noticing, it would prove we could handle any scenario, no matter how ridiculous.

The tragedy was, much good material from the novel got left behind. The novel also contains the death of Rifleman Tongue; perhaps production, having been denied that pleasure, were determined this series to make up for it by murdering Rifleman Perkins. Of even graver concern for the 'franchise' was the possibility that 'Gold', might in television terms 'jump the shark', signalling the beginning of the end, when a show has reached its peak and begun a downhill slide to mediocrity or a moment when an established long-running series changes in a significant manner. The term refers to the painful last episodes of *Happy Days* where the Fonz, coolest dude on the planet – until Sharpe – leaps over Jaws' cousin on water skis. With normal service being resumed with the next two scripts this series would hopefully see Sharpe avoid jumping the shark.

The water cut-offs continued unabated, keeping the office Xerox machine busy spitting out daily water reports; in one week the unit was due to move to Yalta, where we'd been promised this problem would be licked. Shame production neglected also to issue a vermin report as many of us were realising that our mattresses were flea-ridden. It seemed there was less hope for problem child scouse scallywag Phil Dowd, aka Skillycorn, who was still flirting with both the mafia bar babes and disaster. He had even fallen foul of Daragh, who demanded Phil leave the bar even though at 6:30 in the morning it was time *everyone* should have left the bar. Phil declined the order, incurring a kick up the bum from Daragh, much to the approval of all who witnessed it. Only three weeks in and things were looking messy.

CHOSEN MAN DOWN

We were switching location to Chufut-Kale to film a cavalry attack on our wagon convoy involving lots of Chosen combat action, including a moment that would alter the composition of the Chosen Men. Our delivery of rifles to El Casco has been slowed down by the search for Dada Nugent, allowing our convoy to be ambushed by the French. During our counter-attack, Cooper succumbs to a sneaky sabre blow from the rear, sustaining a gash to his upper arm. This injury supposedly puts Cooper out to pasture, a moment everyone knew was coming because of Mike Mears' contract, yet little was made of the incident in the scene. It was bad enough a Chosen Man getting taken unawares from behind, but the strike from the cavalryman's sword barely broke the cloth of Cooper's tunic. Hussars of the Chasseurs à Cheval regularly lopped off body parts with a smart swoop of their sabres, so Cooper coming away with barely a scratch bordered on pathetic, especially if this was the injury that was to sever Cooper from our Chosen team. To add insult to injury, Cooper receiving treatment for his wounds was placed in the rear of a wide shot with no separate set-ups, let alone a close-up for a scene important in the chronology of *Sharpe*.

The scene's aftermath produced a real life 'butcher's bill': Sean smashed his thumb, Mike Mears split the skin on his finger and Lyndon, while trying to hang onto a horse's reins, had a three-kilo cavalry sword dropped on his head, point first. Of course, all bladed weapons on *Sharpe* had blunt points and edges to prevent serious injury, nevertheless the weight of the blade cut into Lyndon's scalp causing plenty of claret to pour forth; no need for fake blood there. Tom got me to take Lyndon's place holding the horse's reins. The stunt choreography mirrored the on-screen chaos of the ambush; there was no way Lyndon's skull should have come anywhere near the cavalry sabre. New stunt coordinator Roy Street cheekily suggested Lyndon had clouted himself with his own rifle butt, highly unlikely as during stunts replica wooden Bakers are issued which are feather-light compared to the genuine article.

With the pandemonium of the ambush behind us, we moved on to Chufut-Kale to the ruins of an ancient settlement, site of our first day filming in the Crimea with Paul McGann. A short distance from the summit lay even older cave dwellings carved into the chalky rock that had been chosen as El Casco's lair where his skin-flaying, Aztec-worshipping men did their open-heart surgery. Our attack on El Casco and the subsequent explosive destruction of his hideout was, for me, precisely what the doctor ordered to get our minds off the problems of water shortages. However, shooting exciting Chosen action wasn't enough to smooth the rumpled fabric of our Crimea tenure; John Tams had basically written a letter of resignation, asking to be released from his contract, or to be allowed to go home for one episode. I was used to profound shocks to the system while out on campaign with Sharpe, but to have such a sober, thoughtful, intelligent and important member of the Sharpe machine really not fancy it anymore was a seismic jolt. Though considering what John's body had battled through these past two campaigns, I could see where he was coming from. John had suffered most from the debilitating gastrointestinal lurgy, *Giardia lamblia*, on some days being unable to leave his room to work. He was also badly missing his family and had realised that cutting his losses and returning home was better for his wellbeing than three more months on campaign in Ukraine.

I read a draft of John's plea to be released, almost bringing me to tears; the powers responded saying maybe he could have two weeks off but no more. Chris had to check first with Sean and Daragh, who had both fought for a small break back home to be written into their contracts, to no avail. Naturally we remaining Chosen Men, whose morale was at an all-time low, and bound to be directly affected by such a move, weren't even consulted. The powers knew Michael would be gone in a week, Lyndon gone a month after that, and I had a home away from home with a beautiful girl in my bed, and therefore had no need to be coddled. Conspiracy theorists might speculate there was a policy to let the Chosen unit self-destruct or wither on the vine. Almost a dishonourable discharge from the job, so fingers could never be pointed at management for annihilating the Chosen Men. I hoped this wouldn't manifest itself in trouble at Sharpe mill.

WHITE RIOT, A RIOT OF MY OWN

That trouble came, on a debilitatingly hot day at Belogorsk as the sun-baked rocks teemed with little lizards. The day started pleasantly enough, apart from the usual on-set delays exacerbated by the unit moving down to Yalta the next day. By the time we cleared costume and make-up, the mercury had reached 35° Celsius, not ideal for shooting a cross-country march in full kit. Before the take, we asked if water could follow us as we went. Attempting to hurry us along Tom retorted, 'Water's been following us, it just hasn't got here yet.' Lyndon, now in a strop, replied, 'If we could do the scene in shorts and T-shirt there'd be no need for constant water'. I was a millisecond from donating my two coupons' worth, when Natasha fixed my gaze with a look that said, 'Don't you dare get involved.' I duly obeyed, mostly out a desire to get the scene shot and get out of my kit. Natasha had reported that our revolutionary spirit was seen as the spoilt behaviour of westerners by the local crew, probably by some of ours, too. I countered that production was supposed to uphold certain standards, including not having to endure sharing your room with a porcelain platform of your own excrement till the appropriate bribe was paid so that you could flush the toilet. Daragh's face was a picture of stunned, silent incredulity; I could see Michael Mears was the most incensed, loudly muttering, 'Never on any film set, anywhere in the world, have I been treated like this.' And we were being bollocked by the director for even daring to request a drink in such heat.

The water eventually showed up, we got the shots in the can and moved on to scenes featuring Sergeant Rodd which went some way to lightening the mood as Peter Hugo Daley is nutty as a box of frogs. That evening, I eschewed the delights of the Red Bar, instead getting stuck into the onerous task of packing for the move to Yalta. Lyndon appeared in my doorway looking stunned: 'Mickey has just handed in his resignation.' He only had a week left on his contract; had Mike tendered his resignation in expectation of a quick refusal from the powers? Apparently, the reply was quick, but one of acceptance; after two and a third tours, forty-four weeks and six episodes, Michael Mears exited *Sharpe*.

It seemed like an avoidable situation, but it wasn't just about lack of drinking water on set; over three campaigns we had been last in the pecking order of respect, appreciation and, this year, the money. It also confirmed the sad reality that management could easily do without us, in part or in total. I bade farewell to both

Mike and the Tavria Hotel, heading to my transport with a heavy heart. The atmosphere on set was unsurprisingly tense; there was a universal sadness among those of us on their third *Sharpe* campaign. Those closer to Tom, crew for whom this was their first rodeo, were saying how stupid Mike was to quit, particularly as he only had a week before he was done. Not to mention Mike would be in breach of contract. Making matters worse, high winds were battering Belogorsk, whipping the dust into every available orifice. Even the camera had to be covered between takes.

With the Simferopol leg complete, Sharpe's army marched south to our Black Sea base. Two days earlier, Russia had removed its remaining troops from Baltic states Estonia and Latvia, ending the last traces of Soviet occupation in Eastern Europe. Just as the Cold War was finally over, Camp Sharpe was entering its very own hot war with the 'good guys' one man down and facing the scheduled loss of another. Aside from Natasha, I was probably closest to Lyndon and it was unthinkable not having him around on location. The three of us drove down from location to the Chernomore sanatorium with our now regular driver, Volodia, whose car was clean, comfortable and safe. I was again billeted to room 406, where I discovered, in spite of production's assurances that everything had been unloaded, much of my clearly labelled luggage, including my portable cooker, video player and CD collection, hadn't reached my room.

WATER, WATER EVERYWHERE

We had only been on tour for a month, but events had really taken the shine off our penny, so taking up residence in Yalta's resort

Andrew Salkey, novelist, poet, broadcaster and teacher. Was the
main topic of conversation at my *Sharpe* audition.

The original incarnation of Sharpe and his men getting ready to shoot the first promotional shot. Paul McGann's son Joe helps with the set-up. Dimerdji, Crimea. August 1992.

Paul McGann returns to work on crutches the morning after sustaining his knee injury. From the background, McGann's stunt double watches on with concern. Chufut Valley, Crimea. August 1992.

Lyndon Davies (Perkins), Paul Trussell (Tongue), Daragh O'Malley (Harper), Jason Salkey (Harris) and Michael Mears (Cooper). Chufut Valley, Crimea. August 1992.

Shooting a marching scene from 'Sharpe's Eagle'. Gavan O'Herlihy (Leroy), Daniel Craig (Berry) and Michael Cochrane (Simmerson) lead the column. Baidar Valley, Crimea. August 1992.

Esteemed director, Jim Goddard, the man responsible for casting me in the role of Harris.

After Force Majeure was called on production we flew home via Moscow. I took the opportunity to do a little sightseeing in Red Square. Moscow, Russia. September 1992.

Sean Bean, previously rejected for the role in favour of Paul McGann, now replaces him as our eponymous hero. The first group shot of the Bean era. Baidar Valley, Crimea. October 1992.

Not a lot of people know Sharpe was one of Daniel Craig's first jobs on television. It was probably Lt Berry's dodgy brown wig that put people off the scent. Dimerdji, Crimea. October 1992.

Before heading out to Crimea for filming, Tim Bentinck (Murray) was instrumental in inspiring my appreciation of the Sharpe novels. Outside Lisbon, Portugal. December 1992.

Never had a guest actor's arrival been greeted with as much anticipation, appreciation and adoration. Moscow Hotel, Simferopol, Crimea. August 1993.

Interpreter Natasha, my love from the Crimea!

By the middle of the second series we'd lost two colossal characters, Haikeswill and Teresa, from the Sharpe universe.

I always looked forward to Bernard Cornwell's annual trips out to location. Yalta Hotel, Yalta, Crimea. November 1993.

Meeting the Parents. Natasha at home with Valentina and Alexi Lakhmaniuk. Yalta, Crimea. November 1993.

Natasha's sister, Lyosya Lakhmaniuk. Lyosya worked in the Hornblower production office when they filmed in Crimea shortly after Sharpe left town. Yalta, Crimea. November 1993.

A scene from Sharpe's Battle shot at the former deer park of Czar Nicholas II, a spectacular location used only once. Red Stone Pass. Yalta, Crimea. September 1994.

Collective unhappiness at the death of Perkins and the exit of Lyndon from *Sharpe*. Dimerdji, Crimea. October 1994.

The ever-ebullient Diana Perez brought a little South American rhythm to proceedings off-camera. Dimerdji, Crimea. September 1994.

In series three I lost my main partner in crime, Lyndon Davies (Perkins). Killed in action during Sharpe's Battle. Dimerdji, Crimea. October 1994.

Executive producer, Malcolm Craddock, often left to deliver doses of harsh reality to cast and crew. Adapazarı, Turkey. September 1996.

Muir Sutherland was the man Bernard Cornwell trusted to take Sharpe from page to screen. Baidar Valley, Crimea. November 1994.

We get some unexpected news. Natasha confirms she's carrying the second 'Sharpe-generated child'. Cidadela Hotel, Cascais, Portugal. December 1994.

In Turkey, Sharpe's new home, with the indefatigable Tom Clegg, director of every single second of Sharpe. Alayna, Turkey. October 1995.

Sharpe-generated child, Daniel Salkey, makes a visit to location at six months old. Silifke, Turkey. December 1995.

In 1992 we began as a magnificent seven; by 1996 we'd been distilled down to a fab four. Adapazarı, Turkey. September 1996.

atmosphere would contribute somewhat towards soothing the perceived ills. Every yin has a yang within reach, and I can safely say I hadn't missed the unashamed, unabashed, liberal use of garlic which added to the olfactory assault sustained on the streets of Yalta. The garlic blended with the stench of cheap, rough tobacco, Crimean red onions and benzene that permeated the air through breath and sweat, somewhat subsided during the cooler months, was nevertheless still apparent. Now that capitalism was king, inflation steamed ahead unabated; since 1992 the coupon/*karbovanets* had soared from tens to thousands of coupons to the dollar which, of course, had a knock-on effect when spending our per diems. After a quick trip to visit Natasha's mum for lunch, I got back to the sanatorium to find a note stuck to my door saying my lost luggage had been found in room 402, making for a happy end to the day.

The following day was Monday 5 September, a date that will live on in Sharpe infamy. The day began unremarkably. As was the custom, I knocked on Lyndon's door when my alarm went off then jumped back into bed. Ten minutes before our 6:30 a.m. transport, Lyndon knocked at my door meekly informing me, 'The water's off and we're not leaving until it's turned on again.' Thinking he was joking, I peered into the corridor to see the surreal sight of John and Sean standing there, Sean propped up against an abandoned fridge with a face like thunder. Realising Beano meant business, I darted back into my room, dumped my work bag and took my kettle and toaster oven out to the corridor, parking them on the fridge to create a notional picket line. The Bacon Riot spirit was back; the revolution to guarantee our water rights was on.

Chris Burt was first at the picket line looking very calm under the circumstances, timidly asking us if we could overlook this little mistake and board the transport for work. We told him there would be no movement from us until our bowel movements could be properly flushed. As the daily water reports had stated, 'If water is off within an hour of your call you have the right to withdraw labour without financial penalty'. Chris, facing defeat, skulked off; he knew he was on a hiding to nothing primarily because Beano was fronting this particular action. We tucked into toast and tea as Daragh joined us at the picket line, the fourth floor by this point looking more like a wing of Strangeways during a prison riot with a fridge, a bed box and other detritus from our move strewn along the corridor.

In due course, Chris arrived with Pavel, wheeled out principally to apologise 'for how fucked up his country is', and to assure us that they would try to get the water back on soon; more empty promises. More lip service solely to ameliorate our fractious spirit in the face of a month of bucket washes and the occasional cold shower.

By now all actors on the call sheet had emerged onto the corridor, Ian Shaw, Jake and two of the other deserter boys looking bewildered and a little fearful, having never gone on strike while on an acting job. We said welcome to life in Sharpe world, assuring them everything would be okay if they stood firm with us. Noticeably absent was Pete Hugo Daley, who had failed to materialise for his call, blissfully ignorant of the drama brewing outside his door. Feeling we should notify Peter, Lyndon and I approached his room. We knocked a few times without reply; not that alarming, we had plenty of heavy sleepers on *Sharpe*. We proceeded to bang on it with our fists and feet intermittently for a full twenty minutes. Eventually our floor lady arrived, opening Peter's room to find him sound asleep draped, fully dressed, over the wooden bed frame. It was a blessed glimmer of light relief on a morning of much heaviness.

An hour later, the revolutionary party was summoned up to Stefan Pojenan's room, the Association's head honcho, who had famously claimed last year he would make chefs pay the ultimate price if they didn't shape up. The same threats would be directed towards those in charge of the mains water spigot: 'I will crack heads to solve the problems of our shitty country.' Perhaps he thought the Soviet Union was still around as we were in Ukraine and he was Russian. Suitably unimpressed, we withdrew to the picket line to discuss strategy; we wouldn't move until the three-hour time difference allowed our agents' offices to open. During that lull in proceedings, associate producer Ray tried sneakily to break the strike by leaning on some of the younger deserter boys. with no result. As we waited the cold water started to trickle thorough the system, allowing us at least to flush the toilet, but we weren't going to budge till we had proper assurances that constant hot and cold running water would be restored.

After agents, agents' lawyers and Central Television's legal team were notified, it was decided we were perfectly within our rights to take the action we had chosen. Sean, John and Daragh hashed out a settlement with Chris, stating we wouldn't have to work if there was no water, with no penalty in terms of money or any other repercussion. The Chernomore water action was over with a total, unconditional victory declared for the good guys, though we had lost a day of shooting at a cost of several thousand pounds to the production. Perhaps had production not tried to achieve everything on less money such actions might not have been necessary.

VIVA LA REVOLUTION

Needless to say, that evening in the KGB bar there was some serious unwinding, with a bit of soul-searching thrown in about what had just occurred; after all, this was the second time we'd taken matters into our own hands and those of less importance to the show might get left behind on the next campaign. Sean, Lyndon and I chatted at length about how our actions would be perceived by the crew; we knew the acting department was certainly on our side but other members of the unit had to dutifully roll into work on time and waited on the side of a mountain kicking their heels the entire day. Props, horses, extras and all that expensive camera and lighting equipment all standing idle while the dollars flowed down the drain.

The next morning, we were reacquainted with iconic *Sharpe* location Dimerdji to shoot the rifles-for-deserters swap scene. I wouldn't say we were greeted like conquering heroes by the crew, but the reception was overwhelmingly positive. I suppose waking up to a hot shower and being able to flush the toilet was met with universal favour; our strike was not being seen as the selfish, entitled, petulant act of pampered thespians, but was being taken in the spirit in which it had been meant, a stand taken for the greater good, for the benefit of all. Even Tom showed no outward sign of resentment; we responded with ultra-efficiency and rapt attention when rehearsing and lining up the shot. The vibe on set was upbeat, I got to display Harris's language skills in a nice scene with Sharpe and the meowing El Casco and we were all entertained by the deserter boys in full flow, playing their parts to perfection with just a hint of slapstick.

With impeccable timing, Malcolm Craddock arrived to hold a post-mortem of the previous day's strike. It was good to see Malcolm, who after all was also a three-campaign veteran and someone we felt we could speak frankly with. I also needed to get a Portuguese visa for Natasha; Malcolm very helpfully steered me towards a person from the production office in Lisbon. He also mentioned Carlton was producing a Sharpe book that might need to use some of my on-set photos; so, there seemed a chance I might make a couple of bucks off *Sharpe* in the future. His arrival was timed perfectly for him to witness a cockroach population explosion at the sanatorium; getting rid of them was a sub-clause of the 'water action' agreement, so while we were finishing up at Dimerdji, they were fumigating the bathrooms and corridor areas. During the strike Lyndon had kept himself busy killing and harvesting twenty or so of the little buggers in a jar before presenting them to the production office. Suitably disgusted, Chris Burt dumped the cockroaches, with the jar, in the Russian production office; I would say that Chris was beginning to be sympathetic to the multi-layered shit storm we'd all had to put up with.

Up at the Valley of Ghosts, we headed towards the end of our first turbulent week in Yalta – who am I kidding, every week out there was tumultuous. From high on the mountain, I got a bird's-eye view of the extended 'Torrecastro' set; gone was the breeched interior wall of Badajoz, now replaced with Spanish-style houses built on a street running off the main square and free from squatters. Dominating the town square sat the church from where we had raised the gonfalon during 'Rifles', now used for a scene where we were to shelter from the rain within the church interior. As we were still gripped by drought, the rain had to be supplied by the Dimerdji fire brigade's pathetic fire hoses, gently splashing us as we took cover with the horses. God help us if there was ever a real fire to deal with. Roy Street got a little heated with Tom at wetting the horses too soon, thinking they wouldn't like repeated dousing; but they didn't seem to mind and the scene went off without a hitch. I couldn't help but notice the Cooper-shaped hole in our Chosen posse; it was demoralising seeing how seamlessly production dealt with discarding a quarter of the gang. For a short time, we would be down to Perkins and Harris as production had finally granted John Tams a two-week break to recover his physical and mental health back in Blighty.

GOLDEN FAREWELL

I had a day off in advance of completing the concluding scenes of 'Gold' at Polikur: Sharpe's showdown with Ayres and the final takedown of El Caso. Lyndon and I spent the afternoon with Malcolm on the hot pebbles of our private beach. The remains of the day were spent with Beano and his motorhome driver Gary at the only place to get draught lager in town: the Yalta Hotel. Daragh showed up later with his agent from ICM, Jane Brand, who was here on a fact-finding mission to determine exactly how nightmarish it really was on *Sharpe*. Shame she caught us having a laugh on a beautifully sunny afternoon, with our shirts off and supping frosty pints of lager. No doubt Daragh would have given her chapter and verse of the catalogue of woes faced out here. If his agent was in any doubt, hopefully she read Rosie Linehan's poetic farewell message printed in the call sheet, stating how she 'wished for more thorns to deal with the day to day existence of shooting Sharpe', a pertinent pun on her own name that neatly expressed her feelings about life on campaign.

On 10 September we moved to Polikur to complete principal photography on 'Gold'. I sometimes mused over what would have happened if we had got to shoot the original 'Gold' script from the first campaign, not the twice-digested story we'd been left with. But we were where we were, with the script we had now, a unique story that employed bundles of artistic licence and was almost completely divorced from the novel. I really shouldn't complain as Harris isn't in the original pre-television incarnation of the novels, therefore my involvement in this great programme owes heaps to artistic licence.

It was Saturday at Polikur, so the atmosphere was very relaxed while we were shooting the final confrontation with El Casco in his sacrificial cave. Even though we still had one more day of 'Gold' on the call sheet due to the Chernomore water action, the end-of-episode party still went ahead. Natasha, Saint and I decided to forgo the first throws of the party, instead hitting a restaurant in town called Venizia where we all had an absolutely delicious meal of grilled sturgeon and chips.

From there, the night went steadily downhill as a series of unsavoury events took place at the bar, starting with make-up chief Jacquetta Levon's bag being swiped; followed by a gangster accompanied by his henchmen striding into the bar. One of them then turned to DJ Lyndon and rather dramatically drew a thumb across his throat. Absolutely out of order in anyone's language; I immediately jumped up, went over to Ray's table, telling him to 'get security to boot these fuckers out'. Disease, starvation, boredom and injury could be endured – we'd proved that over three tours – but threats to our lives in the safety of our own 'home' should not be tolerated. A small fuss was made before our head of security informed me they were the local mafia who either ran the place or had some special significance to the sanatorium. Perhaps there was less money in the budget to pay bribes this year, making surviving out here all the more perilous.

At around 5:30 in the morning, when sensible people were tucked up in bed, horse master Roy Street staggered up to get another drink; sitting quietly at the bar, Daragh sensibly suggested he'd had enough. Roy flipped out, advanced on Daragh shouting drunkenly and threatening him with violence. I slipped between them before Roy made the mistake of laying hands on Daragh, who sat there cool as a cucumber nursing his drink through the whole episode. After Roy jostled with me and anyone trying to stop him, Beano finally took Roy aside for a chat before calmly steering him towards the stairs to our rooms; even when sozzled, Roy had the good sense not to manhandle the main man.

One last day at Polikur and we could finally say goodbye to 'Sharpe's Gold'. First order of the day was pulling Provost Ayre's body from El Casco's sacrificial caves; after lunch we tackled the arrest of Skillycorn. Ian Shaw looked suitably demonic and twisted when delivering his lines; as he shouted 'hang him' it really reminding me of his father, Robert Shaw, one of our greatest actors and a Hollywood legend. The scene took a while to shoot, causing Tom to get quite agitated when the on-set hubbub got too noisy, shouting *tishina* – silence in Russian – at the top of his lungs, putting everyone on edge. The pressure was getting to Tom, which couldn't be a good thing. In many ways Tom was the most affected by the budget cuts. He was ultimately responsible for what ended up in the frame when *Sharpe* was broadcast to the world, and all the foundations he relied on to paint the pictures had been nibbled away.

In part of the action Sharpe punches Skillycorn in the chest as punishment for getting nicked by the Provost; each rather enthusiastic punch made me wince, they were that hard. On the third take Sean managed to hit one of Skillycorn's hefty tunic buttons, sending Phil to the floor and bringing up a nasty bump on Sean's knuckle. Miraculously enough, Phil had made it through the shoot without incurring the ultimate sanction from the Simferopol mob even though he was heard enquiring of one of them 'Hey, are you that mafia geezer?' Blimey. Only five weeks into the campaign and we had already seen so much off-set action.

LUCKY SEVEN

We stood poised at the dawn of another story, 'Sharpe's Battle', our seventh episode, the next novel added to the opus. As a fan of the books it was a privilege to have a crack at filming the episode before it was published, but as a dear friend of Lyndon I was distressed that 'Battle' contained the death of Perkins. A moment we dreaded filming, yet on another level, a brilliant move designed to tug the viewer's heart strings. On the positive side, 'Battle' had a couple of heavy hitters in central roles, Ian McNeice playing Wagon Master Runciman and Oliver Cotton in the role of chief baddie, Brigadier Guy Loup. The screenplay was also a notch up from 'Gold'; it must have been useful for the writer to be briefed on the story while it was still fresh in Bernard's mind.

With a brand-new episode came an absolutely fresh location, formerly the Tsar's deer park, now a nature reserve 'of outstanding beauty set four thousand metres above Yalta' called Red Stone Pass.

At the summit of Red Stone Pass, the view overlooking the Bay of Yalta is breathtaking; grassy hillocks, sprouting with mushrooms and dingley dells abound, giving it an enchanted fairy-tale feel. I didn't see many deer, though I did see plenty of deer droppings scattered everywhere. 'Battle' commenced with the episode's opening scene where we traverse the side of a ridge accompanied by a couple of stunts dressed as Chosen Men hopping like goats from rock to rock. This was production's solution to replacing the hole left by discarded Chosen Men; at this rate budget cuts would result in five stuntmen going into battle with Sharpe at series end. Then it was on to the customary shot of us walking over the hill, shot on a precipitous incline with a seriously vertiginous drop on one side. We capped the day's work with an emotional farewell at Perkins' graveside, a sombre end to the day's filming. A scene from the episode finale, but shot out of sequence as this was going to be the only time we could get access to this location.

Seeing as Johnny had secured a break back home, I had managed to wangle a little break in Kiev for a couple days. Always a bonus to extricate oneself from the bubble once in a while; however, our trip was to secure Natasha a British visa for the flight home at the end of the shoot. Production gave permission to leave location, but they weren't going to help one jot with the logistics, which I thought was fair enough. Instead I went direct to the transportation chief who I knew was scheduling 'Battle' cast pickups at Simferopol airport. With no guarantee of getting a flight, we gladly hopped aboard the transport more in hope than expectation. At the airport we met five of the new intake, most of the cast from 'Sharpe's Battle'. After filling them all in on the joys of life on *Sharpe*, Natasha and I manged to bum a lift on a charter plane taking some Americans on a trip to Kiev, St

Petersburg and beyond. I say 'bum a lift', but we did pay full fare for the seats.

After lots of help from the Americans' interpreter in getting to Kiev, I started to get more than slightly concerned at being only seventy miles from Chernobyl, no doubt still highly radioactive after only eight years since meltdown. Once in town we settled at the Kievskaya, the best hotel in town, only a goalkeeper's punt from the Olympic stadium, home of Dynamo Kiev. What a breath of fresh air Kiev proved to be: it was green, clean and serene compared to the parched, beige and frenetic Crimea. It felt a lot more European and western, so different from everything in Yalta which still seemed very Soviet; even the mafia looked kinder. Day one was spent sightseeing and seeking out the British Embassy; on day two we got down to the business at hand. Pulling my best foreigner-in-his-own-embassy routine to secure an appointment; must have helped that the embassy official had seen *Sharpe* and within two and a half hours Natasha was granted a six-month, multiple-entry visa. Once back at the hotel there was a message from production telling me to get back to Crimea the next day. We spent the evening in the hotel casino where we met some fellow Brits who ran a stable of casinos in Kiev and introduced us to a hip new warehouse joint called Club 200. We got to Borisopol airport bleary-eyed with only two hours' sleep but refreshed after our trip and very happy to have obtained the visa.

Back at Red Stone Pass we wrapped all shots for this location and the blessed weekend was upon us, kicked off with a group dinner at what was becoming the unit's favourite restaurant, Venizia, where much dancing and downing of vodka shots left me completely plastered; at thirty-two was I getting too old for this? We staggered up the road reaching the chintzy, velvety splendour of the casino

777, to find Daragh and Ian McNeice ensconced on high stools. I tailed Daragh from roulette to the blackjack table pretending I knew what I was doing, first finding myself forty bucks up before losing everything and ending up forty dollars in the red. We got a cab back to the sanatorium where we joined the Saturday night rave in full swing. I later learned that Daragh was a grand up on the house before leaving two hundred bucks down. What else were we going to do with our per diem money?

The new working week started with the relative calm of a two-day stint at Polikur; lots of satisfying stunt action, primarily the attack on Loup's men, who we spied sniffing around our wagons. Mr Knock, Harper's seven-barrelled weapon of choice, got an airing, and Sean and I pulled a couple of stuntmen from their horses before dispatching them to hell. As the day wore on, it started to get tense on set, possibly due to the nature of what we were filming: arriving in the aftermath of Loup's attack on the village. In particular Harper rescuing a bloodied baby from a dwelling; throughout the rehearsal the baby slept soundly, but as we went for the take chatting from behind the set could be heard prompting Natasha to shout *tishina*, which woke the baby, making it cry. Tom flashed a contemptuous look of 'why' at her; the baby then proceeded to cry all the way through the scene, making it much more realistic. Shortly afterwards, Tom questioned my pronunciation of 'Loup', incorrectly telling me to say 'loop' because Sharpe says it that way, winding me up further. Had Tom forgotten Harris was the educated one with mastery of French, Spanish and Portuguese, unlike Sharpe? An afternoon to forget; we couldn't wait for the day to wrap.

Back at the sanatorium we were greeted with our first power cut; if it wasn't one thing it was another! Out came the candles along with the spirit of the Blitz as we gathered in the lounge for a party by candlelight. Fortunately, the power returned pretty quickly, triggering a mass migration downstairs to the bar. I went to my room to write letters for John Tams to post back in Blighty as he was off home the following day. Joining John on the plane was Fiona Clegg who required a UK dentist for an infected wisdom tooth; sounds crazy, but I couldn't help thinking 'lucky girl'! Scribbling complete, I left Natasha sleeping while I slipped downstairs for a night cap. I reached the bar to discover Irish night in full swing, oiled liberally with whiskey and Guinness. Much drink was taken as I listened to the absolutely brilliant Phelim Drew entertaining us with his lovely voice and gusto-filled guitar; then again, he was the son of a Dubliner. Thoroughly Irished-out, I eventually staggered to bed at 4:30 in the morning, three and half hours before my call.

The first realisation that I was alive came at 08:17, two minutes after I was due downstairs. After taking Nurofen washed down by litres of water, I grabbed my bag and grabbed my hat, made the car in seconds flat. I needn't have hurried. Daragh was still in his bed showing no signs of budging and I was riding to Polikur in Big D's car. In the end we left without him; he showed up two hours later, but it mattered little as operation 'hurry up and wait' was in action, as usual. Muir was on set with a producer friend keen on shooting a remake of *The Prisoner of Zenda* out here in the Crimea with eyes on Beano for the lead. As there were VIPs on set, the caterers whipped up a delicious lunch followed by truly scrumptious sweet treats at tea break; however, Muir's presence didn't prevent Tom from screaming his head off on set when things got noisy, something that was becoming a regular occurrence.

COUNTDOWN TO DESOLATION

We returned to Dimerdji for the protracted conclusion of 'Battle'; in three short weeks we were to film the death of Perkins, a day I hoped would never arrive. Before work I was able to call Kiev where it was revealed there was a Portuguese Embassy; I wish I had known that as I was now relying solely on the production office to get Natasha a visa. As she wasn't required to work on the Portuguese shoot they were probably going to treat it as a low priority. I got to Dimerdji base camp positively looking forward to the day's work. Natasha had been 'promoted' to make-up continuity and the sticky flystrip hanging in our tent had caught well over thirty of the little buggers. On set, Muir regaled us with tales of how in the early days of ITV he broke the strike at LWT, the now defunct London Weekend Television, by producing the schedule, with Sharpe secretary Cindy's help. I never tired of that oft-repeated tale, though I wondered if it was a veiled threat to those who fancied using industrial action in future. However, Muir playing Sharpe wouldn't go down too well, I thought.

The weather was fine, the mood was light and we put the first shot in the can: a small skirmish at the fort entrance with Loup's men, followed by a scene between Ian McNeice, Sean and Daragh while the diminished flock faithfully stood by in the background. A 25mm lens was put on the camera indicating they were doing close-ups and therefore the Chosen weren't in the frame; however, as we were in such extreme background Tom forgot we were there and left us standing around waiting to be dismissed. After a while we had to ask Tom whether we were actually in the frame, which made it look like we were complaining, when in reality they had simply forgotten to stand us down. After double-checking the script, Daragh realised that neither he nor the Chosen were mentioned anywhere in the 'stage' directions. We really were just being used as background dressing to fill in the rear of the frame; I was dispatched to plead our case to Mike Mallinson. He assumed we had been in the previous scene, so we were there for continuity, but said he would raise the matter with Tom. We waited two hours for an answer; none came. We arrived back in front of camera where my spies reliably informed me Tom had been having a go at us, 'those fucking Chosen Men they're always complaining' declared loudly within earshot of the whole unit. Just as the camera was about to turn over, Lyndon mentioned that we hadn't been told where to stand or which direction was our eye line. Tom stormed out from behind the camera, angrily telling us we'd been told already, then he remembered we'd been away at base camp and backed down.

While the camera was being reset for the scene, Tom grumpily approached us enquiring what the problem was – as if he didn't know. I calmly explained that Harris, Harper and Perkins were not mentioned anywhere in the scene, yet we were on the call sheet, therefore we felt it must have been a typographical error – knowing full well it wasn't a typo. We were just added to the call sheet as they would add horses or gunpowder barrels. Don't get me wrong: our paycheques still rolled in so production could put us on the call sheet every day and not use us. Tom countered asking, 'So what do you want to do?'; we said that if we were not in the scene we should be released, not left to hang about for nothing. 'Then go,' Tom said, turning on his heels and storming off. The subtext was brutally clear; go from the set, leave the shoot, go back to England like Mike Mears. That evening Daragh, Lyndon and I spoke with producer

Chris Burt, demanding a showdown with Tom either tonight or tomorrow, pointing out that otherwise it would happen on set or in the sanatorium bar and, given the mood we were in, it wouldn't be pleasant.

On Thursday 22 September, the three rebels were not included on the call sheet, by accident or design we didn't know. We spent the afternoon of the proposed showdown at the Yalta Hotel downing pints in the hope it might chill us out; funnily enough, the alcohol just served to fire us up in our desire for a showdown. So as not to ruin our day with constant griping about our director, we limited ourselves to a concentrated bout of criticism in the first eight minutes of every hour which turned to more like thirty minutes as the alcohol started to take effect. Sean, accompanied by his driver Gary, joined us on the terrace bar; before things got too sloppy, I made my excuses and went home to prepare dinner for when Natasha came back from work. I also wanted to be as mentally sharp as possible for the confrontation.

The passing of time and food in my belly served to straighten me up considerably; not so my fellow rebels. Checking on Lyndon, I discovered him still drunk and very upset, Chris Burt attempting to console him. I came to Lyndon's aid, restating to Chris our demand to speak with Tom that night. It was arranged: Tom's room, after dinner, a time when Big D was at his most oiled, having declined the opportunity of a pause in the partying. We entered Tom's suite, me at point, greeted by the following tableau: Tom seated at his desk, glasses on, reading over the script with a glass of water in his hand; trying overly hard to present a picture of a thoughtful, abstemious director. As if we were there to question his effectiveness or competence as a director; we were only there to demand respect

170

that was long overdue. I opened up with the specific complaint about the previous day's treatment at Dimerdji; how it was indicative of the way we've been handled by production through the years. Tom replied with absolute denial, innocence and bafflement that we could feel this way.

It made our collective blood boil, causing Daragh to launch into a tirade against Tom, accusing him of stuff unrelated to our grievances. Two minutes into the confrontation, I felt we'd lost focus and were therefore in danger of losing the battle. Daragh continued shouting, poking a finger at Tom to emphasise his points which were becoming increasingly tangential. Trying to play the good cop I sprang from my chair, inserting myself between Tom and Daragh, prompting Daragh to give my chair a good kick before storming out of the suite.

I went to close the door just as a concerned-looking Ray tried to enter. I stopped him and promised that Tom was safe. As Ray left the room, I could see the entire security detail lined up in the corridor outside like a prison riot squad poised to storm a cell. It was left to me to continue the meeting as calmly as possible, but Daragh burst in again, shouted a few choice insults before storming out for a second time. The moment for meaningful dialogue had passed. Shortly afterwards, Beano came up to the suite to guide us to calmer waters while backing up most of our claims and that after three years' service we deserved a little better than this. Tom pathetically tried to excuse himself by turning to Sean and asking, 'Haven't I done all right by you, Sean?' This absolutely irrelevant question showed me Tom had completely missed the point. He really thought our complaints were baseless; then again, I knew if it were up to Tom there would be a different actor in my costume. It wasn't a pretty two hours, but it had been coming for some time; we shook hands at the end, the grip was firm, but it felt hollow in terms of any genuine resolution. Incredibly enough in a classic case of Chinese whispers, I spoke with Cindy Winter on the phone a little time after and she told me she'd heard I had punched Tom Clegg.

The morning after the night before, and the revolting peasants were driven to work in Daragh's car after a suitably late appearance by the big man himself. We still felt fairly shitty at the lack of outcome from our gunfight at the O'Clegg corral. At Dimerdji base camp, Daragh immediately ushered Chris Burt inside our tent to announce he would not be filming our next episode if Tom Clegg was still at the helm. Naturally, Chris had little or no sympathy for such a radical declaration and swiftly left the meeting. On set, things seemed pretty genial; Mike Mallinson took us through the set-up, an action-packed sequence that had us acting like Napoleonic repo men retrieving our rifle-laden wagons stolen by Loup's men. It was exhilarating stuff to shoot, especially steaming down a rutted mountain path riding a rickety wagon; not once that day were we just in the background of a shot. It was a great day's filming; but would the actions of the previous evening result in blowback further down the line?

Day two of a brave new world of respect! The following day, Daragh rode in with Lyndon and me in our dedicated car driven by a chap we'd named 'Boz', who ran a strict no-smoking policy. That policy had to be abandoned at the last minute for Big D who thanked us by smoking five ciggies on the drive; by the time I got to Dimerdji the second-hand smoke made me feel quite queasy, that and the fact that I hadn't bought shares in Rothmans cigarettes. At base camp sickness and squabbles had beset the make-up department, resulting in a divided tent. Already short-handed after Fiona's dental emergency, Sano had banished her Ukrainian assistant to work on the extras, accusing her of shoddy workmanship. Just for good measure, make-up assistant Tanya was showing unwillingness to take instructions from Jacquetta through Natasha; Tanya had done Chosen Man make-up since last year, in that time forging another *Sharpe*-generated romance with Guy Pugh, Sean's assistant. Obviously, Tanya's English had improved significantly with this liaison, but she still consulted Natasha once Jacquetta had moved on to do Sean's make-up, a situation that pissed the interpreters off considerably. It seemed discontent was not solely the province of Chosen Men.

If you weren't particularly disgruntled with your situation, there was now a totally debilitating flu decimating the unit, leaving only four fit available actors: Bean, O'Malley, Salkey and Davies; Sharpe's Rifles to the rescue. Attempts to ameliorate our water woes had led the Association to send for water diviners in the hope of finding a source behind the sanatorium. The idea would be to drill a well and somehow connect the source to the sanatorium's plumbing; pretty much 'pie in the sky' thinking, but an indication of how desperate the water situation still was. Days later, Chris Burt declared success in the water prospecting, but expressed doubts as to whether it was financially viable to pump, purify and connect it. Now there's a surprise.

Unrelated, but not unconnected, news came in that the Alushta checkpoint was about to shut to all traffic, making it impossible to get to Dimerdji from Yalta. Holidaymakers from Moscow had been told not to come down to the Crimea as many of the sanatoria were closing down early. We wondered whether it was due to the lack of water or the more ominous rumour that cholera had broken out in Alushta.

Wednesday 28 September, driving to Dimerdji, Lyndon told me he had befriended the mafia heavies who had invaded our party the other night. He of the cutthroat gesture was a kick-boxing champion, bodyguarding for the chap I mistook for one of the muscle. Rustlan was the boss's name and he'd told Lyndon he could get us anything we need; sounded dodgy to me. I informed Lyndon that Chris Burt had asked if I could make peace with Tom; I couldn't believe I was being asked to do that. Neither Lyndon nor Daragh had been asked to apologise and I was the calm, measured voice of reason during the showdown. On a happier note, first assistant director Mike Mallinson had proposed marriage to Sano, our beloved Portuguese hairdresser; I couldn't say I saw that one coming.

Two weeks before we began shooting 'Sharpe's Sword' I was issued with a copy of the script, adapted by my favourite *Sharpe* scriptwriter, Eoghan Harris, he of 'Rifles', 'Eagle' and 'Enemy'. Happily for me, Harris had a bearing on the narrative for a change, saving the day with his superior intellect and giving me proper lines to learn. Looking back at contract negotiations, production knew my contribution to the series would be increased, yet not a penny in extra pay had been offered. That's what I call life at the Sharpe end. 'Sword' was well within the *Sharpe* tradition, though Eoghan's script seemed to have turned me into a bit of an eccentric. In one scene Harris burned a book because there was a little blood on the pages. Sharpe's love interest was a very young novice nun, which made him a bit of cradle-snatcher, Harper had morphed into a hen-pecked coward and Hagman was much the same as before, but barely figured in the story.

HEAVENLY SHADES OF NIGHT ARE CALLING

We pressed on with 'Battle' at Dimerdji with a stretch of night shoots, thankfully nothing as arduous as on 'Company'; nevertheless, a pain to live 'on the other side of the clock' – a neat saying coined by John Tams. Speaking of the man with the golden tonsils, I had phoned him in the UK to update him on the off-stage *Sharpe* soap opera. Disunity in the make-up department lingered on; one morning Tanya, perhaps a little distracted while doing my make-up, made me look like Placido Domingo's Otello. Jacquetta took one look at my face, quietly followed me outside the tent with the appropriate shade of slap and put me back to normal. Across base camp in the wardrobe department tent, Natasha heard that costume designer Robin Fraser Paye had requested that his two local wardrobe assistants join us on the Portuguese shoot, thus requiring visas. I hoped this meant Natasha's visa would be included in that application or I'd have to stage a one-man revolt.

The first day of October had arrived; we had now been in-country for ten weeks. Oliver Cotton had returned to the UK the previous week with a list of grievances about *Sharpe* for the actors' union Equity. The water, the food, the flies were all mentioned; of course, Equity already knew all about the lax health and safety out here, yet not a lot of changes had resulted. It seemed that one or two of the directives had been implemented: the mobile kitchen had been moved a few hundred yards up the mountain presumably to avoid the Mexico City-like fly population lower down the slope. The kitchen's former position was sandwiched between a disgusting, algae-choked pond and a 'septic pit' for disposing of the army's faecal matter.

On the factory floor, we were filming on a set constructed adjacent to the ruins of a thirteenth-century settlement. Built during our first tour for use on 'Gold', it then became Ducos's headquarters in 'Honour'; its current incarnation was Alona fort, a broken-down fortress located close to the French front line. That day's action saw the Irish Company patching up the perimeter while Harris and Perkins mined the open ground with barrels of gunpowder, giving the scene a satisfyingly epic feel. It took my mind back to the first series at Kamishinka where we blow up the bridge after the Napoleonic clusterfuck Colonel Henry Simmerson loses the colours during 'Eagle'; it wouldn't be long now before we were reacquainted with Michael Cochrane making his reappearance in 'Sword'.

Another sacred Sunday dawned, welcomed with a clear head for a change. Natasha and I had got to bed before midnight – a record on *Sharpe* – falling asleep to a video of Tom Cruise's *Far and Away*, a film as good as any sleeping pill. The remains of the unit partied till four in the morning at a newly discovered haunt, the Italian Disco. Later that day, Natasha took me to some sights around Yalta unseen by many of us on *Sharpe*. As this was my third tour it was about time. Plus, Harris could all too easily meet with an off-screen demise before the next series, possibly making this the last time I'd see Yalta. First stop on the itinerary was a visit to a grandiose Great Patriotic War memorial dedicated to the brave marines who defended Yalta from the Nazis, which was accessed by a funicular cable car, the ascent affording spectacular views over Yalta. With the sombre visit to the war memorial done, we descended to Yalta market to exchange some dollars; if inflation carried on at this rate, we'd soon need wheelbarrows à la 1920s Berlin to transport our coupons. At the sanatorium we welcomed the return of John Tams and Fiona Clegg, respectively rested and repaired, bringing 'care packages' stuffed with goodies from home. The evening was spent having what I thought was a quiet drink with Lyndon and Sean in his suite, where we tucked into what Russians refer to as the 'water of life' – vodka to you and me. As the hour got later and later, we found out Sean wasn't being called till 1:30 the next afternoon, not six in the morning like Lyndon and me. No wonder he kept topping up our glasses.

The next morning, still pretty wasted, we struggled through the morning, grabbing shuteye in the numerous delays between takes. Lunch was a welcome respite from being under the still very hot October sun; Muir was in town so decent chow was served in the mess hall. At one point an exceptionally drunk local carpenter – so unprofessional, showing up drunk to work – started to pile an inordinately huge heap of egg mayonnaise onto his salad plate, presumably to feed a large family when he got home. Muir lashed into the vodka-soaked carpenter, demanding he put the food down and leave the tent. It was an unedifying spectacle, fat cat Muir hauling back an almost emaciated Crimean from a plate of food. Muir pointed out that it wasn't the blitzed chippy's first trip to the salad table; hilariously he came back into the tent and sat slap-bang in front of Muir and Tom's table, before eventually being banished a final time.

Once I'd repaired to the cocoon of my room, had a hard-fought-for shower and a meal in my belly, I finally began to feel normal again. After a mini party in my room, I nipped to the bar where I was immediately collared by a well-oiled Ray who asked me to do him 'a favour, be a big man, swallow your pride, apologise to Tom', dramatically leaning towards me to finish with 'I need you to do this for me.' Blimey. Chris had already asked this of me in a clear, concise manner, but Ray had to lay it on thick. Interestingly, none of the other revolutionaries had been asked to apologise.

Acceding to his appeal, I disengaged from Ray only to be collared again by a couple of local crew, who were eager to have me sample a special bottle of 99 per cent proof vodka. It being the height of rudeness to refuse at least one drink from a Russian, I downed a large shot, scorching the lining of my throat in the process. With the alcohol kicking in almost immediately, one of my new-found drinking buddies declared he wanted revenge for an arm-wrestling reverse I'd inflicted upon him in the bar a year earlier. Now fortified with the water of life, we stepped out onto the bar's patio where I made it two-nil to Harris, much to the amusement of his assembled mates who honoured me with more 99 per cent proof toasts. Ten minutes later, I was completely fucked as I climbed the stairs back to the fourth floor where Daragh, probably as wasted as me, was taking on some of the local crew at chess for money. Thankfully, my room was yards from the fourth-floor lounge as when I woke next morning I had no recollection of walking to my door, opening it and getting into bed. It looked like the health benefits of those early nights had been completely reversed.

In make-up the following afternoon, Natasha recounted my drunken blabbering in my sleep, providing much mirth to those listening. After a bit of a general boogying to Diana's Latino mix tape we headed to set for more scenes of Chosen repose; scenes requiring the reappearance of baby Harper who was being surprisingly mellow until John Tams leaned over the infant and said 'boo', which caused the baby to kick off, prolonging the scene, much to Tom's displeasure. It seemed as though every time I had dialogue to deliver, the baby wailed loudly; coupled with the blazing sun forcing me to squint heavily, I was finding it hard to repose.

It was 5 October, the second anniversary of the Bean era. No work for me that day, allowing for a day of taking on supplies and keeping the body clock in sync with the night shift, achieved by sleeping as much as you could during the day to be ready to party when the unit returned from set at the break of dawn. Though technically it was 6 October by the time Beano got back to the sanatorium, Lyndon and I still laid on a small celebration to mark the anniversary. A note of concern: poor Ian McNeice had completed his night duties but was stuck in Yalta as Turkey was not allowing planes from Simferopol to land due to the cholera outbreak. The checkpoint on the road to Dimerdji still hadn't been shut, so that either meant the authorities had everything under control, or thought they had, leaving open the spectre of an infected host travelling down to Yalta, which gave us all massive pause for thought.

The night shoots were at least all-action; that is, when the camera was rolling; otherwise proceedings crept along at a snail's pace with Harris not seeing combat till midnight as part of a complex action sequence. At three in the morning, Tom gave me potentially the most challenging stunt of the night and certainly the most dangerous to date on *Sharpe*: jump from an eight-foot fort wall and knock a rider off his horse as he trots past. Roy Street instructed me to lightly tap the rider's shoulder as I leaped past him and the stuntman would do the rest. Three takes later, and the stunt looked phoney through the lens; on one of the takes the horse went slower, causing me to bounce off its hindquarters before hitting the dirt awkwardly. The camera position was moved on the fourth take, but the action still looked as real as WWE wrestling. Finally, Roy said 'just pull 'im off the horse, Jase'; something I had wanted to do on take one, Tom too by the looks of it, as on the fifth take it went like a dream. In

Roy's defence, he told me how years ago he had been performing the same stunt and sustained an injury because the actor pulled him awkwardly from the saddle.

Happily, this tranche of nocturnal filming was mercifully short. On the final night, we arrived on set to be told by Mike Mallinson, 'Sorry, chaps, we have no particular plan, not sure when we'll need you.' At last some refreshing honesty from production. In the end our time was used efficiently, and we were packed off home to roam an empty sanatorium. Chris Burt had returned from London fresh from pleading with the suits at ITV for more money to prolong the Portuguese shoot. I hoped he had more luck getting extra cash from the executives at Carlton Television than I had getting an increase in my wage from him. After all, these were the folk who had slashed Sharpe's budget by 12 per cent from the previous year; congratulations, you've made one of the best shows on British television, let's reward you with a budget cut! Rumours were, they'd already rearranged for some the scenes scheduled to be filmed here to be moved to Portugal.

With nights complete, we transitioned back to days, with the whole weekend free to adjust the body clock. Natasha took Siri Neal and Maria Petrucci into town to show them the sights; I spent the afternoon with Saint and the man tasked with slaying Perkins, Liam Carney. Or Liam Carnage as Daragh had christened him due to the trail of destruction he laid in his wake after a session in Bacchus's court. Later, when the girls returned from town nicely merry, Maria proceeded to read Natasha's tarot cards, which was my cue to exit.

Later still, a posse went to racketeer Rustlan's restaurant just outside Yalta; Beano came back slightly agitated after a heated conversation with Ray. While Chris had been home in England, associate producer Ray had been strutting around like Alexander Haig after President Reagan was shot, erroneously claiming he was the boss. Lyndon and I went up to Sean's suite to get the lowdown. At dinner, with Daragh and Johnny looking on, Sean talked about what improvements could be made on *Sharpe* going forward. Ray countered with 'I couldn't give a shit for the future of *Sharpe*,' followed up with 'this is a business, nothing else'. Beano was really miffed; it got us talking about the show, going over the same old ground; *Sharpe*'s ills and why had such a successful show had its budget slashed, how had Malcolm and Muir let this happen. Oh, fuck it, we collectively decided, and headed back down to the bar where Beano was cornered again by Ray, this time apologising profusely one would hope. I sloped off to bed at four in the morning before things got too sloppy.

October the 10th, the eleventh week of this campaign; a week I had been dreading as we were just days away from the unwarranted, unjust death of Perkins. War is hell and soldiers die all the time, and I was well aware, of course, that the death of a regular character would guarantee the heart strings of the audience would be tugged. Arriving at base camp, Lyndon and I immediately repaired to our tents to catch up on our sleep and wait for breakfast; catering had made a right royal hash of the transition from nights back to days, delaying the morning's preparation. Poor old caterers: their organisation seemed to be racked with incompetence, not helped by a continuous conveyer belt of personnel changes. Their most talented chef was nicknamed 'Space' for taking bacchanalian excess to new extremes; he upped and quit the unit because he couldn't hack the Crimea. Mike, his replacement, was no master chef, but he was quiet as a mouse and nice as pie; trouble was, he went AWOL with the petty cash. His replacement was Carlos – name changed to protect the guilty – a bright-eyed chef who cared about what he cooked, but, like Space, was in a permanent state of hangover, a bit like most of the actors. However, the caterers were called to location many hours before any of us. Bless them; they were a good bunch, charged with a hell of a tough job, in challenging conditions for virtually no money.

It was time to move up the hill to the 'Torrecastro' set, to film the street-to-street fighting with Loup's brigade that preceded Perkins' death. After work I headed back home, stopping at the production office to establish if they had secured visas for the girls. The answer was no. Back on our floor I encountered John Tams with fresh intel regarding Chris Burt's trip to London, where his plea for extra dosh to extend the Portuguese shoot had proved fruitless. The mandarins at Carlton Television saw no need to throw more cash at *Sharpe* and had no regard for the health and safety of the unit. After lunch, Lyndon and I became courtiers to my lord Bacchus, embarking on a session that lasted till a disapproving Natasha came back from work. We were well and truly wrecked; no surprise, for we knew what was coming tomorrow: Perkins' removal from our band of brothers.

October the 12th arrived with the definite hint of moisture in the air, confirmed by the tell-tale evidence of overnight rain remaining on the road outside. Boz, our driver, dropped us at Dimerdji predicting further rain as he could feel it in his bones. As Tanya dabbed the last bit of powder on my face, I could hear the first dull splats of rain hitting the roof of the make-up tent; by the time we reached our tent to 'don our frocks' the skies had opened, unleashing torrential rain. It hadn't rained for four months and, boy, did the skies make up for it; was someone up in the heavens trying to delay the inevitable? As a fervent non-believer, I knew the rain had to come at some point and here it was, coincidentally on the day Perkins was to die.

After a three-hour delay, urban warfare continued through the streets of 'Torrecastro', covering a section where we were pinned down under terrible crossfire, seemingly doomed. Harper hatched a plan to play possum and we were to fall from our firing positions, apparently dead. It felt very peculiar filming my own mock death as I fell next to Hagman's prostrate body. You never knew, with it being open season on the Chosen Men, if Harris could be croaking for real at the beginning of the next series. Cheaper still to open the next series with:

Sharpe: 'Where's that bloody Harris.'

Harper: 'Oh, didn't you hear? He's dead.'

The excitement of shooting that sequence kept our minds off the inevitable and inescapable murder of a Chosen Man. First up was Harper carrying Perkins' bayonetted body into the church, followed by the most emotional scene I had ever shot in my three tours on *Sharpe*. Everyone felt the emotion; what could only be described as a solemn hush descended upon the unit as Harper laid Perkins down on the straw-covered wooden floor; Lyndon and Daragh giving incredibly convincing performances. Many a tear was shed on both sides of the camera. It felt good to have actually done a bit of proper acting for a change; Tom looked very pleased. The episode finale would leave very few dry eyes anywhere. I could see the pain and disenchantment on Lyndon's face; Perkins was dead, the non-stop party was over, he was going home.

The death of a Chosen Man heralded a change in the weather; the Crimean summer was over and cooler winds began to sweep through the Valley of Ghosts. The day after Perkins' ghost ascended to heaven, we arrived on set feeling fully deflated after the previous day's emotional exertions to continue the street fighting prior to

Perkins' death. Forgoing lunch, I went to sleep in the tent, bundled up against the cold winds forcing their way under the tent flaps, hoping to awake to find Perkins' death was merely a horrible nightmare. I filmed my last bit of this sequence and shuffled home for an early night.

October the 14th was the final day of 'Sharpe's Battle' and our last day at Dimerdji that series. Worst of all, it was Lyndon's final day ever; with one stab of a bayonet the average age of the Chosen Men shot up dramatically. Overnight gale-force winds had pulled down part of the set, further evidence that even Mother Nature frowned upon killing off an innocent regular character. The downed set provided plenty of time to hurry up and wait; we filled the void reading newspaper clippings Daragh had received as part of his press service, including a chart of the year's best TV shows. *Sharpe* polled fourth behind *Absolutely Fabulous*, the game show *Play Your Cards Right* and customs and excise drama *The Knock*, again achieving a 50 per cent share of the available audience the night *Sharpe* aired. A larger share of the audience than the three higher-rated shows and still ITV wanted to squeeze the budget year on year. One review thought 'Sharpe's friends were ugly gargoyles', terribly uplifting for those of us classed as Sharpe's friends. Possibly that was why production was so keen on culling the Chosen Men?

The first action saw us charging from the church, firing our Bakers and screaming in pain at the loss of our beloved comrade-in-arms. The gulf between how we felt yesterday, straight after Perkins' death scene, and now was enormous; it was really hard to recreate that feeling. I just had to concentrate on the overriding objective: death to the French! Post-lunch, after rescuing our tents from a sudden gust of gale-force wind, we resumed filming the denouement of 'Battle', where Harper, flanked by Hagman and Harris, carries Perkins' dead body sombrely across the courtyard to Sharpe, whose face registers suitable horror. And that was it, the episode was wrapped, one more added to the canon; then it was onwards to 'Sharpe's Sword' and, hopefully, more placid, sedate, uneventful times ahead.

At the Chernomore, most of the unit were readying themselves for a threefold reason to celebrate: the end of an episode, a goodbye to 'Battle' actors and a melancholy farewell to one of Sharpe's leading lights. Yes, I had Natasha; yes, I was about to shoot potentially Harris's best ever episode in 'Sword'. Yes, I was a Chosen Man in this legendary series, but losing my main partner in crime was a big blow. Down in the bar the party was in full swing; Daragh was talking to a new accountant freshly arrived from London. This was ITV's response to our request for more cash; send out another accountant; made sense. I sat with Sean and John Tams, who were in deep discussion about the 'Sword' script, namely the big question: how would Sharpe reconcile having sex with a sixteen-year-old postulant nun. I supposed we would have to put it down to it being a time of different morals.

Earlier, Johnny and Daragh had had to talk Richard Moore out of resigning from the show. During the final skirmish of 'Battle', Rifleman Moore was seen to be severely injured, which he took to mean he'd been killed off on the sly, like so many other Sharpe stalwarts before him. There was no need for Richard to worry; in front of camera he and armourer Will Whitlam had been filling in the holes left by vacating Chosen all through 'Battle'. Sometime later, I left Sean drinking vodka shots with friendly neighbourhood gangster Rustlan in the bar and slipped upstairs to Lyndon's room. Where we inevitably got around to talking with Sam Craddock about *Sharpe*'s predicament, namely why was a top-four-rated show getting no extra financial assistance from ITV? Sam summed it up like this: had we been a Central Television, in-house production like *Peak Practice* or *Cadfael*, we'd have ascended through the ranks getting bigger budgets year on year. Since Malcolm and Muir were independent producers they weren't trusted with loads of dosh, the sort you'd need to do justice to a show like *Sharpe*. I suppose calling *force majeure* and initiating the largest insurance claim in British television history can't have helped the cause.

The circular conversations carried on for a while before bed beckoned; Lyndon's transport was set to leave at eleven and, seeing as I was his default alarm clock, I would need to be ready. My mind turned to the first *Sharpe* when his electric alarm clock kept going off at different times as a result of power cuts. Lyndon's room was above Dan Craig's and within earshot of the alarm. One day Daniel had had enough and strode into Lyndon's room, unplugged the alarm and threw it off the balcony, where it disintegrated on the pavement below.

I rose with great difficulty fifteen minutes before departure time and scrambled to Lyndon's room, finding him still fast asleep. Used to fast turnarounds, Lyndon arrived downstairs where Natasha, Daragh and Johnny were there to see him 'packed in his box' and returned home. Some said Lyndon had aged considerably over three tours; possibly it was just that phase of life, early twenties, when you start to grow up. I'd spent a fair few hours with Lyndon and I would say that he started with an old head on young shoulders; still prone to the odd bout of childish hyperactivity, but sometimes surprising us all with his maturity of thought and action. Phelim Drew, travelling with Lyndon to the airport, was last seen stumbling from the bar to get his guitar, only to find bacchanalian excess had prevented the normally talented Irishman from singing and playing at the same time; in fact, he couldn't talk too well either. He finally made it downstairs to the transport after our production secretary Felicity went to wake him; once everyone had assembled, we exchanged hugs, made arrangements to meet back home and said goodbye to Rifleman Perkins.

WHO'S THE DADDY? I'M THE DADDY!

We got back to our room for what I anticipated was going to be a chilled-out Sunday; instead it was the day that changed my life forever – for the better. Natasha emerged from the bathroom declaring she was late; it took a beat before I realised what she was implying. I could feel the blood draining from my face as she said she must be pregnant. It certainly made me totally lose faith in tarot cards, if ever I had any; how did Maria Petrucci reading Natasha's cards completely fail to predict this huge chunk of life-changing news? Well, there might not be a fourth *Sharpe* campaign, but there would certainly be a second *Sharpe* baby, production designer Andrew Mollo and interpreter Oxana being the proud parents of the first. I remember the conversation when we first heard about their situation; Andrew's circumstances were potentially more awkward compared to mine as he already had a family. This led to their baby, Dascha, being born in Yalta. I remember scoffing at this, declaring 'Any child of mine will be born in London!' Well, it looked like I would be putting my money where my mouth was on that one.

The news, coupled with the previous night's partying, sent me into a spacey, almost floating mood; until we had done another test we were going to keep our little secret for a bit longer. At lunch we popped over to the dining hall to meet members of the 'Sword' cast, Emily Mortimer playing Lass, and Patrick Fierry, this episode's French baddy, Leroux. Lass was the postulant nun love interest who had given Beano much pause for thought. He needn't have worried. Emily was in her early twenties, so perfectly grown up enough for the audience to accept her as an object of Sharpe's affections; although her voice did sound very young and girly-like, she didn't speak for vast chunks of the script; a bit like us Chosen Men.

Sunday 16 October felt like the first day of the rest of my new life. I spent the morning seeing off the remaining 'Battle' cast from the Chernomore forecourt, bound for Moscow. Coming the other way was Phelim Drew, who had mislaid his Russian visa, preventing him from entering Russia for the onward flight home; instead of making him pay for a new visa, they'd sent him all the way back to Simferopol, poor bugger. Also departing was Andrew Mollo, off to sort out anything needed for the Portuguese shoot. With him was Oxana, his interpreter and mother of the first *Sharpe* baby – that we know of! Very funny I should bump into them so soon after learning our own little secret. Later on, we visited Natasha's mum, not to break the news she was going to be a grandma; that would have to wait a little while. I spent the afternoon playing football before taking advantage of the recently made available swimming pool and sauna, where I was introduced to slapping my sweaty body with birch twigs. It was so nice to have this facility at our disposal: a good swim, sweat and slap really helped to iron out the creases of life in the Crimea.

Now my first thoughts of the day were: 'Fuck, I'm going to be a father!' Plenty of the cast were parents, including Beano and Johnny, so why should it be so scary for me, already thirty-two years on the planet? It did put all the problems we'd been having on *Sharpe* into perspective; I certainly wouldn't have as much energy for the eternal struggles. With 'Sharpe's Sword' on the doorstep, I was getting exactly what I'd always craved on *Sharpe*: more action for Harris and a bearing on the narrative. A great episode for me by all accounts, but the cynic in me knew to wait till it was broadcast the following May before declaring victory. I'd witnessed many a brilliant Chosen Man scene consigned to the cutting-room floor; cynicism aside, I did have some very nice scenes coming up in this episode.

Twelve weeks in-country and I was starting to succumb to Sharpe's belly. Oh well, only three years of my life so far dealing with my digestive tract getting a kicking. To make matters worse, my toilet needed constant tinkering to stop the water trickling down from the cistern, turning me into a bit of a toilet whisperer. Thankfully I wasn't on the first call sheet, not just for the proximity to the toilet, but also for some extra revision of Voltaire's *Candide* so that I could appear to speak with a bit of authority in my scenes. Not that *Candide* was an immediately comprehensible read.

October the 18th saw the commencement of 'Sword' with four consecutive night shoots; the first night, I had some nice scenes with Beano, so part of the morning was spent rehearsing, something we'd never before felt the need to do. It was very low key, consisting of a couple of read-throughs followed by tuning in the shortwave radio to get the previous night's footie results. No poncing about discussing motivations or subtext for us; we knew exactly what our characters were about at this stage of the game. In the news, the Queen was visiting Russia with the main channel showing her touring St Petersburg. Apparently the royal visit was playing havoc with the flights in and out of Moscow, having a knock-on effect for *Sharpe* actors reporting for duty.

The bulk of 'Sword' would be shot at Baidar Valley, a bread and butter location for *Sharpe* that had provided many a backdrop down the years. Riding to work with Emily Mortimer, I discovered she lived around the corner from me in London, we knew people in common and she had a Russian boyfriend who went to school with Chelsea's goalkeeper Dmitri Kharine. Evidently, she was also fluent in Russian, having attended the prestigious Moscow Art Theatre (MHAT) founded by Konstantin Stanislavski in 1898. I had almost embarrassed myself at the bar the previous night, seeing Emily surrounded by stuntmen, who were in no way intimidating, but I could hear them firing lots of questions at her in Russian. Ignorant about her command of Russian, I began to edge towards her table to heroically 'rescue' her with my minimal translating skills; I was stopped in my tracks upon hearing Emily's youthful voice speaking perfect Russian. What a gal. I had clearly underestimated her.

I CAN READ, SIR!

The next night, we filmed the scenes Sean and I had rehearsed: Sharpe walks through the camp, encountering Harris burning a copy of *Candide* in the campfire. When I first read this, I thought how bloody ridiculous; why was a supposed bibliophile incinerating a perfectly good book because it was bloodstained? It made Harris look like a bumbling fool; quite strange that Eoghan Harris, normally the best screenwriter for Harris, should have crafted a scene like this. Otherwise it was great for my character, explaining the plot of

Candide to Sharpe, giving him the idea there was a hidden code; Sean and I popped it swiftly in the can without a hitch, which was handy as the freezing Baidar winds were super-cooling the location. With the workday done, I retired back to the Chernomore for a breakfast beer with Stephen Moore who was playing the role of Berkeley. The part was written as Colonel Wyndham, last seen at Badajoz's breached wall in 'Company', a role played by Clive Francis, but he hadn't liked how the part was written nor the fact that he got blown up halfway through the piece. Though I liked Clive, I was so happy Stephen had taken over the role as his son Guy, also an actor, was in my class at secondary school, so I had known Stephen half my life.

Night two of 'Sword' and we were shooting a night of setbacks for Sharpe during our attack on the French fort; chief baddie Leroux escaped custody, Berkeley got blown up and our leader was badly injured in the retreat. Talk about a bad day at the office. Things got a little tetchy behind the camera as well, when Tom discovered that the South Essex weren't fitted with boot mufflers, something he had specifically requested as we were filming a stealthy, silent night attack. It had been a day to forget on many fronts; luckless Phelim Drew was still without a visa to enter Russia, and flights via Istanbul were still suspended, thus extending his stay at Camp Sharpe, where he was nonetheless having a ball in the process. Trouble was, Phelim was due to start a job in Prague, which he was in danger of missing, a minor tragedy for an actor. We asked production why he couldn't fly out through Kiev, which was, after all, in the same country as Simferopol. They said there were no flights available; more likely it was a more expensive option. The final calamity heaped upon my person was my shortwave radio smashing to bits after falling off my balcony railings in the high winds. My instant connection to the outside world was gone; no more listening to BBC World Service in the privacy of my own room. I did have Russian and local television, which went some way to filling the news void and, of course, there was Paddy World News, still with his shortwave radio intact.

Due to the plunging temperatures up at Baidar, base camp was moved from the dried-up pond over to the Orlynoye cultural centre where we'd spent many an hour while filming the latter part of 'Honour'. The interiors looked the same, spartan, almost no furniture bar our camp beds, a fold-up table and a clothes rail for our costumes. Already ensconced was fresh meat, James Purefoy playing the treacherous, one-arm spy, Captain Spears. He seemed a pleasant enough chap; curiously and cleverly, James had brought with him an oak burr, knives, chisels and other tools to fashion the oak into a lidded cup; James must have been forewarned about the colossal waiting times on night shoots.

On a call sheet came a faxed message from Johnny Goodman of Central Television, declaring on behalf of head honcho Ted Childs that they 'really appreciate the fantastic job of work' we were doing. He described the 'circumstances' of working in the Crimea as 'some of the most difficult you are ever likely to encounter on a foreign location', adding that he knew from his short stay during the first campaign what we were going through; except that he was here for three short days, staying at the far more comfortable and well-heeled Yalta Hotel. He signed off somewhat patronisingly with the suggestion 'turkey and Christmas pudding will taste even better this year because we carried on in the face of constant adversity', a roundabout way of saying sorry for slashing the budget and denying emergency cash and potentially compromising our health and safety. Again, it brought to mind Harper's line in 'Sharpe's Rifles': 'We don't have a proper officer so we get pushed around like pot boys.' ITV/ Central were the military brass pushing around the Sharpe Film pot boys, Malcolm and Muir.

With night shoots over, storms started to batter the Chernomore and I renewed my focus on making sure production secured Natasha's Portuguese visa. I wanted it settled, now that we were three. Good thing I reminded Chris; he was under the impression I had sorted the visa out myself. What a shambles. The notion of fatherhood was slowly sinking in; Natasha's pregnancy was confirmed by a tester bought at Boots the chemist by Saint, now returned after a snow delay in Moscow. Due to the gastrointestinal aggro we were experiencing they had also flown out a proper medic, Dr Tim Nuthall, which was a comfort considering our unborn child was now part of the *Sharpe* unit.

With the weekend upon us, we went to see Natasha's mum, but Nat was still too nervous to give her the news. After lunch we headed back to the sanatorium for the Saturday night revelry. There were fewer racketeer types in the bar that night, though we did have more freshly arrived 'Sword' cast, including John Kavanagh playing Father Curtis, Matthew Pannell, a non-actor, in the cast for his horsemanship, and the crown prince of bacchanalian excess, one of the most hilarious and mischievous actors to have graced any *Sharpe* cast, a *Sharpe* icon after just one episode, Michael Cochrane. As a fellow traveller from the first campaign, he knew exactly what we had to put up with and what you had to do to survive it. Party!

On Saturday evening we hit the Italian restaurant for Saint's birthday celebrations, but didn't stay long as Natasha started to feel sick; she appeared to be skipping morning sickness in favour of evening sickness. Once at the sanatorium, I let Natasha sleep while

I hit the bar to embark on another night of excess. The big three, Sean, Daragh and Johnny, were lined up along the bar, and across the room I spied Michael Cochrane, who appeared to be in conversation with Slava Burlasko, our top horse stuntman. Only thing was, I knew Slava spoke no English and Cockie, our name for Michael, was no Emily Mortimer. As I got closer, I could see the baffled look on Slava's face as a fairly inebriated Cockie babbled away at him. I helped him up towards his room whereupon he insisted we have a joint for a nightcap, as in the old days. I lied and said I was going to crash out and that he should do the same. Leaving Michael to his slumber, I popped along to Saint's room with Beano for a nightcap, where I told Sean the news about Natasha's pregnancy, which he seemed very pleased about. Only the previous week Natasha had said Sean had told her it was about time she had kids; steady on, Beano, she's only twenty-two. As the night wore on, the two of them proceeded to expound upon the joys of fatherhood with Beano saying it would bring me luck. Not if I kept partying till five in the morning it wouldn't; thank God Sean and I had a day off. Saint wasn't as fortunate.

It was three weeks till we were to depart for Portugal; it crossed my mind that these could be Sharpe's last days in the Crimea. Not for me, of course; I was to become embedded forever, for better or for worse, as Natasha and I had plans to get spliced once we were back in Blighty. I took a trip to the Yalta Hotel for some light shopping and a swing through Yalta market to convert my dollars. Current rate being eighty-eight thousand coupons to the dollar, a massive hike from our first year when one dollar only got you four hundred coupons; a textbook case of hyperinflation if ever there was one. Now Ukraine was in the free market economy, a lot of the goods came from Turkey, making everything uninteresting and homogenous;

a far cry from the curious, ex-Soviet tat that had appealed to me previously.

On the way back to the sanatorium, I stopped at a new Italian café that served excellent French fries; it was also where Natasha's grandma – the dead spit of Natasha – worked and I chatted intermittently with her, still managing not to let slip that she was going to be a great-grandma. Back in my room, Beano joined me to watch a tape of *Match of the Day* hot off the plane. Sean told me he was going to eschew the delights of the Sharpe charter to Lisbon, instead opting for a twenty-six-hour train journey to Moscow, where the trusted British Airways would fly him back to civilisation. John Tams and Michael Cochrane would join him; an option open to me as well. Natasha contended that I wouldn't like a long train journey on the ex-Soviet rail network and nor would Beano.

Back at Baidar, we were filming the march on the squat little wooden fort for a revenge attack, our leader newly having recuperated from his near-death experience with a combo of Lass's love and freezing cold baths. Looking fit and happy, Malcolm Craddock was back in-country with the news that 'Battle' was three minutes short and we would possibly need to conjure up a new scene. A situation the Chosen found to their advantage on the first campaign when 'Rifles' was also discovered to be short.

After a languorous morning of prep, the camera rolled on our column marching towards the fort; but it wasn't long before problems arose. Baidar Valley was pretty huge but we were shooting at one of its fringes encroached by a road; several times we had to stop for vehicles, aircraft overhead, hammering in the distance, fluffed lines and a broken telescope, all of which conspired to interrupt the flow with one take having to restart seven times. I lunched with Daragh, who met me with his customary opening gambit, 'Well?'; a sort of rhetorical question in the guise of a greeting. Normally it was met with a perfunctory 'Not much.' This time I hit him with the news that Natasha was pregnant. Suddenly I remembered the story he had told me of the actor who found himself in the same position on that calamitous production Daragh shot in the Arctic. He seemed pleased at the news, if a little confused; not sure why, he must have known Nat and I weren't playing chess in my room the whole time.

I got released straight after lunch, riding back to Yalta in Malcolm's car; for some reason I didn't feel it was time to tell him my big news. He mentioned *Sharpe* had been sold to Australia and Germany, but neither executive would be getting residuals. Cue the violins! Malcolm also confirmed Central Television would require three more films next year; we would probably have to shoot it on an even more reduced budget, too. I reminded him Sean had firmly asserted he wouldn't be returning here for more *Sharpe*s; Malcolm laconically replied it would be one of many obstacles between now and another series. I spent the evening entertaining some of the 'Sword' cast in my room, Stephen Moore, James Purefoy and John Kavanagh in attendance. John told me about his wild night in Red Square followed by a seven-hour wait for a flight to Simferopol at one of Moscow's domestic airports, aided by liberal doses of vodka to ease the pain. He couldn't fathom how we put up with this for several months at a time and wondered why they didn't film where he lived in Ireland. I imagined the pounds, shillings and pence might have a bearing.

Fog at Baidar had made it impossible to complete the scene started the day before in the blazing sunshine, so I was at the Chernomore taking advantage of a desolate sanatorium, hogging the phone room to call family and friends around the world, managing to avoid telling anyone my main news. I caught the news on Russian television; peace had apparently broken out in the Middle East with pictures showing Hosni Mubarak, Yasser Arafat, Bill Clinton and Shimon Peres smiling broadly while shaking each other's hands. There was movement on the visa front, production having called for the passports of Ukrainian crew needed in Portugal; no need for the midnight train to Moscow. Phew!

Over at the cultural centre, or 'kloob', as Boz my driver called it, Paddy World News had done his best to disseminate the news of the new Sharpe baby with John Tams and Michael Cochrane, both of whom congratulated me as I arrived; l should probably have just got them to put the news on the call sheet. On the valley floor with the last shafts of the winter sun to illuminate the scene, bagpiper Bob White piped out a tune for a wild track – recording for sound not vision. As the shadows lengthened, the plaintive sound of Scotland wafted across the valley; a truly beautiful if slightly melancholy end to the workday. Once home, we all chilled out watching 'Sharpe's Honour', which for me gets better with each viewing.

It was 28 October and it was 'Jack Spears riding day' as part of the action covering our advance on the fort. In this section, the perfidious, one-armed Captain Spears atones for his treachery with a suicide charge on the French fort. Most of the hard work was done by our senior Russian horse stuntman, Slava Burlatchko, but that didn't stop James looking very satisfied with himself. With Spears martyred, the column continued the advance towards the squat wooden fort with even more gunfire, explosions and stuntmen being thrown hither and thither; great fun to shoot and an amazing spectacle that kept the onlooking locals riveted.

Daragh had been pumping Sam for news of the Portuguese schedule; apparently our contracts would expire a few days before the end of the shoot, meaning they would try to clear us, then ship us home before the wrap party, which seemed slightly cruel. Daragh had also discovered the rough cut of 'Battle' wasn't three minutes under, as had been reported; it was twenty-six minutes over, requiring some hefty editing, which could mean Chosen Men scenes scattered all over the editing-room floor. We wrapped the work week with more of our explosive advance towards the fort before retreating to the sanatorium for the weekend's shenanigans. This was the time we finally plucked up the collective courage to inform Natasha's mum of her impending grandmotherhood; but not before I went through the charade of asking Valentina for her daughter's hand in marriage, something Natasha insisted on. We arrived suited and booted, nervous as hell to deliver the news. We needn't have worried; Valentina had sort of guessed that might be the case when Natasha told her she was giving up smoking; mums always know! I supposed it was time to call my parents in Massachusetts to let them know the good news.

Back at the Chernomore bar, the unit were celebrating 'Drivers Day' with our Moldovan friends. On a normal evening these guys party like madmen, but this celebration was like several Oliver Reeds with a legitimate excuse to get paralytic. Unfortunately, in an attempt to escape the amorous advances of Sano's Ukrainian assistant at the party, one of them hid by perching himself on the wrong side of the balcony rail, slipped and fell almost two floors onto the hard concrete below. Our nurse Suzanna, Giles and others rushed to his aid, finding him with compound fractures of both legs. Dr Tim was summoned from the bar at three-thirty in the morning, interrupting his drinking session with James Purefoy. Nevertheless,

Dr Tim, ably assisted by James, stemmed the bleeding and applied a splint and went back to their bacchanalian excess.

James told me when they got back to the bar, the sun came up and they realised their clothes were spattered with the blood of the unfortunate Moldovan. Perhaps because he was so drunk, he escaped death; but that was quite a price to pay to avoid a drunken snog.

With my increased involvement in 'Sword', the shooting schedule got progressively kinder; no longer was I part of the Chosen flock, in fact the flock no longer existed as there were only two of us left. I was called in to do my bit and released when done; no hanging around in case I was needed to fill in the background of a shot. After a morning chilling in my room, I made a trip to the Yalta Hotel. On the way back to the Chernomore the minivan popped a tyre on a steep incline in front of the Rossiya sanatorium. With the minivan now perched on an upward slope, the driver proceeded to give a masterclass on how not to change a tyre on a hill. Once safely back at the deathly quiet Chernomore, I hit the phone room to call the British Embassy in Kiev to ask for advice on marrying a Ukrainian, but got no answer. I then called Lyndon, who wasn't home. Typical. I had the bloody phone room all to myself, but I couldn't get through to anyone.

When the crew started to arrive back at the sanatorium, we discovered there would be a new addition to the passenger manifest for the Lisbon flight; Sano had bought a devastatingly cute French bulldog from the bootleg pet market in front of Yalta bazaar. Chris Burt was furious with her, telling her there was no way he could get the dog on the plane. In honour of our esteemed producer, Sano had named the dog Burty! It would be interesting to see how this dispute got resolved.

The first day of November arrived, with rain clouds threatening to soak the valley, but just in time the sun appeared, blasting away the clouds and causing it to get pretty warm as we prepared to shoot our first appearance in this episode: the hunt for the dastardly Colonel Leroux. The scene continued after lunch with more Leroux-hunting and a bit of dialogue from Harris. With work complete, Boz drove me and Natasha back to Yalta; he was driving aggressively fast, which I didn't mind, but on the drive through Orlynoye he hit a little white Scottie dog crossing the road. He didn't stop the car. I turned back to see the poor little dog writhing in agony as its horrified owners rushed to its aid. I didn't know what to say, I felt sick. How could Boz be so callous? It was an extremely quiet ride back, the image of that stricken dog burned onto my retinas. At home we got news of the Moldovan driver who had slipped from the balcony. The damage to his ankles was so bad he might have to have his feet amputated. What a sobering end to the day! What a country!

LORD OF THE SWORD

The next morning on the drive to work I half-expected angry villagers to be lining the road pelting the car with bottles and stones, or maybe a dog-shaped ghost flying through the windscreen to bite Boz, causing us to crash. I was hoping the dog was still alive with just a broken leg, but if the Moldovan driver's feet couldn't be saved what hope did the dog have? When I got to base, another canine was the centre of attention with the unveiling of Burty, a chunky, cute, scrunched-faced pooch being paraded around the cultural centre by Daragh; it looked like there would be no end of babysitters for this new addition to the unit.

Up on location we continued the pursuit of French spymaster Leroux, who we caught trying to hide his identity. Patrick Fierry was brilliantly cast as the devious French spy, full of evil intent and mock innocence, with a face you'd love to punch; the audience was going to relish seeing him dispatched. Upon wrap, I jumped into the dog-squashing-mobile with a live and kicking Burty on my lap as I was now the designated dog sitter. I was rewarded with dinner cooked by Sano accompanied by the newly arrived Diana Perez; the remains of the evening were spent watching one of the endless Alan Delon films broadcast on Russia's main channel.

Dog sitting continued the following morning; Sano had even arranged for Natasha to have the day off to help with Burty. I visited the production office to check on the Portuguese visa situation, a state of affairs that was quickly turning into farce. I had speedily filled out Natasha's visa application for immediate dispatch to Moscow; the application had sat in the office since then, waiting for Helen Khramova, Russian wardrobe mistress, to complete her application. Though Helen was nice as pie to me, she was quite tough on her subordinates and there were some in the costume department who wouldn't have minded if she didn't travel to Portugal. This had all the hallmarks of a titanic Sharpe cock-up. Not securing a visa for Natasha would cause no end of hassle.

Our third Guy Fawkes Day in the Crimea rolled around with the pyro boys promising a few bangs later in the day. My late call automatically put me on Burty watch; at 5:45 a.m. a frisky pup was let loose into my charge. Luckily after a little while we both curled up on my bed and dozed off to a Steven Segal movie unfinished from the night before. After a nap we bounded up to the production office where Burty was lavished with attention before jumping into the lift. On the next floor, Chris Burt, who made a big show of hating Burty, got in; for a few moments we had the two Burtys face-to-face. Little Burty wanted to lick big Burt's face, Chris was trying his hardest to feign enmity towards the cutest member of the unit since Lyndon's departure. Big Burty was on his way to Lisbon, with a lovely stop at his London home worked into the itinerary, I imagine. That would give Ray 'Kray', his associate producer, licence to repeat his Alexander Haig act.

Riding into work with me was the impressively large figure of Uldis Veispal, joining us to put the finishing touches to the various sword fights in this episode, starting with the choreography on the Father Curtis versus Simmerson duel. Uldis was an Olympic-class instructor and had really honed Beano's fighting style; he had also played a small role in 'Sharpe's Honour' as the duelling marquis whose murder was subsequently pinned on Sharpe. Arriving at the 'kloob', I discovered that someone who knew we were soon leaving the country had decided to liberate our expensive silk thermal underwear. Fortunately, Harris's scenes were all set by the campfire, where the possibility that *Candide* could hold the key to the French spy code was discussed. Sean was on great form and displayed great comic timing when he delivered the line to Lass, 'I want you in my bed by the time I get back.' Realising what he'd just said, he quickly added, 'and I'll be sleeping out here by the fire', handled with deft, expert timing. I couldn't wait to see it when broadcast.

When Saturday came it was time to pray to the god of football. With my shortwave radio out of action I stood on Beano's balcony to get the football results; dressed only in a towel and jacket, Sean's outfit would have ladies' hearts beating that bit faster – and no doubt a few gentlemen, too. We froze our arses waiting for the Premiership results; elsewhere in the sanatorium grounds five loud bangs were heard, but witnessed by hardly anyone. Apparently that was our

Guy Fawkes firework display. The evening was saved by a seventies-themed disco replete with coloured lights and smoke machines creating a great atmosphere. Natasha came down to the bar at three in the morning after feeling nauseous, prompting my 'early' retirement from the fray as she had to be up early to go in search of the correct papers to export Burty to Portugal. Sano's seemingly crazy notion looked like it was coming to fruition.

Overnight, while we were boogying on the dance floor, there was a fire at the wooden fort set constructed at Baidar. First reports claimed the entire construction was burned to a crisp. At lunch, set builder Grant Montgomery reported it was only the guardhouse next to the fort that got torched. Apparently as temperatures dipped our location security guard had decided to keep warm by lighting a fire inside the wooden set; the Sharpe jinx at work again, or just Crimean stupidity, or were they inextricably linked? Whatever the state of the fort, it looked like the schedule would be elongated; Sean, John and the train posse would have to leave the following Friday to make the journey feasible and Sean was adamant that was the only route he'd be taking home.

One week till we decamped to Portugal. After walkies with Burty, I made another attempt to get through to the British Embassy in Kiev to ascertain what documents would be needed for marrying Natasha, a certificate of no impediment being one of them. Where on earth did you get one of those from? I returned to my room with a two-day-old – fresh by our standards – copy of the *Independent* newspaper, which I lovingly read from cover to cover, drawing out the enjoyment as long as I could. Once every word of the newspaper had been devoured, our other reliable source of inside information rolled in for an afternoon cuppa. 'Well,' Daragh intoned, 'what's the news?' I told him of my plans to marry Natasha as soon as we returned to the UK. Daragh reported there would be no change to the schedule due to the burned portion of the set; Sean was standing firm that he would not film past the coming Friday, which was in five days. The Portuguese consulate had reportedly said it would take three weeks to process the visas; it was abundantly clear the production office had made this a low priority. I really should have gone to sort it out myself like I had done in Kiev. I spoke with wardrobe chief Robin Fraser Paye, who told me he had seen a fax sent from Muir to Chris Burt telling him to squash the Portuguese visa procurement as other local crew members would be jealous and it would set a dangerous precedent for subsequent UK productions shot out here. To Chris's credit, he had binned the fax, ignoring the advice from London; nevertheless I went to Felicity to inform her that, should the girls' visas fall through, I'd need Natasha's passport back and our travel booked through Moscow, where we would stop off for a visit to the Portuguese consulate. I hoped this would concentrate a few minds in the production office.

DASVIDANIYA UKRAINE

Wednesday 9 November saw our last day out at Baidar this tour and possibly the last time we would ever see this vast valley perched at the top of a mountain. Predicting the demise of *Sharpe* in the Crimea had proved wrong in the past, though this time the show's prized asset had refused to return to film more episodes here. Then again, he did say on this campaign he would only come out to Yalta for eight weeks and we had already been there almost fourteen; so, we would see.

At the fort we were putting the finishing touches to the episode's denouement, including the now iconic 'over the hills' shot. Harris was first up in front of camera to lower the tricolour, making way for the victorious Union Jack, a fairly simple shot one might think, but Tom wanted the flag to flutter once it had been raised. We'd experienced some unrelenting, biting winds in the past up here at Baidar, but on this occasion, when we required an intermittent gust, conditions were as benign as the doldrums, necessitating a few retakes before an adequate puff of wind made the flag flutter majestically.

With four days left of our Crimean leg, the sanatorium was positively brimming with an end-of-term, demob happiness; apart, that is, from the cleaning ladies, who had a forlorn look on their faces knowing the dollars garnered from their entrepreneurial (yet illicit) laundry service would soon dry up. Riding into work with me on my last workday was a bleary-eyed James Purefoy, lying crumpled in the back seat having become the latest victim of accumulated bacchanalian excess. Polikur would house us for the final two days of Yalta with the cloister set last used on 'Honour' and 'Enemy' convincingly transformed into Father Curtis's mission, now a makeshift a hospital. Strewn around the set were soldiers convalescing from various injuries, including one genuine amputee extra, which really created a chillingly realistic environment. We began with the Chosen posse's entry to the mission with Spears, Simmerson, Lass and Ramona as part of the group, where Father Curtis told the remaining Chosen men that even God wouldn't choose us; had Tom made them add that line? In the wait between takes, Roy was actively encouraging us to be photographed on horseback; my first time in the saddle in all these years. After posing for one shot, Roy began to let Beano have a little ride on a horse, but that was quickly blocked by Mike Mallinson who reminded Roy that Sean wasn't insured for such activities.

After work I went with Natasha and her mum to a local clinic to have a low-tech inspection of the developing baby. We had known for almost a month now and Natasha still hadn't told her dad, saying we should do it once we had announced our wedding date. Hint, hint! We got back to the Chernomore to begin the colossal task of packing my stuff and the tat accumulated over the campaign. Once I'd tired of packing, I left my future bride sleeping while I popped to Beano's for a mini wrap party where Sean told me of his vision for future *Sharpe*s. He wanted a year off with a return to action in the spring of 1996. filming anywhere but the Crimea. Pain in the arse though it might be, I couldn't see us completely ignoring a small stint out here. After all, the Crimea had provided a perfect backdrop, and the hardships of existing out here had given our faces a combat-hardened veneer. In the end it would be down to how anxious the suits at ITV were to get a fourth series of *Sharpe* underway.

November the 11th dawned, exactly fourteen weeks since we had touched down at Simferopol International Airport on that roasting hot day in August; two and a half months that had changed my life forever. Upon rising I continued packing my trunk, then John Tams and I took the transport to Polikur for the unit photo. With a few clicks of the stills camera, Beano was done in the Crimea, free to begin his epic train, plane and automobile journey to Lisbon via Moscow and London. A huge sigh of relief was let out when the Portuguese visas arrived for the girls, obviating the need for Natasha and me to join Sean on the ludicrously circuitous route to the next location.

With our Crimea stint now complete, we had the whole weekend to get out, lock stock and barrel, ready for our charter at noon on Monday. I spied Muir going to his room, and, as I had some photos for him, I went over. As a thank-you, he suggested I 'make peace with Tom Clegg'; I had to stop my jaw dropping with stunned surprise as I had already made peace with Tom. The day continued with a final farewell to my gold-toothed journalist friend and sometime father, Sacha from Simferopol. He had alienated the production office with his article in a local paper asserting Ukrainian crew members were being exploited and underpaid. A perfectly reasonable claim, but it wasn't the evil English capitalists taking advantage of the locals; it was the East-West Creative Association who set the salaries of locals, often only a fraction of the money they received from Sharpe Film for local crew wages.

On our last day in the Crimea, the sanatorium, now shorn of Sean, Johnny, a few other 'Sword' cast and all the Muscovite crew, felt eerie and empty. With everything packed away, the only entertainment was conversation, more getting wasted and listening to the shortwave radio. News came in of the first passengers traversing the newly opened Channel Tunnel; *sacre bleu* would surely be heard emanating from Napoleon's Tomb and anyone else opposed to Entente Cordiale. A little further north, Sweden had held a referendum to join the European Union; the dream one day would be for Ukraine to be offered EU accession, which would certainly make our lives a hell of a lot easier when travelling. Of course, 259 months and 12 days from this diary entry Brexit would ruin that particular dream; it wouldn't matter, though, as Ukraine appeared even further from joining the EU in June 2016.

The final fracas of the Crimean leg came late on the Sunday night, while watching television in the lounge. All of a sudden, Sveta, the bar manager, accompanied by several mafia heavies, came striding down the corridor and proceeded to knock on Daragh's door. After several minutes the knocking turned to banging, which eventually roused a dazed-looking Daragh from his slumbers; I slid down the couch so as not to be seen. Sveta translated for the heavies explaining to Big D that he still owed a hundred dollars on his bar bill and by the tone of the voices they weren't going anywhere till they had collected. Daragh put up a half-hearted, unconvincing defence, claiming first that he had given it to one person then to another; even I was confused as I surreptitiously listened. Needless to say, the greenbacks were produced, the mob retreated and Daragh resumed his beauty sleep.

LEAVING ON A JET PLANE, DON'T KNOW WHEN I'LL BE BACK AGAIN

Monday 14 November, a day many had been looking forward to for three and a half months: liberation from Crimea day! That year's withdrawal found me in a completely different head space from previous departures; year one I had been desperate to exit, year two I had been forlorn at leaving Natasha behind, but this year my sole focus was returning home to start my *Sharpe*-generated family. Natasha's mum came up to say goodbye and collected anything useful we didn't want to take with us. Normally I would give any unwanted stuff to our floor's cleaning lady; however, the mean boss of the 'chambermaids' had given them the day off so she alone could reap the rewards of our leftover bits and pieces.

We arrived at Simferopol airport to find it still undergoing a facelift; normally chaotic on a good day, today the terminal building showed signs of construction but no workmen and scaffolding everywhere. Throw a film unit, Burty the dog and the first *Sharpe* baby, Dascha Mollo, into the mix and it was instant pandemonium. Once we had cleared the excuse for airport security, fixer Igor Nossov informed us we couldn't fly over Spanish airspace, adding an hour to the normally four-hour flight. Igor disappeared to loud noises of displeasure from the unit, returning with an offer to wait inside the warm plane sitting on the runway, an offer we couldn't refuse. We sat on the runway for two and a half hours, eventually taking off at five in the afternoon; fairly standard for *Sharpe* in the Crimea. If Beano had his way this would be a thing of the past. As was the custom, catering had baked one of our special charter flight cakes; Ray and Felicity tucked into a slice, but when coming back for seconds they were tipped off as to the contents, so they declined. I doubt they would have felt anything due to the high level of alcohol normally in their systems.

Having to avoid mainland Spain meant that we traversed the length of the Mediterranean, passing the bright lights of Marseilles, Toulouse and San Sebastian along the way; I know this because I went into the cockpit where the co-pilot let me peer at his flight maps. I did wonder why we had to avoid Spain; I bet some sort of baksheesh failed to cross the appropriate palm yet again. It was a pleasant flight, though; Air Ukraine served up a hot meal for the first time ever. The food was absolutely horrendous, but at least they tried. Allowing for the two-hour time difference, we got into Lisbon at eight in the evening local time. Natasha and I were whisked to Cascais by car along the shiny new road I remembered being built back on the first tour. Understandably, Natasha felt tired and melancholy, partly because she is a Slav, but mostly because, at the tender age of twenty-two, she was leaving home, unsure of when she would return. After I'd tucked a sleepy Natasha up in bed, I went on a little walkabout in the hotel where so much drama had unfolded during our first stay.

From landing in Lisbon to my first workday was four days. I drove to location in the pitch-black Cascais morning with Emily Mortimer and Michael Cochrane to film what, on paper at least, looked like one of the funnier scenes from 'Sword'. As we drove to work, Cockie regaled us with stories of the marathon train journey from Simferopol to Moscow. Much carriage-hopping and bacchanalian excess eased the journey along, Cockie even managing to introduce a train stewardess to the delights of a Sharpe party. Natasha's best mate, Igor, had accompanied the lads to interpret, ensuring a smooth crossing at the Russian border; the only hairy moment had come when a border guard decided to double back towards Michael's cabin just after he had lit an illegal 'cigarette' and had the associated detritus spread over the table in front of him. As the door opened his cabin mates quickly lay back and feigned sleep, leaving Cockie in a fug of smoke, joint in hand. Michael told me he thought, 'Oh, fuck. Looks like I'll be heading to the gulag for a long stretch,' but the machine-gun-toting guard merely popped in his head, took one look at Cockie and went on his way, never to return. Blessed Cockie, he's a character both off screen and on and an absolute gift to the Sharpe family.

Today's location was a spectacular country estate called Bom Jardim, with immaculately tended grounds dotted with stone statues. In a courtyard facing the house was a long rectangle of grass encircled by the driveway; we were told that on this lawn the first ever football match in Portugal took place around 1883. To pay homage to this event, we had a kickabout with a deflated football against the three dogs belonging to the house. A suitable distance away stood a calm, well-organised base camp with a motorhome just for me. Shame I had only four working days in Portugal under these new rock-star conditions; unfortunately Harris's upgrade had come at the price of the loss of two of my Chosen comrades. I was experiencing a sort of survivor's guilt. It seemed that on *Sharpe* negative events had to occur before positive outcomes could transpire, like Paul McGann's injury landing Beano the greatest role of his career so far.

The first scene captured was Harris's obsessive search of the library for a copy of *Candide*, interrupted by Simmerson's pursuit of Lass. I thought it rather ridiculous Harris spending hours forensically combing the library for a copy of *Candide* only for Simmerson to find it on top of a pile of books within seconds of entering the scene. Again, it made it look like Harris was either blind or a bumbling fool. I didn't have dialogue with Simmerson on the first *Sharpe*, so it was a delight to do a scene together, even if I did have great difficulty in keeping a straight face as everything Mike says or does is usually hilarious. Next up I shot a scene with Daragh inside the house, Tom adding a couple of touches giving the scene a good-humoured feel. The good humour continued through lunch, helped by the caterers having beer and wine available in the drinks section; I shuddered to think of the mayhem that would have ensued having alcohol served at mealtime in the Crimea.

Our first week in Portugal passed swiftly and soon it was only a week till I wrapped on the third series. Not required for work, we had a leisurely breakfast with the luxury of reading English papers the same day they were printed. In the afternoon more damage to my credit card was done at the shops and restaurants in Lisbon before a few of the lads went to watch Beleneses versus Guimarães in the Portuguese football league. The next day Beano and Johnny arrived back on set looking a little ragged after a week back home; their absence from Camp Sharpe made Daragh and I the longest-serving actors on *Sharpe* with almost fifty-two weeks continuous service over three tours.

Bom Jardim base camp was teeming, with the order of filming meaning that many of the 'Sword' cast returned from the dead after biting the dust in the Crimea. Escaping the pleasures of Yalta was Vernon Dobtcheff, playing Dom Felipe; he'd been in so many UK and European films and television series since I was a kid, I was almost star-struck in his presence. The cast of 'Sword' and 'Battle' was so far superior in terms of heavyweight actors compared to little old 'Sharpe's Gold', I wondered if it would look weak or disproportionate compared with the other two. Tom had set up a long tracking shot up the drive, through the iron gates, finally alighting in front of Don Felipe's house. Tom's job was made slightly more challenging as the occupants of the house had their entire extended family in attendance to view the shooting, with kids and dogs swarming everywhere.

With the exterior shots in the can we moved inside, to cover Harris's adventures with Voltaire's *Candide*. As we were approaching wrap, Bernard Cornwell had flown in to treat the department heads and a chosen few actors to dinner at a fancy fish restaurant on the outskirts of Cascais. Before departing I met Sean at the hotel bar while waiting for John and Daragh to emerge as it was always best to be a little buzzed at those events. As Bernard waited for his taxi, I sidled up to him to say what a good episode I thought 'Battle' was, apart from the death of Perkins; he pleaded innocence, categorically stating that Perkins' death was not in the finished novel and that it was the idea of the management and scriptwriter Russell Lewis. In fact, he seemed a little hurt that I could have thought he would have written such a thing. I wanted to remind him he killed off Hagman in his book *Waterloo* and Tongue in 'Gold', but I wasn't quick-witted enough.

Both Daragh and Johnny declined to join us, so I jumped in the car with Sean for the short ride; after our driver sped out of Cascais, crossing into neighbouring Estoril, I began to get a little worried, wondering if this was a kidnap attempt on Beano. I reminded the driver that Baluarte restaurant was in Cascais, and he went into head-slapping mode and turned the car around. We arrived at a very posh fish restaurant to a group starter, a huge platter of shellfish that in London would have set you back a pretty penny. I sat next to Muir's wife, Mercedes, a charming woman who knew how to pull Muir's strings like a virtuoso, gently putting him in his place whenever necessary; seated on my other side was director of photography Chris O'Dell, who kept me amused most of the evening with tales of Crimean incompetence. We headed back to the Cidadela Hotel stuffed with hundreds of pounds' worth of seafood; I got up to my room to find Natasha watching *Scarlett* on telly, a television imagining of *Gone with the Wind*, one of Sean's less heralded projects. Immediately following *Scarlett*, the main Portuguese channel broadcast a Yuppie stockbroker film called *Dealers* which, in a bizarre twist of coincidence, starred Paul McGann. All roads led to *Sharpe*? I was beginning to think they did.

November the 25th arrived, exactly sixteen weeks since leaving Stansted and my final shooting day this campaign. Taking into account the friction and turbulence experienced on this tour, I could well have been next up for the chop. Surely Hagman couldn't be on the endangered list; it might be slightly awkward as he was also in charge of the music, not to mention one of the best characters in the show. Having only one Chosen Man running alongside Sharpe would look ridiculous, so maybe I'd still have skin in the game next time, whenever that might be. As I was staring down the barrel of parenthood, I would need to maintain my place on *Sharpe* more than ever; a far cry from the dark days of misery on the second campaign when the Chosen Men vowed never to do *Sharpe* again.

My last day of taking the King's shilling would be spent filming Harris making haste to the 'Mirador', to declare the code had been broken, only to be barred by Harper acting as a bouncer while Sharpe received 'post-operative care' from Lass. We had used two locations as Don Felipe's house, the gorgeous Bom Jardim and now the rather less pleasant Quinta Do Bulhaco, formerly a farmhouse, but now some sort of riding school stuck between two major motorways to the north of Lisbon. The set decorators had done a great job on the house's back balcony, transforming it into the Mirador, where Sharpe was being treated for his wounds. The scene went without a hitch: Harris sprinted up the Mirador stairs, chest puffed out with pride at finally cracking the code, babbling like a demented professor. Daragh had decided he was going to take over directing this scene himself, giving me notes on when to catch his eyeline and cutting a line laden full of sexual innuendo about the sort of position Sharpe was in. Once that scene was done, we had to say goodbye to our Russian/ Ukrainian costume team, who had to leave the shoot early due to there being only one scheduled flight a week from Lisbon to Moscow. Most of the unit filed off set to bid them farewell; many tears were shed on both sides. Would this be our final farewell, would we see them or the Crimea ever again?

We broke for our final delicious lunch cooked up by our amazing caterers, joined by Sean's wife, Melanie Hill, who had arrived from London the day before. After mealtime, the shoot proceeded at a snail's pace; it being Sharpe, Harper, Harris and Hagman's last day on set, Tom seemed to draw everything out a little, a far cry from the hurry up and wait we were used to. Fairly soon, Bernard Cornwell arrived on set, and, as it was likely to be the last time I would see him for a while, I took the opportunity to lightly pump Bernie about any more *Sharpe* novels brewing in his head. Last year he had intimated the possibility of a prequel story set in India, tentatively titled *Sharpe's Curry*, which I guess would cover the time when Sharpe was a private or a sergeant. Bernard hinted that the *Curry* story was mooted to possibly be a feature film, so we could find ourselves shooting in a place where cholera was practically invented.

On the Mirador, the four of us reconvened under the warm winter sun for our final scene together, Sharpe rising from his sick bed with the aid of a cane to inspect his men – what was left of them. As Sharpe passed along the line, exchanging words with his men like the Queen at a Leicester Square film premiere, each of us proffered a gift: Harper the repaired cavalry sword, Harris the key to the code with a well-thumbed copy of *Candide* and Hagman a bottle of paraffin with some 'best brown paper'. The last bit of business, Hagman's leitmotif, was not originally in the script but added by John at the last moment with Tom's blessing, kind of stealing the scene from Daragh and myself. The director called cut on a medium shot of Sharpe and Hagman, thus ending the Fab Four's involvement in this year's production. A series of pronouncements confirming when each of us was done prompted applause from the unit; when the entire scene was complete there was a further outpouring of emotions, especially from Tom, who declared it to be the perfect way to end.

We dried our eyes, stepped out of our costumes one last time and joined the rush-hour traffic through Lisbon to prepare for one last departure the next day. In the evening the wrap party was again held at the Coconuts night club; Natasha and I put in a brief appearance, I took advantage of my free drink before we headed home early, stopping for some Chinese food on the way back to the hotel. One of my most abstemious wrap parties; then again, 'we' were pregnant.

Saturday 26 November 1994 was demob day for Sean, Daragh, John and me, ahead of the rest of the unit. They were rushing us out early as our contracts had expired the previous day, protecting production from shelling out another week's wages for the four of us; not such a big deal if you're on my lowly wage, but punitive if you're on leading-man wedge. Trying not to let the end-of-show blues hit me, I went with Natasha for a last stroll along the Cascais seafront where fisherman were repairing their nets in readiness for the next catch. On the rocky high ground at a bend in the coast road lies Cascais army barracks with a statue of a Napoleonic-era Portuguese rifleman leaning on a boulder as he surveys the ground ahead. I obviously dwelled too long videoing the statue because I attracted the sentry's suspicions; I didn't feel like explaining myself, so we swiftly exited and headed back for the final send-off and our taxi to Lisbon airport.

Tom, Chris Burt and Ray were in the hotel lobby to bid us all farewell. Considering the often fractious relationship between the regulars and the production office, the farewell and thanks for our hard work were sincere. With that out of the way, our cars sped towards the airport; for one last moment Sharpe and his Chosen Men stood together in front of British Airways check-in desk, only to be forced apart as reality set in with Sean and Mel going to first class, John, Natasha and I to standard class and Daragh onto a separate flight direct to Los Angeles. Last glimpse I got of Daragh was of him attempting to explain why he was taking an antique Baker rifle on board for the flight.

It had been sixteen weeks and a day from when we had landed in the Crimea for the third tour, but it felt like much longer. We had learned to keep grinding on despite the continual obstacles thrown up; three years in the Crimea had thickened our skins, we took everything in our stride. The success of *Sharpe* in the Crimea walked on the crushed bodies of those who could not hack the attritional nature of life on campaign. With Sean's rising star power, the *Sharpe* tour cycle might be interrupted. The smart money said this juggernaut would ride again, over the hills and far away, at the same time, but possibly not in the same place. For Sean, *Sharpe* was like Hotel California: you can check out, but you can never leave.

INTERBELLUM III

The campaign was over with no great outpouring of relief on my part, possibly because I had become used to the *Sharpe* cycle; mostly, though, because of the life-altering event Natasha and I were about to face. The hedonistic lifestyle was over, gone the frivolous, devil-may-care, fun-chasing attitude of the past; in came marriage, parenting, financial frugality and no longer solely looking out for number one. Those past two years, *Sharpe* had been my entire world, it had subsumed my life; all roads led to *Sharpe*. I wanted to go forward with it, relished being part of a very special team and was proud of the fact we had taken all the Crimea could throw at us, coming out the other side having created television gold. Of course, Natasha and I were part of the greater family unit which had built up over three campaigns, and in our first days back in the UK we were inundated with well-wishers. But, like all families, sometimes they had dysfunctional tendencies.

In early December a dinner was held at Joe Allen's to say goodbye to Bernard before he headed back to the States, and I attended for a post-meal drink. After a short while I went to use the toilet; on my return Diana Perez intercepted me looking concerned about something she'd just heard. Bernard had asked her what she thought about getting a new husband. She wasn't sure what it meant, but I had a bloody good idea; Bernard had inadvertently, possibly deliberately, let slip there were plans to replace Daragh. Back at the table I was unable to corroborate this with Bernard as Muir was within earshot. The polite conversation continued, I finished my drink and headed home, shaking my head in dismay at the Machiavellian manoeuvrings of the powers. Of course, as I was merely a couple of rungs up from the horses in importance, these matters were way above my pay grade. I possessed not one jot of power or influence over this potentially disastrous decision made in the corridors of power, but I knew a man who did.

I called the Bean residence. Sean was still at the pub, but I filled Mel in on the latest developments; well after closing time, I got a call back from Sean. I told him about the sequence of events, how Daragh's expulsion wasn't explicitly spelled out, but despite Diana rambling a little drunkenly, I got the gist. Sean agreed this shouldn't happen; we knew Daragh could be a right old handful sometimes but replacing him wouldn't be good for the show. Long ago Daragh had identified *Sharpe* as a buddy picture and, after reading all the novels, we knew that the Sharpe–Harper relationship was an essential strand of the formula. When Daragh was on form he was the warmest, most charming and engaging soul, capable of huge generosity and wit; but there was also the scary-as-fuck Daragh, who didn't suffer fools, was never shy of a ruck, especially if there was the mere whiff of his rights being violated. For me, though, Daragh *was* Harper; he was the first actor to be cast on *Sharpe*. Thoughts of dumping him were absolutely bonkers. On a not totally unrelated matter, I wrote the letter of apology to Tom that Muir urged me to write; no longer interested in all-out revolution against the powers, I meekly handed over my testicles.

DING-DONG THE BELLS ARE GONNA CHIME

The dust had barely settled on the third campaign and we were already facing our first skirmish; I shouldn't have been surprised, this was all part of the landscape on *Sharpe*. With the main man heading off the problem at the pass, I concentrated on my own upcoming engagement. As Chosen Men prefer a tavern to a church, I was preparing for a register office wedding and I chose the Chelsea Register Office, famous for celebrity marriages including those of Judy Garland and Paul McCartney. With our certificate of no impediment applied for, we signed the register at 3:30 in the afternoon on 18 January 1995. Naturally it was a Sharpe-dominated reception back at our flat although I studiously avoided the inevitable bacchanalian excess that unfolded around me.

The first snippets of news started to filter down the grapevine. Apparently, we would be hopping across the Black Sea to Turkey for the next chapter in our *Sharpe* odyssey. What a difference that particular switch of location would make, like doing a whole shoot in Portugal; there would also be one episode, 'Sharpe's Regiment', set in England. Cashing in on our success, Malcolm was putting together a book, a Sharpe annual; I had been interviewed as part of the research. When the book's author discovered I'd written a diary, she was very interested in having a look. I told her I was reserving it to one day write my own account of *Sharpe*: a warts-and-all, no-holds-barred version recounted by someone who actually had boots on the ground.

The year started to zoom along as we keenly awaited Natasha's due date; the third series aired to great acclaim with viewing figures in the region of ten million. A review of 'Sword' spawned one of my favourite quips to date: the *Sun*'s Gary Bushell asked if anyone had noticed Mick Hucknall was playing Harris; quite hilarious as I had been mistaken for the Simply Red frontman for years. Things were good in my world. But, as so often happens in the cycle of life, I got some extremely sad news: 'Jason, Dad died', three words uttered quietly down the transatlantic line by my mum. I tried my best not to freak out Natasha with my response; I knew my dad had lived with ill health, having suffered from diabetes for years, but he was only sixty-seven and this news came like a bolt from the blue. In many ways I was emulating my father when writing a diary on *Sharpe*; two of his published books are *Havana Journal* and *Georgetown Journal*, documenting his time in Cuba and Guyana respectively. At my audition for *Sharpe* the director barely mentioned the Napoleonic era or Bernard's novels; my father was the main topic of conversation, so I felt he was crucial to my *Sharpe* narrative.

At this point of the cycle, I would usually be solely focused on getting prepared for the upcoming campaign. That year, I had been spliced for better or worse, awaited my firstborn child, lost my father, welcomed my mum home to London after twenty years away and had to plan my dad's funeral. A fair bit to have on your plate, even for a Chosen Man trained to improvise, adapt and overcome. It was now late May and, crucially, a couple of weeks before our baby was due. Alejandro Sutherland visited my flat, providing some juicy intelligence on the upcoming campaign: 'Regiment' would be followed by 'Siege' and there would be an entirely new story not in book form called 'Sharpe's Mission', which was shaping up to be a good episode for Harris.

On the downside, confirmation that the Chosen few would remain the same in number became apparent with no reappearance of Cooper – I knew leaving *Sharpe* voluntarily was a bad idea – but at least Sean had prevented us being Harper-less. I had witnessed how, on year three, Rifleman Moore and armourer Will Whitlam had filled in the space formally held by Chosen Men; why would production bring back more expensive frame fillers? There were rumours Hugh Fraser might not be available for a fourth series, but I bet that was just his agent playing hardball in contract negotiations. Another blow to my heart was the choice of scriptwriter Charles Wood for 'Regiment'; undoubtedly a legend in his field, his penchant for writing semi-coherent short utterances for the Chosen Men really irked me. I hoped the script of 'Mission' was as good for me as reported.

FAREWELL TO SLEEP

At St Mary's Hospital, on 17 June 1995, at eight minutes past ten in the morning, the stresses of career, *Sharpe* and supporting Chelsea suddenly paled into insignificance as Daniel Alexander Salkey came into the world. Funnily enough, Dan was born exactly two years to the day after Dascha Mollo, the first *Sharpe*-generated baby, came into this world. The first few weeks were as challenging to my system as a month of night shoots on *Sharpe*; popping over to help with the new delivery was Valentina, Natasha's mum, so now our chosen baby had both his grandmas taking the strain.

Some days later, we were invited to lunch along with Tom Clegg at Sean and Mel's place. When asked about the rumours of replacing Daragh, Tom claimed he had nothing to do with it; thanks to Beano, Big D was still part of the team so we didn't delve too deeply into the matter. By June there was still no call to my agent about *Sharpe*; I made an emotional trip back to the USA to clear out our belongings from the family home in Amherst, Massachusetts. As Bernard Cornwell lived in the same state, I put in my customary call to his Cape Cod home for a bit of *Sharpe* chat. He told me the Indian *Sharpe* story was coming along nicely, but it sounded like there was no Harper or Chosen Men. By the time I returned it was late July; in the three previous campaigns I would have been signed and sealed at this stage of the cycle, but, as I was barely in the first episode shot, they had no need to contract me yet.

In early August my agent got *the* call from Hubbard casting with details of my *Sharpe* contract; it was confirmed I would only be required for one of the four weeks needed to shoot 'Regiment'. Further rubbing the shine off my penny was discovering that Ray

Frift would resume his role as associate producer after a visit to the Bromley Place office on a script-seeking exercise. My request was rebuffed, with Ray telling me to wait till the 'Regiment' read-through later in the month.

At the end of August, the regular cast re-formed for a read-through of 'Regiment' in Holborn, joined by supporting cast and a new regular, Abigail Cruttenden, playing Sharpe's wife, Jane Gibbons. I felt like a bit of a spare part, pained at reading the inarticulate grunts given to Harris by the screenwriter; I was happy when my newly purchased mobile phone rang during the read-through, allowing me to slip out of the hall. It was my agent calling me with an audition, demonstrating to the powers that I did have a career outside *Sharpe* – just!

TURKISH TASTER

With a Crimean return ruled out, we decided Natasha and Dan should stay in Yalta for first part of the Turkish tour, only joining me towards the end of the schedule. Transiting through Istanbul on the way to Yalta would prove a handy reconnaissance mission to dispel or prove some of the Turkish stereotypes I had in my head from watching films like *Midnight Express*; worryingly, there was even something in the paper about the militant arm of a group called the Kurdistan Workers' Party (PKK) orchestrating bombing campaigns against tourists, threatening more in the future; not ideal as we were filming in a resort town. However, the Foreign Office hadn't advised against travel.

My first, brief taste of Turkey was pretty positive; being apart from the family would be a wrench but they would be well taken care of by Natasha's mum. Though missing the family, after my Istanbul jaunt I made up for three months of interrupted sleep, as well as making final preparations for the campaign, keeping in mind the arrival of the family on location. We were heading into a different, unfamiliar world for *Sharpe*; before us novel delights and possibly new dangers. What would an Anatolian *Sharpe* hold in store? I sure as hell was going to find out.

4

TURKISH DELIGHTS

On 5 October 1995, the fourth act of my *Sharpe* drama began at Gatwick with our Monarch Air charter flight to Antalya, Turkey, on the Mediterranean coast. Gone were the excitement and anticipation of previous campaigns, and the fact that I wouldn't see my family for a couple of months didn't help. Still, it was nice to be back at my fellow Chosen Men's side; the previous campaign had been brutal, reducing our Chosen band of brothers from a Fab Four to a Dynamic Duo. Lacking Lyndon, my chief partner in crime, on location would be very strange indeed; *Sharpe* wouldn't be the same without him.

Sharpe Film naïvely thought Monarch would allow equipment cases into the cabin as we were accustomed to with our previous carriers. Unlike Air Ukraine or Aeroflot, Monarch freight crew obeyed the rules of the Civil Aviation Authority and left several boxes of equipment sitting on the tarmac. We were not in Ukraine anymore, Toto! With thirty-three of us scattered through a hundred-odd-seat cabin it felt very rock 'n' roll, even presidential. We touched down, quickly clearing immigration with a payment of £10 each;

what a difference from the labyrinthine process of visas and entry checks every time we entered the former Soviet bloc.

We left Antalya airport in two buses; one vehicle took crew members directly to our first base outside Alayna, another 130 kilometres down the highway; the other bus, with producers, directors and cast, took the shorter ride to our base for the middle section of our tour, the vast Antalya Sheraton Voyager which sounded very like a NASA probe sent to Mars. It was reputedly owned by a fugitive from British justice, Asil Nadir, wanted for embezzling investors' dosh; perhaps some of that money built this place. Waking up in my plush hotel room the following morning, I felt disoriented as hell, in desperate need of some nourishment and hadn't a clue where anyone else was in the hotel. I ordered a light snack from room service, gasping at the ten-pound charge for a sandwich, fries and Coke. We *seriously* weren't in Ukraine anymore, Toto. The Sheraton was enormous, luxuriously appointed with bars and restaurants on several floors, everywhere clad in glass, chrome and marble. On the downside, the towering hotel had hundreds of rooms on several floors; you could probably go for days in this place without seeing other unit members. The complete opposite of our situation in the Crimea where the lunatics took over the asylum; I was hoping our base in Alanya would be on a more human scale.

YES, WE HAVE NO BANANAS

We waved goodbye to the Sheraton and headed along the coast to Alanya, our base for the next two weeks. The coast road was reminiscent of both the Crimean and Portuguese coastlines; we partied and told tales of past *Sharpe*s to the new 'Regiment' cast, eventually pulling into the Alanya Alarapark Banana. So-called because this whole area had once been covered in the bent yellow fruit; in fact, an entire plantation had been razed to make room for our complex. At the border of the property you could see huge banana trees growing in neat lines; yup, you know the deal, Toto.

After a drink with the crew, I got settled in my room; even though I was completely knackered, sleeping in the cloying heat with incessant attacks from mosquitoes was impossible. Two nights, two different beds; no wonder I awoke feeling a little detached and out of place. Hoping to find something recognisable, I went down to the pool/bar area for breakfast. Pretty soon the recognisable rolled up in the shape of Daragh, dressed all in black and pale of face in the heat of a 30° Celsius morning. We sat out of earshot on the children's swings, where Daragh told me the latest gossip, including a minor verbal ruck between Ray and Tom which had concluded with Tom declaring, 'That's it. It's either him or me!' Malcolm had been seen shifting his taut little body up to Tom's room to mediate. Daragh always reported with the inside info; it seemed inconceivable that a move had been made to take him out of *Sharpe*. Rumour had it they had been going to create a new character called O'Hennighan, or some other cliché of a Irish name; it was only a rumour, though, never substantiated.

Over by the pool bar more familiar faces started to gather; the Russian/Ukrainian crew members, stunt, costume and pyrotechnic chaps had all just arrived. It was almost a culture shock to see these guys in such salubrious surroundings – well, salubrious compared to the Crimea. Soon we were joined by Gary Fiddler, Sean's Winnebago driver from the last campaign; this year, Gary had been promoted to Sean's personal driver, bodyguard and secretary. He ordered food and told me to cheer up: 'I'm picking up the governor this evening.' Hopefully Sean's arrival would make things seem a little more normal. I skulked back to my room. Unfortunately, my room didn't have a fridge, nor had my trunk arrived at the hotel. Apparently it had been taken to the set despite my name being clearly marked on it; John Tams had two trunks, both were delivered to his room.

A few hours later, my trunk arrived in the lobby, a fair old schlep from the building I now called home; when the hotel porters saw the trunk, they swiftly disappeared for a coffee break. The combined efforts of both English and Turkish production offices failed to winkle the porters from their shells. In truth it was quite a load, but if this had been the Crimea strapping lads would already have transported the trunk to my room; here in Anatolia I was on my own. I returned to the bar with a sore back and rewarded myself with a beer; if *Sharpe* had given me anything it was the ability to order beer in three different languages: Russian, Portuguese and now Turkish. The governor duly arrived looking a little reticent in our new surroundings; it wasn't long before we repaired to my room for a welcome party.

SHARPE'S ANATOLIA

October the 8th saw our inaugural shooting day in Turkey; the next three days we would be shooting all the scenes from 'Regiment' set in Spain. Our location, Alarahan Caravanserai, was truly impressive, the base camp dominated by a giant pointy piece of rock that once served as a fort with a crenelated wall spiralling around it all the way to the top. When checking out the location earlier in the year, Malcolm had thought we might be able to shoot 'Siege' here as well, but after it took super-fit Sam Craddock almost four hours to walk to the top, they shelved that idea.

We accessed the shooting location along a dry riverbed; the huge rock forced a bend in the river, raising the water to waist height. In the next couple of days, we would be criss-crossing the fast-flowing water while shooting all the battle scenes. Before that, we'd be filming Sharpe exhorting his newly arrived regiment on the parade ground to be brave, to stand and fight and die if necessary. The 'parade ground' was roasting hot (we were quite a way south of the Crimea, and it felt so much hotter), made worse by the complete lack of natural shade or a constructed sun screen. I supposed we would need the extras, hired locally, to look as tanned as possible like soldiers kissed by the sun of the Iberian Peninsula; the re-enactors used as extras in the UK portion of the 'Regiment' shoot were all British and were far more pasty-faced. Plus the ranks had thinned down from a hundred and fifty busting-at-the-seams-with-enthusiasm UK re-enactors with their own costumes and weapons to about eighty lacklustre lads from Alanya, only in it for the Turkish lira. This year military adviser Richard Moore really had his work cut out.

October the 10th was our last day on 'Regiment'; when complete, we were to concentrate on exterior scenes from 'Sharpe's Mission'. As Harris was consigned to Sharpe's household wrongly accused of murder, a ten-day break in the schedule had opened up which I was hoping to use for a trip to Yalta. It would depend on wrapping 'Regiment' that day, starting with an impressive-looking set-up of the South Essex wading into battle across the river. Dodging musket fire and cannonballs, the regiment broke into a charge as the shore beckoned; in my haste I tripped on a hidden rock, propelling me forward into the water, where my knee struck another rock. Worst of all, I submerged my Baker rifle, getting water down the barrel, one of the cardinal sins you were taught to avoid at Chosen Man school; the disdainful look I got from Richard Moore said it all. I was mortified, but at least the soaking kept me cool in the fierce heat.

CRIMEAN CALLING

I had lunch the following day with Daragh; he had managed to get eight hundred quid for the use of his image in the forthcoming *Sharpe* book confirmed by a fax from his agent, which he laid on the table. I'd been offered a paltry £30, the same amount already accepted by John Tams, Lyndon and Pete Postlethwaite. I finished lunch and went straight to call my agent. She told me Carlton Books had reiterated their offer, claiming 'We've so many actors to clear we really can't offer more.' Obviously, if Pete had accepted thirty quid, who was I to ask for more? I didn't need their *Hello!* magazine version of the *Sharpe* story; would it include a section on Crimean enema doctors, or the complete absence of effective health and safety that laid waste many a unit member? Perhaps not, but the Harris diaries would.

A large break in the shooting schedule had allowed me to arrange a trip back to Yalta. I arrived in Istanbul in the evening so that I could catch a flight to Simferopol early the next morning. All the nice hotels were still full at that time of year, so I had to stay in the twelve quid a night Sentral Hotel just behind Taksim Square. Probably quite nice sixty years ago, now it made our Simferopol hotels look like the

Ritz. Doing my best to ignore the depressing surroundings, I got my first look at the 'Mission' script, a completely new story written by my favourite Sharpe screenwriter, Eoghan Harris, but not adapted from one of Bernard's novels. Daragh hadn't been too impressed with the story; hardly surprising considering Harper got his head kicked in and Ramona questioned his conjugal prowess, or lack of it. I, on the other hand, was overjoyed at the prospect of some nice scenes that would require some proper acting for a change, a relief after the one-line utterances given to me in 'Regiment'. To complete Harris's overall upgrade in the narrative, he even had a love interest in the shape of Gypsy girl Conchita.

The newly created Air Crimea delivered me to Simferopol airport on the same type of twin-prop plane we had taken to Kiev a year earlier; coincidentally, this flight employed the same stewardesses we had on the past Air Ukraine charters, ensuring I got special treatment. Going through immigration I got my first taste of visiting Ukraine without the protection of Sharpe's all-encompassing umbrella. I made the mistake of mentioning my visit was to see my wife and child, which requires prior invitation; businessmen just had to pay on arrival. The militiaman at passport check began getting particularly difficult; I was in danger of not being allowed to enter the country until Igor, Natasha's best friend, came to my rescue. He had been waiting with Natasha on the other side of passport control; I relayed the problem to him, Igor spotted a higher-ranked militiaman who had previously dealt with Sharpe matters, who then gave the okay for me to enter.

The drive down to Yalta was tinged with nostalgia and sadness as we traversed the Moscow Hotel roundabout in Simferopol, on past the majestic sight of Dimerdji, the Valley of Ghosts, maker and breaker of many a unit member and on to the coast. With the family reunited, we went for a stroll along Yalta's seafront, where even more shops and kiosks had sprung up. Gone were the hard-currency shops and money changers; now they had semi-official bureaux de change everywhere; in Bradley's of London, they even allowed you to convert British pounds into the ever diminishing Ukrainian *karbavonet* – or our old friend the coupon.

As well as there being more in the shops there had also been an upsurge of mafia-related activity; the much-frequented German hard-currency supermarket at the Yalta Hotel had been bombed: no more $10 boxes of Kellogg's Frosties. Of more concern, Natasha's upstairs neighbour had been accidentally killed in a drive-by shooting; Yalta was becoming like Al Capone's Chicago. On a happier note, there was now a greater variety of decent places to eat; it felt like Sharpe had arrived in Yalta three years too early, but we were the mavericks, the pioneers, the guinea pigs in the great Sharpe experiment. In a delicious stroke of coincidence, the main Russian channel, Ostankino, was airing the entire series of *Sharpe*, broadcasting an episode each weekend, shown over two nights. Watching *Sharpe* dubbed into Russian seemed entirely appropriate, if a little humorous, but there was nothing funny about Ostankino's broadcasting footprint, which included the ex-Soviet republics with a potential audience of two hundred million.

Coming back to Yalta was a real tonic, reminding me of my true purpose in life. After an all-too-brief stay, I said my final farewells at the Yalta Hotel, where I hitched a lift to Simferopol airport with a party of Turkish gentlemen on a weekend trip to the Crimean Riviera. At passport control I crossed paths with my favourite border guard who had obviously watched *Sharpe* at the weekend and was a lot more pleasant this time, I heard him say something that I didn't quite understand but I could make out the words 'Sharpe' and 'film'. Still rather miffed at the way he had dealt with me on the way in, I wanted to make a narky comment but I thought better of it as I would probably come this way again in future. I have been recognised all over the place, but this was the most far flung.

WHO ARE YOU?

Back at the Banana Alanya, John Tams informed me that a film company from Ireland's RTE broadcasting company had been on set making a documentary; as it was their last day there, John suggested I get up to location or Harris wouldn't be in the film. When I enquired from Ray, he told me the documentary crew were by the hotel pool and he introduced me to the director. I offered to do an interview for the film, but their equipment had already been packed away, so the offer was declined. Never mind, I thought, I've only been in the show four years, and turned disdainfully on my heels. I suppose being in Yalta I had made myself unavailable for interview, but I hadn't been told there would be a film crew making a documentary. So, Rifleman Harris wouldn't get a mention in a film about *Sharpe*. You wondered if the documentary maker had actually seen any of the films?

Finally getting my hands on the script for 'Siege' was at least one small crumb of comfort; it was another effort from Eoghan Harris. He had written one nice two-hander with Sean; always good to be seen next to 'the money'; in the rest of the script the Chosen Men were mostly relegated to one-liners. My only gripe, born of getting the scripts at the last minute, was the references to Wordsworth and Milton in both 'Mission' and 'Siege'; poets I, shamefully, had never read. Had I received the script earlier I could have swotted up on the quotations used in the text as I had done the previously with Voltaire's *Candide*; some would call it method acting, I call it doing your job properly.

October the 19th saw only my fourth working day in two weeks. Daragh had been turning it into a running joke, introducing himself as I arrived on set as if I were a day tripper; I played along, in turn introducing myself to Tom, Sean and Johnny. I was solely in to shoot the 'over the hills' end section of 'Regiment', uncompleted because of failing light; I probably worked for all of an hour before I was wrapped, generating more ribbing from the boys. I was grateful for the short working day as we were leaving Alanya the following day for Antalya and the longest leg of this tour; I'd spent the last three weeks packing and embarking hither and thither, I didn't know whether I was coming or going. Coming in for our last day at the Banana was our favourite day tripper Diana Perez, in-country to shoot the closing scenes of 'Mission'. She had flown out with Mark Strong, the baddie from 'Mission', Colonel Brand; he had just completed a TV series, *Our Friends from the North*, with another baddie from this parish, Daniel Craig.

WHAT THE BUTLER SAW

With the unit packed and loaded we waved goodbye to the Banana in Alanya, bound for Antalya. Along the route we stopped at Ulugüney Old Town to shoot the exonerated Harris being reunited with the gang. Old Town aptly described the place. It was much more traditionally Islamic than any other place we had come across; all the men had facial hair and all the women wore headscarves covering their hair. The houses were very basic and ramshackle, constructed from large stone blocks with incredible gnarled, age-old wooden roof tiles keeping out the elements; on one corner a house lay in ruins having completely collapsed, a victim of an earthquake the epicentre of which was a hundred miles away in Dinar.

The first action of the day saw Harris reporting back events to Sharpe, the kind of scene we usually knocked off in a single take. The menagerie of Ulugüney's farmyard animals scratching around in every villager's front 'garden' had other ideas. Take one, Sharpe asks: 'Anything to report, Harris?' Before I could get a word out, a cow replied with a loud 'mooooo'. On take two, a goat bleated, sending everyone into gales of laughter, including the watching locals. Third time lucky we all thought, but just before I could respond with my line it was a sheep's turn to pipe up. Maybe Sean was a shepherd in a former life and the livestock were just responding to his velvety Yorkshire tones; especially if they were females. This theory was disproved when the assembled animals piped up even louder as Daragh and Diana tried to shoot the Harpers' reunion scene immediately after; the cacophony was soon mixed with calls to prayer from the local mosque.

Those were some of the day's lighter moments; at one point, a large mustachioed Turk repeatedly interrupted the shot by marching into frame angrily shouting. Set security tried several times to calm him down, to no avail; the local machine-gun-toting gendarme finally had to come and drag him away. Instead of ploughing on through the interruptions, lunch was called early; I ate then went for forty winks in the motorhome till they needed me again. My action was cancelled, but they forgot to inform me, so I slept on, missing my ride to our new base. I waited till wrap to make the long drive in Daragh's car, which meant a painfully slow journey while being suffocated by cigarette smoke. True to form, Daragh freaked out several times at the driver for driving at what I felt was a perfectly reasonable and safe speed. In the end he slowed down to a snail's pace just to spite Big D, resulting in a very late arrival into Antalya.

ALL AT SEA

Our first week in Antalya coincided with Bernard Cornwell's customary visit. Accompanied by his agent Toby Eady, Bernard had arranged a lunch excursion on the Mediterranean. Only heads of department, principal artists and partners were invited for the jaunt, with a manifest that included Muir, Ted Childs, controller of drama at Central Television, and director of programmes, Andy Allan. In short, the money men, the chaps who would decide the future of *Sharpe*; possibly the men who decreed it might be good to have a Harperless *Sharpe*. And with Big D himself aboard things could have got interesting, in the Confucian sense of the word. My invitation came late, but only because Beano had been told to invite John and me, but forgot to tell us; John said he wanted 'nowt to do with it' and I entertained thoughts of blowing it off, but I liked hanging out with Bernard. So, ten minutes before departure I ironed my best shirt, polished my loafers and slicked back my hair and made my way down to the vast hotel lobby to meet Sean. After a short wait I spied him in the glass elevator descending through the Vegas-style atrium dressed in a cut-off T-shirt, jeans and trainers, as if dressed for a day of fishing down by the canal. This was what I love about Sean: he really doesn't give a fuck about appearances. This was his day off and there was no one aboard he needed to impress. However, when Beano saw how I was dressed he about-faced and headed back up to his suite to upgrade his attire, arriving a little later with Gary his driver. Sean had made sure Gary got on the guest list; the sight of a tattooed, West Ham-supporting skinhead thrown in among such refinement warmed my heart; even more reason to love Beano.

We got to the marina to see Bernard had hired *Dedeman II*, the largest, most impressive boat in the harbour. Once aboard, the plebs constituted of cast and crew filtered to the sharp end of the vessel while the executives occupied the stern. After downing a few beers, Sean and I emerged from steerage to mingle with the first-class passengers. Daragh, I noticed, stayed resolutely anchored at the prow with his wife, Gabrielle. As we circulated, Ted Childs initiated a conversation with me which was pleasantly surprising; he seemed an absolutely normal bloke, nothing high and mighty about him. I sucked up to him, making sure he knew how much I loved doing *Sharpe*, while trying not to brown-nose excessively. Bernard seemed to lack his normal boyish enthusiasm; perhaps the thrill of seeing his baby come to life wasn't such a big deal anymore. I quickly found out that he was far from happy at the way 'Gold' had turned out.

Dedeman II made her way out onto the calm Mediterranean, sedately following the mountainous coast, past caves and spectacular waterfalls, finally dropping anchor at the spot where the Cyclops fell into the sea. Sean climbed to the top of the boat and executed a perfect dive, causing the powers to hold their collective breaths.

After joining Sean for a dip, we reboarded and settled down for lunch; as we ate a speed boat glided past with a topless blonde adorning the deck, prompting Andy Alan to shout, 'Will you marry me?' Pretty hilarious at the time, though possibly not for his wife, who was sitting next to him. We weighed anchor as the sun started to dip below the horizon and headed back to harbour just as the last beer was drained; it had been one of our most enjoyable days out on Sharpe, one to remember, particularly as we hadn't partied through the night in our normal fashion. The perfect day was rounded off by a Saturday evening Sharpe ritual: settling in front of the shortwave radio for the BBC World Service football reports.

UPSTAIRS DOWNSTAIRS

October the 22nd kicked off an extremely busy week for Harris the butler with all household duties shot at a carpet warehouse in Antalya Old Town. Sharpe was a major now with a wife in tow demanding he hold dinner parties as part of her quest for culture while on campaign. In 'Mission', Harris is accused of garrotting his Gypsy girlfriend, Sharpe protests his Chosen Man's innocence, arguing house arrest would be sufficient until the murder is solved. Harris is assigned to domestic service, partly to keep an eye on the unctuous Shellington, sent by a London newspaper to illustrate the war, who is making amorous advances towards Jane Sharpe. As the scenes are set at night, the windows had been blacked out, making the air stultifyingly hot; this, combined with regular breaks for the muezzins' call from the local mosque, made for challenging filming.

It was a long, sweaty, but satisfying day; after a nice long shower – no problems with the water at the Voyager – I headed down to the unit's chosen bar for a well-earned beer. Before long Abigail and Warren Saire, who was playing Shellington, came looking for me requesting we do a little rehearsal of the next day's scenes; Geordie grip, Bob Dixon, not used to seeing Chosen Men actually rehearse, teased me for being such a swot. In truth I was grateful for some rehearsal time with the dialogue as Tom was normally too busy with the 'geography' of the scene and getting things done in the fewest number of takes.

Day two at the carpet factory and we were shooting my largest dialogue scene to date, Harris's heart-to-heart with Jane Sharpe. During the scene Jane asks Harris: 'Do you love him?' referring to Sharpe; in the script Harris responds in the affirmative: 'Of course we love him.' Sean wasn't comfortable with this line, but I assured him I would deliver it without making it sound like we were lovers. That morning Tom paid a visit to my motorhome, informing me the line had been cut; in its place, I was to respond with an indignant and embarrassed 'Ma'am.' Tom seemed very keen for this scene to go well; after breakfast we were called to set for rehearsal even before we'd been through costume, hair and make-up for lighting and dialogue rehearsal. I knew the additional care being paid to the scene was mostly due to Abigail's presence, but, hey, I was part of the scene, too, so I was happy to bask in the extra attention.

In the evening we celebrated Saint's birthday at a restaurant in the Antalya harbour called the King's Table, very swanky surroundings and presentation, but nouvelle cuisine had taken hold and the portions weren't enough after a hard day at the carpet factory. Back at the Sheraton most of the party piled into my room for some serious

Sharpe-style bacchanalian excess; it looked as if my much-vaunted resolve to be more abstemious had vanished in the haze. The next morning, I was completely wasted after the night's partying, which I guess was nothing new; I didn't have a lot of dialogue, but enough to need my wits about me.

Unfortunately, by the time the camera pointed towards me, burning the candle at both ends began to bite. Fortunately, we were filming exteriors in the carpet factory courtyard, so my fragile state wouldn't deteriorate further by sweltering behind blacked-out windows. Our set dressers had done a fantastic job of turning the nondescript space into a Moorish-looking courtyard area aided enormously by the presence of citrus and pomegranate trees; the whole effect was rounded off with a prop wishing-well plonked dead centre of the courtyard. Populating the set was a Gypsy encampment where Harris got a glimpse of his future girlfriend Conchita, played by Aysun Metiner, an actress from Istanbul. Tom's unerring eye for casting pretty ladies had provided Harris with a bit of eye candy for a change; take that, lover boy Richard Sharpe.

The scene was set, Harper fraternised with our Gypsy friends in the background, jollity and lightness abounded; Sharpe peered out of his bedroom window to enquire what the hell we thought we were doing. Our hero then asked whether Wordsworth was a philosopher or a poet; Harris, as always, provided the answer then went off to flirt with Conchita. The camera then turned around for my dialogue with Sharpe: 'Beg pardon, Mr Sharpe, but you're to report to General Wellington's tent at ten o'clock.' A simple line to deliver that tripped off the tongue with ease while the camera pointed at Beano; after a couple of rehearsals with the lens pointing my way, in my head the lines began to sound strange. Everything was made ready for the take, Tom called action, I got as far as 'Wellington's tent ...' before my brain stopped communicating with my tongue. On the second take I fared no better, stumbling just after 'Mr Sharpe'. Tom called cut. That sparked much amusement among the crew, my status as a one-take wonder evaporated in the heat and mortal shame consumed me.

I WANT A HOLIDAY IN THE SUN

October the 25th began an eleven-day absence from the call sheet, a period that would test my ability to stay on the straight and narrow. Lyndon used to joke that *Sharpe* was just an 18–65 holiday, but this year really was turning into Sharpe's Vacation for me.

Paddy World News had come up with some interesting inside information after receiving a misplaced fax concerning 'the mooted feature film, *Sharpe's Tiger*', the prequel story Bernard had mentioned with the working title 'Sharpe's Curry'. Set in India, where Sharpe's a private fighting at the Battle of Seringapatam with one Obadiah Hakeswill as his superior. The fax contained no reference to Harper, Hagman or Harris – it seemed we were surplus to requirements in this vision of Sharpe's past. There was a chance none of the original cast would be appearing in *Tiger* as there was talk of casting a different actor as the young incarnation of Sharpe, a lad called Ewan McGregor. The fax also revealed particulars of the money secured for *Tiger* with a promise of exactly twice the budget of any *Sharpe* film so far, about £1.6 million an hour. All revealed because a fax mistakenly landed in Daragh's letter box. Oh, the delicious irony.

The freedom of a long stretch off can be a double-edged sword; at first, you're luxuriating in waking up whenever you want, watching telly, reading, listening to music, writing your diary and generally letting it all hang out. That year, though, I was on my lonesome trying to kill time without Natasha or chief partner in crime, Lyndon. Ensconced at the Voyager with its thousand rooms, you were liable not to see any other unit members unless you got up really early for breakfast or paid a trip to the production office. On the positive side, I won a little victory on the *Sharpe* book negotiation front; I had told my agent not to accept the measly thirty quid fee for the use of my image. I would now get a hundred and fifty.

October came to a close and the unit switched to night shoots, making things a little livelier around the hotel; Sean was currently negotiating with Malcolm to fly out for the New York premiere of *GoldenEye*. He thought his agent had secured permission for this, but Malcolm was apparently now making it difficult. He had gone to the department heads asking them to work a seven-day week to make up for the loss of Sean; also asking them to do it for no extra pay as a favour to Sean. In addition, Malcolm was claiming compensation from EON, Bond's production company, for the expense of rebooking actors due to Sean's absence. This really incensed Sean as he felt it made him lose face with the Bond people; I could see he was irked so I suggested we have a drink or two. He declined the offer, arguing that he shouldn't be seen to be enjoying himself in case Malcolm saw him; the bottle of Absolut cooling in my fridge high up on the Voyager's east wing won the day.

My diary told me it was the ninth Sunday before Christmas. On this day in 1923 the Turkish republic, led by Kemal Atatürk, had been established; all week Turkish flags flew everywhere, and television channels featured a graphic of a flag fluttering behind Atatürk's face in the top right of the screen. Back in the Sharpe Bubble, I braced myself for re-entry to night shoots with a day of sunbathing, swimming and lunching on the Sheraton's outdoor Tropic Terrace along with a few of the 'Mission' cast. Talk soon turned to the contrast between life on the Crimean Sharpe with its reputation for bad food, disease and hardship and our, so far, delightful Turkish campaign. Shooting in Antalya was pure luxury in comparison to our occupation of Yalta, but veterans of previous campaigns had noticed a lack of unit cohesiveness.

Diana Perez, recently arrived for night shoots, definitely noticed the absence of the old Sharpe spirit. In the Crimea, our accommodation had fewer or no other guests. Here at the Sheraton with its hermetically sealed rooms, the inmates were separated and scattered among the general population of the hotel, so it was a whole new ball game. Nigel Betts, playing the leather-masked explosives expert Pyecroft, came up with an interesting assessment of the situation: the Crimea was like the Wild West and much more free, with hardly any rules and certainly no one there to enforce those that existed. Turkey, although thoroughly westernised, was, after all, still an Islamic country despite Atatürk's thrust towards modernisation and the rule of law wasn't as easily bent with a kickback. So, where in the Crimea we basically did what we liked, often illegal in most countries, Turkey was a much different proposition. In a sense we were so battle-hardened we couldn't function without conflict, having been through so much before arriving in Turkey. We needed that grit in the oyster shell to produce the pearl.

HISTORY REPEATS, FIRST AS TRAGEDY
THEN AS FARCE

November the 2nd saw my name back on the call sheet to film Harris's discovery of Conchita's garrotted corpse just as the weather had started to turn inclement; it was as if the sun's heat had suddenly been switched off. In the afternoon, we experienced a power cut; nothing new for Crimean veterans thoroughly used to loss of electricity at regular intervals. A time when we would gather around the candle light engendering a snug sense of togetherness; here at the Sheraton I was left sitting alone in the darkness wondering how a sophisticated five-star hotel failed to have its own emergency power.

All the while, a huge storm was brewing outside, producing scarily dramatic thunderclaps followed a split second later by spectacular bolts of lightning. Power was eventually restored as I set off for my evening call; I stopped off at the production office on the way to speak with Malcolm about Natasha and Dan's planned arrival on location. My contract specified 'suitable accommodation for wife and child' during the shoot, but I also wanted to ask for Lyosya, Natasha's sister, to accompany them to help with Dan. The mighty storm continued to lash the Sheraton with more thunderclaps peppering our discussions, I half expected Malcolm to break out in a maniacal cackle as lightning illuminated his face denying all knowledge of promises made. In the end he enthusiastically granted all my wishes, saying, 'Daniel is a Sharpe baby, that I feel a certain amount of responsibility towards,' although he did ask me to keep my plans 'on the quiet'.

With that matter out of the way, I breathed a sigh of relief. All was good in Sharpe World. I made my way down to the foyer.

Standing there I saw Gabrielle O'Malley anxiously peering through the window at the storm buffeting the building, having just seen Daragh off to location. I tried to reassure her, telling her there was no way they would film in the midst of a hurricane. Yet here I was, practically hydroplaning towards our location, one of many nature reserves in Antalya. Getting to a rain-swept base camp, I dived into my motorhome fully expecting a colossal wait before being called to set. Within minutes Sam had popped his head into the motorhome to tell me that Daragh, Diana and Andrew Schofield, playing Colonel Brand's enforcer, had been called; considering the ark-floating deluge falling from the skies I thought it madness that they should even entertain the thought of setting up the camera, let alone start shooting.

Pretty soon, though muffled by the hammering rain, outside I could hear the sound of car doors being urgently slammed, followed by vehicles hastily exiting base camp. Minutes later Sam re-entered my motorhome to give me my five-minute warning. 'Already?' I grumbled, surprised the previous scene had finished so quickly. Sam calmly explained that Daragh had been injured during the fight scene and had been rushed to hospital, hence the rapid exit of vehicles. It was written in the scene that Pope kicks Harper in the head; I remember alarm bells ringing in my own head when first reading that direction. It was ironic that this should happen to Daragh of all people; he was always so careful when approaching action scenes that involved fights or big bangs, knowing full well that film is a mendacious art.

The rain eased as I made my way down through the trees to Conchita's bivouac, past a small waterfall, the site of Daragh's accident. Tom came straight up to me to explain what had happened, describing how 'Drew slipped as he swung his leg,' causing his boot to miss Daragh's defensive hand, smashing squarely into his face. I suggested the downpour wouldn't have helped with Drew's footing, but Tom, ever paranoid about schedules, had to be clear of this location that night, so cancelling was never an option. With Daragh now admitted to a Turkish hospital, this was a high price to pay for maintaining the shooting schedule. Those of a suspicious inclination might remember shortly after the last campaign when talk of taking Daragh off the wage bill was in the air; fodder for the conspiracy theorists. Sharpe without Daragh 'Learjet' O'Malley didn't bear thinking about.

Not ideal preparation for performing my scene, but the show must go on; I was hoping Daragh's injury only amounted to a nasty bruise and some swelling, with no real damage done to his face. The cameras were set for Harris's discovery of the garrotted corpses of his girlfriend and her Gypsy chums; a grisly sight even for the war-worn Harris, promptly causing him to vomit. Thankfully I only had to fake throwing up a couple of times before heading back to the hotel to get an update on Daragh's condition. It felt depressingly reminiscent of the mood in the immediate aftermath of Paul McGann's knee injury, a lot of uncertainty and helplessness, but this time the injured party was rushed to hospital with an injury to his head. Was this the return of the Sharpe jinx, thought to be the sole province of our time in the Crimea? I put in a call to Lyndon to report the news; later, as I sat watching BBC World Service television, a news bulletin came in of flash floods in Anatolia, Turkey, that had caused the deaths of thirty-three people, immediately putting the trials and tribulations of the Sharpe Bubble into perspective.

The next morning, a bulletin from the hospital brought bad news: Daragh's cheek had been broken in five places. The doctors planned to operate the next day at Antalya's sole private hospital; fortunately, Daragh's wife Gabrielle was still in Turkey to be at his side during this ordeal. I felt like such an idiot for having reassured her that they wouldn't be shooting during the rainstorm. Malcolm could be seen dashing in and out of the Voyager dealing with the fallout from the accident; when would Daragh be available to film again, would he be able to carry on at all? With Sean already committed to his New York trip for the Bond premiere the schedule was looking very fragile.

November the 4th, and tomorrow we were to transition back to day shoots to cover Harris's wrongful arrest. After breakfast I put a call into Daragh's hospital room; he said they were treating him well and had held off operating until the swelling receded. The doctors had told him the exterior of his face would basically look okay after two weeks; Daragh was thinking of popping home in that time to see specialists and Sharpe's very own medic, Dr Gaynor. I had to say, Daragh was sounding very positive about his situation. I imagined he was saving his wrath for the appropriate moment. *Sharpe*: the show that launched a thousand lawsuits.

HARRIS IN THE FRAME

Another Guy Fawkes Day spent on *Sharpe*, an actor in hospital, fierce electrical storms and power cuts having exploded the myth that we'd be safe and more stable with our switch from the Crimea to Turkey. The previous couple of days had left me pretty ragged having completely slipped back into bacchanalian mode. On location we had moved to another area of the vast Antalya nature park to shoot more of Harris's wrongful arrest and Sharpe persuading the Provost he was rushing to justice. Mike Mallinson, our first assistant director, donned the Provost costume, robbing an actor of a job and saving more money for the company; although as Mike used to be an actor in the old days, I guessed I would let him off.

The increased rainfall had turned base camp into a motorhome-studded sea of mud; at six in the morning under thick, dark clouds, base camp was just about the most depressing place on earth. I loved playing Sharpe's butler, getting to shoot lots of dialogue in scenes with a bearing on the narrative, but I had longed to be back among the muck and bullets, dressed in green with a rifle in my hand. Trouble was, being back in uniform required returning to the background where I'd been assigned to hold the reins of Sharpe's horse. Stunt coordinator Dinny Powell had told us horror stories about the behaviour of Turkish horses, but since I was merely leading Sharpe's nag out of frame, I wasn't too concerned. Boy, was I wrong!

The action saw Sharpe arrive, pass Harris the reins, then walk across the camp to the Duke's tent. Sean's first rehearsals passed without incident, then a column of redcoats forming part of the background action was directed to march past our position. The first take went without incident; on take two Sharpe's horse became a little skittish, forcing both Sean and me into a hasty retreat. Dinny calmed the jittery beast, allowing us to take up our positions in front of camera; just as the background action was being repositioned my equine mate stamped a hoof straight down onto my left foot. Now, I've taken my fair share of knocks on campaign, laughing them off with fake machismo, but this time I was in agony. Tom swiftly took me off horse duty, putting me in the background to flirt with

Conchita; not before Nurse Suzanna had treated my foot with some special gel designed to bring out the bruising, reassuring me there was little else she could do even if the toe was broken. At least I could still walk without too much of a limp.

Tuesday 7 November, a week that was to see us transitioning between episodes; Hugh Fraser was in town for all of Wellington's interior tent scenes. Joining him was French actor Christian Brendel, playing the nemesis from 'Siege', the Comte de Maquerre. I felt I knew him already because Malcolm had shown me his audition tape; he was hot property at that moment, fresh from playing the lead in a French television movie about King Charlemagne. Though not required for work, I had popped up to location for a free lunch and to say hello to the new arrivals. During a pause between takes, I squeezed into the back of Wellington's tent, set up my video camera and took in a screen-acting masterclass delivered by Hugh Fraser. He was very interesting to watch at work, dropping and raising his voice with authority, intelligibility and clarity; he was also a stickler for getting it right, asking for several retakes, something Tom liked to avoid at all costs.

Back at the Voyager, John and I waited for Sean to wrap before heading to hospital to visit Daragh. We found him sitting up in bed looking pretty good if you overlooked his left cheek and eye which understandably looked swollen, but still not as bad as I had anticipated. Daragh took us through his ordeal, starting with his arrival in emergency where he had sat being examined by the specialist with Malcolm hovering in the hope it was just severe bruising. Daragh proudly showed us his cat scan, consisting of several slices of his skull, highlighting the six fractures and a pool of blood in his eye socket. He went on to praise the doctors, saying he would never have expected to be so at ease on a Turkish operating table. Finally, Daragh aired his disquiet about events leading up to the incident and the varying accounts on the accident reports. Blimey, he'd had time to root those out already? He said there was only one rehearsal and Tom choreographed the action because Dinny wasn't there; the plot thickened; should there be need for litigation it could prove messy.

HARRIS GONE FOR A SOLDIER

Completion of 'Mission' had yet again thrown up another long stretch of inactivity for Harris; it would be a miracle if I was seen in the episode at all. I was wondering if I'd have enough time to fly back to England to stock up on supplies and equipment for when my family joined us on location. I broached the subject with Malcolm, asking as nonchalantly as possible for permission to leave the unit again for my trip home. To my surprise, he gave his blessing immediately. Good old Malcolm. I would try to get a flight after I had shot the first scenes of 'Siege' at the end of the week, when I knew other cast members would be returning home.

Taking a break from my resort holiday, I reported to set for the opening shots of 'Siege'. A cold wind was whipping across the nature park; Wellington's camp with its neat lines of little white tents and campfires lined with redcoat extras was very like Baidar Valley. John and I were deployed in the extreme background of a shot; in the script it said 'the Rifles are seen by Wellington sat at his desk through a tent flap as it's opened to admit Sharpe'. A shot we were kept waiting literally hours to shoot. With our scenes done, Sean, John and I were chauffeured home by Gary Fiddler in time for lunch at one of the poshest eateries at the Sheraton. It had been a while since we had all sat together blowing off steam and shooting the breeze; it was a shame Daragh wasn't with us. At least we still had Daragh in the band after Beano's intervention. Speaking of which, Diana was starting to press me on how news of replacing Harper had got out; so far I had spinelessly managed to avoid confessing it was me who had let the cat out of the bag, hoping her merry state on the night in question might have blurred her memory. I was sure that one day I would have to man up and admit it was me who had leaked the news that they were thinking of expunging Daragh.

The weekend was here and time to attempt getting a seat on the Saturday morning transport out of Antalya airport with Hugh and Abigail. That flight was full, but it seemed I was guaranteed a seat on the more convenient flight direct to Stansted instead of via Istanbul. Abigail had learned I had been writing a diary while on campaign, asking how personal it got after I referred to a divorce-inducing episode that had occurred on the first Sharpe. I told her if it happened on *Sharpe*, I wrote it down in my journal. She basically told me off, saying I was wrong to include that sort of stuff; I replied that I was involved in all sorts of incriminating acts, therefore I was the one who should have the most fear, implicating myself with a written account of my time on Sharpe.

My flight to Stansted was confirmed, flying out with Diana Perez by my side, which promised to be interesting. It felt extremely strange to be travelling back to England while the shoot was still in full swing; Chosen Men were 'lifers', sentenced to be ever-present yet seldom used. John Tams did have a spell back in Blighty the previous year, but that was to ward off an impending health meltdown. With international and domestic flights more reliable and frequent here in

Turkey, it was a lot easier to pop home. We just about made it onto the flight as the taxi to the airport was late; arriving at the terminal, check-in had closed and nobody seemed to have a clue about our flight. Eventually we were spotted by a walkie-talkie-toting airline official, who rapidly checked us in, ushered us through passport control and onto the plane, which took off with only minutes to spare.

High above Turkish airspace, Diana rekindled the topic of how production's moves to replace Daragh had been divulged. She was still somewhat perplexed after Daragh spun a tale about a friend overhearing her talking about it at the restaurant that night, which she patently didn't buy. Back in Alanya, Diana had mentioned she felt uncomfortable around the powers who wanted Daragh out; she was convinced they knew the leak came through her. Poor girl, she obviously wanted to get to the bottom of this. Her conversations with Daragh at the hospital had led her to believe that only one person could have leaked the info – and that was me. Back-pedalling as fast as possible, I took partial responsibility saying, 'It doesn't matter how it got out, but it was me that alerted Sean to the situation and it was Sean that raised strenuous objections,' implying she should be proud of her part in heading off a disastrous outcome for *Sharpe*. That, I hoped, would put the issue to bed for Diana.

Being in London on a dreary November day was quite a novelty, having barely seen one since 1991 after my life collided with *Sharpe*; I managed to fulfil all the tasks I'd set myself, including stocking up on baby supplies, doing various bits of paperwork and ordering two director's chairs, their backs embroidered with John's name on one and mine on the other. Colin Thurston from props gave me the contact at Pinewood Studios to get them done; I cheekily allowed them to be charged to Sharpe Film as a way of sticking two fingers up to Ray, who thought we didn't merit them. So far, he had a point, with my contribution this tour standing at eleven days' work in five weeks, but after four years' sterling service and a two-year pay freeze I felt we deserved the £16.50 outlay for each chair back.

I hung out with Lyndon as well as other *Sharpe* veterans who had all heard the news of Daragh's accident, which seemed to be common knowledge in the film UK industry. After three days R&R, I was at Heathrow for my flight back, laden with a pram, two suitcases packed with nappies and the customary bag of Sharpe mail to take out to location. I had found myself a cheaper return flight on a Turkish Cypriot airline banned by the UN from flying direct to Cyprus, therefore necessitating a stop in Antalya. The flight back was also empty, making two short-haired army types stick out like sore thumbs; were they SAS on a secret mission? No, they were United Nations peacekeepers travelling to Cyprus on a UN-embargoed flight. As they were *Sharpe* fans, I didn't report them to Boutros Boutros-Ghali.

ON THE MARCH AGAIN

November the 16th: one week until we upped sticks for the reportedly less luxurious town of Silifke, quite some distance east of Antalya, uncomfortably close to the Syrian border. That was where I would be taking Natasha, Dan and Natasha's sister for the final leg of our tour. Beano had rejoined the unit looking extremely spaced-out from jet lag after flying from New York to Istanbul. Unsurprisingly there was a huge buzz of anticipation about the new instalment of Bond. I saw the trailers for *GoldenEye* back in London and Beano looked amazing; much more impressive than Pierce Brosnan, in fact. We sat having breakfast with Daragh, newly discharged from hospital and still showing no obvious signs of the trauma he had undergone. Amazingly, Daragh was on the next day's call sheet; it seemed Malcolm wanted to rush him back into action using the convenient pretext of Harper having a swollen face due to toothache in the 'Siege' script, giving him a handy excuse to be holding a hanky to his face while it was still puffy. Dr Gaynor was hot-footing it from London to give Daragh the final insurance company check-up before filming resumed.

With Sean back in the fold the remaining scenes of 'Mission' could be put to bed, including the opening episode flashback where Brand appears to rescue a dying lieutenant of the South Essex. A flashback sounds good on paper, but three years earlier we would have had Tongue, Cooper and Perkins in our ranks; production had remedied this by instructing hair and make-up to slap Cooperesque sideburns on armourer Will Whitlam. It had to be said, while standing slightly behind him looking at Will's profile, there was a passing resemblance to Cooper; however, I was sure the camera wouldn't be anywhere near Will so all you would see would be a blur of green in the background like a good member of the flock.

Switching between two episodes was slightly confusing but had echoes of our first Crimean tour where the McGann injury required us to chop and change between 'Rifles' and 'Eagle', producing hotel encounters with actors from both episodes. Newly arrived in-country was a veteran of past campaigns, Phil Whitchurch, reprising his role as Captain Frederickson, last seen in 'Enemy'; after reading the script of 'Siege' I couldn't help but notice a lot of Frederickson's lines were the sort that usually emanated from our Irish sergeant. Possibly this was a remnant of the move to minimise or indeed remove Harper from the picture with Frederickson filling the 'buddy' void.

Daragh's face got the go-ahead to resume working from Dr Gaynor on the condition he wore a Phantom of the Opera-style mask to protect his cheek whenever he was not in front of the camera. I never did see him wear it. This meant we could begin to shoot 'Siege' in earnest with another scene of troops marching in column; at the tail of the convoy a wagon carries Harper concealed under a blanket. The Chosen Men were tasked with pushing the heavily laden cart along, made harder by our Turkish donkey interpreting our shoves as its cue to dig in its heels. Harper cried out in pain when the cart hit a bump in the road, prompting an officer to investigate the noise. Harris limped forward in mock pain uttering Irish clichés, such as 'bejesus' so that Harper's hiding place wasn't rumbled. It was very enjoyable to shoot, especially as I could get away with taking the mickey out of Big D. Daragh made his triumphal return to action in front of the camera after lunch for the burial of Reilly scene, Eoghan Harris's homage to Shakespeare, except the grave diggers in this scene had no lines and offered no comic relief. Harper's action dug out a chuckle or two; after delivering the benediction over Reilly's burial place he retrieved a buried bottle of brandy from the grave to relieve his aching tooth. Both scenes confirmed my preference for Eoghan Harris as *Sharpe*'s chosen screen writer.

Daragh's reappearance in front of camera had concerned John Tams. I got down to the bar later that night to find the man with the golden voice rather well oiled in heated discussion with Tom. John argued that 'the powers', including Tom, were guilty of rushing Daragh back to work for the sake of schedules, neglecting his health and safety. Tom took exception to this and walked out of the bar; I was fairly amazed Tom did that to Johnny, but, then again, I hadn't seen John so fired up before. I stayed drinking with John past the witching hour, acting as a sounding board for his fuelled protestations before slumping into bed.

GET ME TO THE CHURCH ON TIME

The final pick-up from 'Mission', delayed due to Sean and Daragh's absences, had been packed in the can and flown home to England to be stitched together. We had now moved into double figures on the episode count; they can now show *Sharpe* marathons on one of those late night-stations in the States with 'I can read, sir' and Sharpe shouting 'bastard' washing over future generations of couch potatoes. Today we were shooting a sick parade scene, something novel for *Sharpe* and making a refreshing change; Hagman and Harris had two tiny lines of dialogue thrown in and I was grateful for that in light of the previous day's session with John Tams. With 'Mission' wrapped, we said farewells to Aysun; she was a lovely girl, and I'd seen her quite a bit in commercials on Turkish telly, most recently in an advert for Ajax. Aysun was determined to win an Oscar by the time she was thirty; only nine more years to go. It was a crying shame that as soon as Harris got a sweetheart she got bumped off. No such problem for our eponymous hero as he was to marry fiancée Jane Gibbons on the next day's call sheet; naturally since it was 'Sharpe's wedding', we celebrated the occasion with a 'stag do' as befits a groom the night before nuptials.

Set dressers had created a wedding marquee out of an officer's tent specially opened out with an altar at its centre. It was just like the morning of a real wedding; the groom looked suitably nervous, everyone dressed in nice togs apart from the Chosen, and ITV network photographer Tony Nutley was with us, all providing a genuine matrimonial atmosphere. Plans to film in a church were shelved but the tent set-up worked nicely; I was surprised they could even find a church in this part of Turkey. Diana Perez was over for the day to do her last scenes on this campaign; again, I swerved owning up to being the mole who exposed the clandestine moves to eliminate Daragh from *Sharpe*. I supposed there'd always be the fifth series.

With the novelty of the wedding scene over, we recommenced shooting the column marcing towards the besieged castle at the focal point of the story. The next location was a mighty trek through the nature park; once there, the scene took forever to set up. Johnny got a nice featured bit of performing using his poacher tracking skills that Hagman did so well. Handy Harris was left near the head of the column desperately trying to act useful while searching for the camera lens. Finishing a little early, I had a late lunch with Malcolm at the hotel, and we discussed Cooper's brief reappearance in the flashback sequence, 'Mission'. Malcolm claimed that Mike Mears was asked if he wanted to come out to shoot the scene and to be in one episode. Mike had turned down the offer as he had his one-man show planned, rendering him unavailable. Malcolm also mentioned he was being sued for a hundred thousand dollars by the owner of the carpet factory, the location of Sharpe's villa. He was apparently claiming the building had been damaged during filming, which was ridiculous as it was so dilapidated to begin with. Blimey, you could knock down the whole place and rebuild it for less dosh. Malcolm said he wasn't fazed as he was used to being sued; take note Mr McGann and Mr O'Malley, I thought.

BACK TO LIFE, BACK TO REALITY

The unit's move along the coastline to Silifke, the final destination of this tour, would be made predominately by road for the eleven-hour car journey as there were no direct flights from Antalya. The other alternative was to fly north to Istanbul for a connecting flight back in a south-easterly direction to Adana, Silifke's closest airport. Natasha and her sister were arriving into Istanbul from Simferopol so I'd opted for the circuitous, two-flight route.

The final evening was spent at a damp squib of a farewell party held at local nightspot the Falez, attended by a small, hardy group. I ducked out early, hoping to get some rest before my flight at the crack of dawn. My conscientious behaviour didn't save me from being completely knackered as I sat waiting in the deathly quiet Voyager lobby for my ride to the airport. I longed to get on the plane to catch up on sleep. I even started thinking an eleven-hour drive in my motorhome might not be such a bad thing after all. As I got towards critical plane-missing time, I realised I had been left to my own devices by production for a second time this tour; I raced out to the taxi rank, woke the driver and sped towards Antalya airport.

I got to the Holiday Inn at Istanbul airport and took a nap knowing flights from Simferopol weren't famed for their punctuality. After precious little rest I made my way to the part of Atatürk airport where flights from exotic locations touched down; Dubai, Damascus, Tripoli, Samarkand and Baku read the arrivals board, all with either 'on-time' or 'landed' next to them. Of course, next to Simferopol there was no information whatsoever. One year on and Ukrainian Airways still hadn't got its shit together. Eventually I spied Natasha holding Daniel in her arms as they stood at passport control; soon the whole party taxied back to the hotel to wait for the flight down south to Adana. Having Daniel sitting on my knee in the cab made everything seem all right, reminding me once more of my purpose in life.

After chilling at the hotel, we met up with John Tams and Phil Whitchurch back at the airport for the flight to Adana. Phil had experienced trouble even getting on the flight; the combined efforts of the English and Turkish production offices failed to reserve a seat on the plane for him, making a dip into his own pockets necessary. Conspiracy theorists might say this was more proof that those opting for the flights were being punished for turning down the less expensive road trip to Silifke. Phil was lucky to get a seat at all as the flight was packed; I sat next to an extremely irritating, fidgety Turk who kept picking up my newspaper when I was out of my seat. As I was exiting the cabin an enthusiastic chap informed me that I had been sitting next to one of Turkey's foremost popstars. Hopefully someone told the restless popstar he was sitting next to one of Sharpe's foremost Chosen Men.

Getting into Adana reminded me we were far from our safe European home; every brick exuded third-world, the street outside the terminal looked dark and unwelcoming and a game of 'spot the westerner' could last a long time. The two Turkish helpers sent to pick us up had no idea who they were supposed to collect other than look out for a group of lost white people; at least they knew the number of passengers they had to round up: seven. I did a mental head count; the four of my group, plus Tamszy and Phil, which still didn't add up to seven. Was Daragh supposed to have been on the flight? As our chaps spoke not a word of English and my Turkish hadn't progressed beyond ordering beer and counting to ten, I tried to call Alejandro Sutherland, but his mobile was switched off; using mime, I then asked the lads if they had producer Ali's number. They just shook their heads at everything.

While this comedy of errors played out, a western-looking woman approached Natasha asking if she was from Sharpe Film; luckily Natasha was wearing her Sharpe tour jacket. The woman just happened to be the seventh passenger, Nicola Murray playing farmer's daughter Brigitte, who might well have been stranded here, a hundred kilometres from the Syrian border, but for Natasha's Sharpe tour jacket. It was amazing our two greeters couldn't work out she was one of the Sharpe party they were supposed to pick up; it wasn't as if Adana airport was the size of Heathrow. Eventually we hit the road for the supposed two-hour drive; a little way into the journey I called Cindy in the London's office. She told me Daragh hadn't gone missing, he had just decided to stay an extra day in Istanbul; I began to tell her about Nicola's lucky escape but lost phone signal before I could outline the sheer incompetence of our pick-up.

There wasn't a lot to see on the dark highway. After about two hours we passed a big town or city called Mersin; at this point John Tams reckoned we should be nearing our destination, situated seventeen kilometres from 'downtown' Silifke. Shooting Hagman's tracking and scouting scenes must really be rubbing off on John. Our greeters pulled into the first hotel complex they saw, both alighting from the van to see if this was our endpoint; they returned none the wiser. Here we were in the pitch black, deep into the continent of Asia relying on a couple of clueless Turks; no problem, I thought, I'll just whip out the mobile to call Alejandro or Cindy again to get

Ali's number and he will guide us in. Not a problem if there was mobile phone signal; alas, this part of the world seemed to have none. I sensed a mini crisis coming on.

The next place we stopped looked to have seen better days, but it did seem a little livelier than our previous stop; as we drove along the pitch-black driveway, I started seeing a long line of large trucks. As we got closer to the main building, there standing in the prime parking position was the British-number-plated Beanomobile. We had arrived in one piece, our little chosen man hadn't cried, much to the relief of already stressed parents, but the darkness, the freezing wind and the haphazard nature of our journey here filled me with a sense of foreboding. Our hotel, the Altınorfoz, or Golden Fish, had obviously been mothballed since the summer season, allowing a nasty smell to have built up. It had a generally filthy air, the fixtures and fittings were knackered, the carpets, threadbare in some places, were well past their use-by date; to cap it all the heating system, dormant for some months, could only offer cold air and water. I knew we had just come from the luxurious, ultra-slick Sheraton, but the Altınorfoz was already in danger of taking last place on our list of Sharpe's hovels; Tavria Hotel in Simferopol, come back, all is forgiven!

Malcolm had promised multiple fan heaters would be produced as 'Daniel is the most important member of the unit'; Malcolm also claimed he tried to call me to dissuade me from bringing the family here when he first laid eyes on it. However, I knew from experience Sharpe's budget normally plumped for the cheapest option in the accommodation stakes – Sheraton being the exception – so I wasn't expecting the Ritz. In the light of a sunny Saturday morning everything looked a lot more pleasant, the Golden Fish was located on a picturesque inlet with a decent strip of beach on which to frolic. There was one positive aspect to this place: we were the only guests there, meaning we'd have the run of this place without offending, shocking or disturbing any other guests, so this hovel near the Syrian border would have its advantages.

After a five-day gap, we returned to work with a bump. Mercifully our first location was only a ten-minute drive; the bulk of 'Siege', however, was to be shot on the other side of Silifke, a forty-five-minute commute from our hotel. We were shooting in a steep-sided ravine scattered with seriously old farmers' huts and even older ancient Greek or Roman ruins. On the call sheet, we were attacking a French convoy, a set-up that took an age to prepare, allowing an almost fully recovered Big D to update John, Sean and me on any news. Apparently, the tour would go on a little longer as production was at least one day behind, pretty good going considering the problems we had faced. Daragh also reported that the night before, around midnight, hotel staff had woken him up with an order of four plates of spaghetti bolognaise. Was this a kitchen malfunction or some brave person playing tricks on Big D?

The convoy attack stretched into a second day as the sunlight slid quickly behind the steep-sided ravine, limiting the amount of shooting time post-lunch. Once wrapped, we moved up to one of the dilapidated huts for the 'sheep pen' scene where Brigitte's papa takes umbrage at Rifleman Robinson's amorous advances towards his daughter. Quite a cute scene that sees Sharpe, desperate to retain the hearts and minds of the local populace, act as both lawyer and judge, sentencing Robinson to hang for his misdeed. Frederickson objects to losing one of his best men; employing Harris's translating skills it's revealed the fumble was consensual, so the sentence is commuted, to a good whooping from Harper.

The dipping sun put paid to us completing the scene, so we returned the next day, giving us lots of time to kill waiting for matching lighting conditions. Giles Ashton over in catering provided the best laugh of the morning; base camp had been set up on the grounds of a small rural school, the mobile kitchen sitting directly opposite the main school building. Normally not a problem, but Giles had a massive mobile stereo on which he liked to play pumping house music at maximum volume. That morning the headmaster had to come out to ask Giles to turn down the volume as the entire student population were bobbing and gyrating to a Paul Oakenfold mix instead of concentrating on their lessons.

HELLO DARKNESS, MY OLD FRIEND

Meanwhile we braced ourselves for night shoots. I played with Daniel before heading off to work; it was such a pleasure having the family close at hand to escape Sharpe's aggravations. And those were never far away. I left for my 7:30 call knowing the first night shoot at a new location never ran smoothly. At one in the morning, Sharpe, Harper, Harris, Hagman and Frederickson were gathered to shoot the Harper tooth-pulling scene. The scene was lit, the actors rehearsed and, just as we went for the take, the sound department detected a low buzzing coming from a generator somewhere in the background. Several adjustments were made but the interference was still being picked up; Tom told us to adjourn to base camp while they fixed the problem. Two hours later, just shy of four in the morning, we returned to resume the scene; as the clock struck four the crew had done their twelve-hour shift, so we were forced to wrap for the night. Oh well, only two more weeks of this lay ahead.

I got to the hotel around five in the morning, just as most of the unit were retiring to the bar for a breakfast pint. I was now leading a double life at this end of the tour, so I had to avoid hungover mornings; payback was waking with a clear head to find Daniel and Natasha sitting on my bed. I hated nights, but Natasha preferred them as it meant I could spend time with them in the daylight hours. The day before, we had spent a lovely morning collecting sea urchins with Féodor Atkine, last seen being killed at the end of 'Honour'. Today we made our first exploration of downtown Silifke, taking Oxana, mother of the first Sharpe baby, with us as a guide. Oxana had been out here for months interpreting for the Crimean set construction team who had built the largest set ever used on *Sharpe*. There wasn't a lot for a tourist to see downtown, apart from warehouses full of grains and beans plus other produce grown locally, but just being there was a fascinating journey into the unknown.

That night, the Chosen Men were involved in every single bit of action, so I was hoping the time would fly by; first order of the night was to complete the Harper tooth extraction scene. Daragh was at his best playing the abused Irishman, garnering sympathy then amusing us all with mock fear at the prospect of Frederickson's medieval dental tools being utilised. All the while John and I struggled to hold Daragh down, more than once getting crushed into the boulder doubling as the dentist's chair; talk about finding yourself between a rock and a hard place. The next scene required an extensive re-light; so, four hours later after 'lunch', Sean, John and I shot a delightful little fireside scene about the preference for tea or soup. Shortly after, Tom called a premature end to the night due to director of photography Chris O'Dell being taken ill on set; he had been experiencing kidney pain of late, but now the problem had become acute. Probably an infection or kidney stones; either way I was sure it must have been extremely painful.

Saturday night saw a double birthday celebration in the drab bar area now transformed by balloons and coloured lights for Gary Fiddler and stuntman Colya's party. Natasha decided she didn't want to party, leaving me to be the irresponsible one; I was joined by her sister, Lyosya, who spent most of the night ably fending off the attentions of a chap who turned out to be a US Navy scuba diver. What the hell he was doing at our party just down the coast from Syria in a country that borders Iran was anybody's guess. The undoubted highlight of the party was the evening's live entertainment, the obligatory belly dancer. After much swishing of hips, she beckoned unsuspecting male victims into a human circle where they were stripped to the waist, laid down on the floor and playfully abused. Birthday boys Gary and Colya were the first willing victims; then, obviously tipped off as to who the real main man was, she turned her attentions to Beano.

Sean and Chris Villiers were duly stripped to the waist in no time, then they waited with trepidation as the dancer gyrated around them. It came time to lay them down; Beano looked nervous as he allowed his shoes to be taken off, but he drew a line when she started to loosen his belt, pushing her off and climbing to his feet. She took this as a serious affront to her professional integrity, and hurled one of Sean's shoes at him, catching him squarely in the groin. Sean wisely chose not to react, instead gathering his clothing and retreating to his safe place at the bar. It was a memorable party for many reasons, but, crucially, signs of the old Sharpe spirit came shining through.

We were now less than three weeks till the end of the fourth campaign. Muir had flown in via Vienna to relieve Malcolm; he had been location spotting in Eastern Europe checking suitable places to shoot battle scenes for a fifth series. He attended a battle re-enactment in Austerlitz where he met many *Sharpe* fans only too willing to provide their services as extras. Muir thought we'd be able to shoot most of the next series in Turkey, with the Czech Republic used for major battle scenes. It sounded interesting to me, but whether Beano fancied another jaunt through Eastern Europe was another matter; either way it looked like there'd be no return to Yalta. A real shame as they were the best of times and the worst of times, but most of all the Crimea was the making of *Sharpe*.

On set we were filming one of the many exits we made from the castle. At last the generators were cooperating and it was my first chance to get a close look at Andrew Mollo's castle construction. The existing ruins of Silifke Kalesi had been extended with two huge walls and massive wooden front gates; no wonder it took so long to build. When it was illuminated the castle sat up on the hill like a glowing, indomitable mass of rock looking awesomely scary; there would be no need to act in awe of this place when we first approached it in the story.

Back at the Golden Fish I had left Big D in my room watching 'Sharpe's Sword', which he still hadn't seen as he was in LA when it was aired. Daragh had wasted no time in pumping Muir for information regarding *Sharpe*'s future; apparently the network wanted three more episodes next year. They also wanted *Sharpe* to have a fresh look with a new director in for one episode and disposing of the services of

Eoghan Harris. Presumably that meant more Charles Wood, bad news for me as he was the man with no regard for a Chosen Man's back story. The following night I lay beside the campfire with John and Phil waiting for a lengthy relight while supping a cuppa, when Muir slid up for a chat, possibly after a few sherries in the officers' tent. We were in no mood for executive producer small talk, but he got my attention when he announced, 'Hello, boys, don't you think we need some more Chosen Men?' I wondered if he meant instead of Hagman and Harris or in addition to. I guessed I'd find out sooner or later.

COUNT DOWN TO UNEMPLOYMENT

Only two more night shoots remained on the schedule and more actors had arrived to do their parts in 'Siege'; Amira Casar was here to play the Comte de Maquerre's sister, Catherine. On the other side of the camera trouble was brewing at t'mill with industrial action threatened. Ray Frift had asked the crew if they wouldn't mind working into the seventh day after working six nights; traditionally after a week of nights the unit is supposed to have two days off so the body clock can reacclimatise to daylight hours. He'd also asked them to do it for a nominal payment and not the full day's pay plus overtime that would normally be due. Members of the sound and camera department had denied the request; Ray countered by saying, 'I will sack the lot of you.' Ray, pissed with power, had even gone as far as having a Turkish camera crew standing by in Istanbul should the boys make good on their threat to down tools at one minute into the seventh day. I would be keenly watching how this situation developed.

My penultimate night shoot started well with our arrival at the French fort deploying a sort of 'Trojan Horse' ruse to gain entry, claiming we were Westphalian troops – allies of Napoleon – needing help with a wounded soldier. Frederickson and Harris's combined language skills manage to bluff our way in by revealing a post-dental surgery, blood-soaked Harper. The fort doors swing open and we storm the courtyard, forming a circle of rifles pointing in every direction. Fantastic stuff to film; Tom came up with some great ideas for this scene. From then on things went downhill; to alert the troops outside the castle to advance, Harris made a bugle call. I liked to think of myself as multi-skilled, but getting a note, let alone a tune, out of the bugle proved almost impossible; in the end they had props man Colin blow the right tune off camera for a wild track. In the finished episode it wouldn't be me you'd be hearing; had they given me a week to practise, even a couple of days, I might have been able to get a tune out of that bugle.

December the 7th, two weeks till we were scheduled to formally wrap; customarily production handed a letter to the unit giving two weeks' notice of contract termination. Tomorrow at midnight the crew would go into the seventh shooting day. Ray had done a deal with the whole crew apart from the two camera boys, who were holding firm. In true Sharpe jinx fashion, Ray had made a typo on the letter of notice stating a date four days earlier than the anticipated last day of shooting. A letter with the correct date was reissued; the camera boys, disgusted at the way they'd been treated, had decided they would abide by the first letter, which meant they would be shipping out with four shooting days remaining on the schedule.

The atmosphere on set felt tense; two-tour veteran camera operator Martin Hume looked very pensive. Obviously the situation was weighing heavily on his mind, but he had the sympathy of those most affected by the walk-out, director Tom Clegg and DP Chris O'Dell – now recovered from his kidney problems – who both agreed Ray had handled the situation inappropriately. Ray, in addition to having the relatively cheap Turkish camera crew standing by in Istanbul, would also have to contract two UK crew on far higher wages, making the whole dispute much more expensive than paying Martin and Sean a full day's pay for going into the seventh day.

Praise the Lord, it was the last time I was required on set in the middle of the night; after much thumb twiddling down at base, I was called to set at three in the morning. By now, icy winds were battering the castle as I trudged up to the battlements to shoot Sharpe and Harris surveying the enemy. Harris quotes Milton as a way of reassuring Sharpe his men are firmly behind him. The two-handed scene went swiftly and smoothly despite the conditions and the late hour, mainly due to the bond Sean and I had formed down the years. And that was my final night on *Sharpe* this tour, possibly my last ever.

I eventually managed to get to bed, but at four in the morning Dan decided he wanted to get up and play. After getting dressed we headed down to the bar area which was still humming with all the die-hard drinkers in attendance. Daniel really seemed to like the party atmosphere, only momentarily freaking out when I tried to sit him on Tom's lap. Tom told me the camera boys had made good on their threat to down tools with only three more takes remaining; Ray had activated his standby camera operator and focus puller. Martin Hume and Sean Connor would definitely leave the following Saturday, as per the first mistaken letter of notice. We had experienced continual trials and tribulations on *Sharpe*, but nothing like this had happened before. It left a very nasty taste in the mouth. Thanks to Ray's obstinacy the closing period of this tour would be spent under a cloud of discontent and recrimination.

WHY CAN'T WE ALL JUST GET ALONG?

At least the sun shone brightly on most days here in Silifke; there wouldn't be any weather delays from here on in. The switch from night to day shoots gave me my first glimpse in daylight of our beautiful base camp location adjacent to a strip of beachside bars and restaurants thirty yards from the gently lapping Mediterranean. An extremely pleasant spot to while away the huge waiting times thrown up by incompetent scheduling. I made the fatal mistake of checking the scenes on the call sheet against the script, which revealed that neither Harper nor the Chosen had any lines or stage directions. When we approached Tom about this, he got very bolshie; shades of infamous incidents from last year which hadn't had a very pleasant outcome. However, all revolutionary fervour had drained out of me, so I was resigned to huge swathes of inactivity or lots of standing in the extreme background.

December the 14th signalled it was one week till we departed from Turkey. That morning, called to set egregiously early, I spent most of the morning standing around in the chilly air chatting and drinking tea. Eventually we took up our positions, peering over the battlements at an advancing French column of such numerical superiority it would surely obliterate our absurdly small force of defenders. Sharpe exchanged glances with his trusty Chosen; would this be our last stand? Would Sharpe and the boys live to fight another day? Not if the discontented rumblings at the way Malcolm had handled Sean's Bond premiere trip were true, casting doubt on a fifth outing. In the bar the previous night, Daragh had told me the sole reason we were out doing a fourth series was to help Beano pay for his new £1.2 million mortgage. When I came to think of it, I decided I wouldn't mind a little sabbatical from the show I loved and the chance to get my face seen in something different; of course, unlike Beano my sabbatical from *Sharpe* would probably be bracketed by lengthy spells of unemployment.

From high on the battlements, the camera came down to the courtyard for Sharpe's final face-off with Maquerre, who offered Sharpe's troops the choice of languishing in a French prison camp or certain death. Christian Brendel played the slimy French nemesis to a tee, wringing every drop of Gallic deceit from the role. It was quite a long scene to cover with dialogue being shot from multiple angles. As time wore on, Maquerre's horse became fractious. Dinny's off-camera horse calming methods kept us entertained. Every time Maquerre's horse shifted it hooves, Dinny fixed the horse's gaze with a stern look on his face while holding his index finger aloft; a true horse whisperer in action.

The following day's light workload allowed me to take the family up to location for the afternoon to see Harris delivering the Jesuit's bark to Catherine Maquerre's fever-stricken mother. In the story, Sharpe is torn between saving the bark, with its fever-taming quinine, for his own similarly stricken wife Jane or giving it all to Grandmother Maquerre. A gesture Sharpe must keep secret as it signals to his men that he feels we won't be getting out of the siege alive. Amira Casar, playing Catherine Maquerre, had arrived fresh out of drama school; having once graced the pages of French *Vogue*, she still retained the air of an impetuous, capricious model. Already in Natasha's bad books for resembling my ex, Amira had further transgressed by saying to Natasha, 'You look really beautiful in those pictures from the last series,' implying that was not the case now, patently not true.

Amira did her best to elongate the shooting of this scene, pondering each word, movement or gesture as if she was still in the classroom; Tom started to get a little tetchy, but, seeing as she was a pretty face, he indulged her a bit. At the close of scene Catherine quietly sobbed at her mother's bedside; Tom decided we didn't need the shot. Amira got wind of this and appealed to Tom, manipulating him with real tears to change his mind; rumour had it that film wasn't loaded, or the camera wasn't turned over for the take.

THE BEGINNING OF THE END

The final Friday in-country was designated as wrap party night; drinks were free till four in the morning; shame the staff were rumbled watering down the vodka and replacing the Courvoisier with Turkish brandy. No self-respecting Turkish party could be without the mandatory belly dancers and ours arrived this time accompanied by a live band. Wrap parties were usually the time to meet crew you'd not encountered before, but by the sheer weight of numbers every crew member must have invited their uncles, brothers, cousins and any other available male relative from all over Turkey. It seemed women weren't invited unless you were a belly dancer. The overabundance of males got a little tedious when their appreciation of the belly dancing started to get a little disorderly as the crowd encircling her closed in tighter and tighter, like animals closing in on their prey.

The poor dancer tried to break from the frenzied circle by snaring Tom for a bit of ritual humiliation; unusually for Tom he pretended to demur, his legendary love of young females suppressed for the moment. Poor Tom; even he was slightly fazed by the exuberance of our new-found Turkish friends. The tension was broken when Gary Fiddler suddenly appeared on the dance floor wearing a superhero costume with the words 'Super Driver' emblazoned across his chest, stealing the focus more skilfully than a Brian Cox snuff-induced sneeze. Once Gary had swept the room jiggling his bits along the way, the atmosphere in the room lightened considerably, allowing us to relax into our own brand of bacchanalian excess. Natasha and I had left godfather Saint in charge of Daniel, permitting us to join in the fun. Even Dan waking up at two in the morning didn't dent our enjoyment. We simply popped upstairs, lay back and watched ace babysitter Saint put Dan in the harness then sang, danced and tapped on the drum to lull Dan back to sleep. With that job done we retired next door with other campaign regulars for toasted sandwiches. It was just like old times.

The next morning it was evident the hotel staff couldn't handle a Sharpe-style party; the Altınorfoz was a ghost town when I came down for breakfast. We found a young kitchen helper looking rudderless in the absence of the head chef who hadn't made it into work. With previous form in taking over the kitchens of Crimean sanatoria, we simply asked the kitchen lad where everything was and got to work whipping up a batch of Menemen, a traditional Turkish dish like scrambled eggs with vegetables. After serving up chow for the early-rising crew, I took breakfast in bed to Natasha. A short while later we waved goodbye to the rebellious camera boys. The production office had somewhat unsurprisingly abandoned the usual farewell protocols – they were either still mad at the rebels or supremely hungover, probably a bit of both.

Sunday 17 December, one week till Christmas Eve and six months since our Sharpe-generated child had come into existence. All we had left to shoot was the successful repulsion of the attack on the fort by a huge French column led by our old friend General Calvet. In the story a plan is hatched to defend our position with what amounts to chemical warfare by dropping lime, created by crushing burned oyster shells, on the advancing column. In order to get the 'lime' to drift through the air a plane propeller had been mounted on the back of a truck to send it in the appropriate direction; much fun was had watching Tom and Andrew Mollo testing the prop by throwing their hats into the updraught. Soon anyone with a hat was chucking it in the air and watching a gust throw it quite some distance away.

It transpired we had shot 'Siege' in record time; 'Company' took thirty-eight days to shoot, 'Siege' was on course to take twenty-seven shooting days to complete. Management was thinking of scheduling an extra day of filming so that they wouldn't be expected to bring all future episodes in inside that shorter time frame – probably for less money as well. Why the money men at ITV consistently tried to scrimp and save to make this show, I'll never know; why couldn't they accept it took around thirty days to shoot an episode of *Sharpe*? That extra shoot would have been on the day Sean was promised he would be wrapped on this series, so the idea was rapidly squashed.

On our penultimate shooting day Sean, Daragh, John and I sat in our motorhome, window wide open letting in the glorious sunshine and listening to the sound of the surf lapping against the beach. I suppose that was our end-of-term chat, the last time we would all be together undisturbed as our departures would be staggered over two days; Daragh first, off to Los Angeles, then Sean and John plus other actors, followed finally by my group leaving on the last transport out. Daragh rather dramatically informed us this would be his last *Sharpe*; upon returning home he would initiate legal proceedings against the company for damages sustained to his broken cheek.

After waiting the whole morning, we were finally called to resume our defence of the fortress. It just so happened to be Gobi, our pyrotechnics expert's birthday, which meant that, to celebrate, all explosions would be slightly beefed up. It took my mind back to Badajoz nights when a particularly large birthday blast injured a couple of soldier extras; Daragh had flipped out, accusing those in charge of coordinating the stunts of being slightly merry from liquid fortification, and causing a verbal ruck between him and Dinny. As we were mostly concentrating on pouring sustained rifle fire onto the French column the chances of someone being blown up this time were minimised. In the story Sharpe's gunpowder supply has been compromised with sawdust, severely limiting our firepower and making it impossible to kill the numerically superior enemy. This time it looks like we're done for, but in true end-of-episode, against-all-odds tradition, Sharpe and his dwindling bunch of men repel the irresistible force with the help of 'lime' and machine-like rank firing.

We had now arrived at the final call sheet of the fourth campaign. Sanity had prevailed with the management, who had decided we would not be shooting an extra day to gain a greater budget on any future *Sharpe*s. The phantom shoot was called off, not out of concern for a unit which had toiled for a quarter of a year, but due to the five hundred quid cost of feeding the unit for a day, which says a lot for the compassion of the management. The sun shone brightly on our final shooting day, making it very hard to get my head round the fact that it was six days to Christmas; news from home told of the UK experiencing a severe cold snap sending temperatures plummeting to zero, so a rude awakening awaited us on our arrival home. Natasha and I were more excited about Daniel experiencing his very first Christmas Day; at six months he'd have no recollection of it, but it was a milestone for new parents.

Our last day brought another promotion for Sean's driver Gary, who had been cast as Sergeant Waters, an injured redcoat guarding the wounded in the sick bay. Gary's rapid, Sharpe-like rise through the ranks had seen Tom giving him a close-up with a line of dialogue. It had been a lucrative tour for Gary; not only did he draw wages for driving and the security of Beano's motorhome, he also got paid for driving Sean to set. Now he had reached the exalted heights of extra with dialogue, we'd have to start calling him four-jobs Fiddler.

As it was wrap day, we shot the customary unit photo, supped our last free lunch then repaired to our motorhome to appreciate the beautifully blue Mediterranean Sea one last time while getting probably the last bulletin from Paddy World News. Big D had been told by the accountant that, as he was domiciled in Los Angeles, he had foreign entertainer's tax status and would be subject to having a third of his wages withheld. I would miss the bulletins from PWN once I was back off tour in Civvy Street; I'd have to get any breaking news down the transatlantic phone line until we met again. That was, of course, if Beano's elevation to mega-stardom allowed a fifth outing of *Sharpe*; with the industry raving about Sean in Bond and taking the lead in his football movie *When Saturday Comes*, possibly feature films and not more episodes of *Sharpe* would be foremost on his or his agent's mind.

And so, to the concluding yards of celluloid exposed on *Sharpe*'s fourth series: on the fort's ramparts Sharpe tricks the remains of the lime-dusted enemy into thinking we are about to let loose another volley of rifle fire. As Sharpe raises his sword to signal us to shoot, the French turn tail and run; but it's a supreme bluff as our rifles are out of ammunition. After seeing off the frogs we walked back into the fortress to survey the damage wrought and tot up the butcher's bill; Sharpe is triumphant yet remorseful as he weaves through the bodies of dead defenders. As with last year's closing moments of the shoot, the final take of the campaign involved Sean and John; by the time they had called 'cut' Daragh had already changed out of his costume and was waiting in his car to zip him to Adana airport. It was a truly fractured departure from this year's campaign; gone were the Crimean years where we did most things as a group, brought together by the often extreme nature of our circumstances.

At 6:45 a.m. on 21 December 1995 the remains of the unit were waved off from the Altınorfoz forecourt for the marathon trip home to London. Most of the crew had been slogging away for sixteen weeks, eleven of them away from their families in the UK, so everyone was in a good mood. Fortunate to have my family out on location with me, I was in no hurry to be back in London. Natasha was dreading the journey for fear of Daniel kicking off, but as soon as the rubber hit the road, he crashed like a baby despite the customary *Sharpe* party also kicking off at the back of the bus. On the short flight from Adana to Istanbul, Daniel was a little less cooperative and was more interested in being carried around the cabin or banging on Saint's mini drum than letting his parents have a rest. I had to say that, although I did grumble about pay rises, lack of respect and everything else on *Sharpe*, Malcolm had done everything he could to accommodate having my family out on location with me.

The onward flight to London was blissfully uneventful, as one would expect from a scheduled flight with British Airways. Then again, *Sharpe* was now four years old, we'd matured and we'd had to grow up. The question now was, had Sean outgrown *Sharpe*? The Yorkshire Lad held all the cards as to when or if we rolled again. At this point, I wasn't duly bothered if we took a break as long as I was fully included in what would probably be our swansong campaign, but I was sure when spring turned to summer my whole being would fall in with the *Sharpe* cycle again. Keeping an ear out for snippets from the grapevine, rumours and preparing everything you needed for another long tour away; wherever that might be, over the hills and far away or maybe a little closer to home.

DUST IT OFF AND START AGAIN

Arrival in London was, of course, a relief, but gone was the absolute joy of emancipation when coming off campaign; then again, previously I'd been battered by several months of Crimean quirks and complications. This time there was a new, more important focus in my life. For the first time my world won't be solely focused on *Sharpe*, particularly if Beano did take a sabbatical from the role and I was left with a longer stretch between campaigns. Also, we had almost reached the conclusion of the Sharpe story; yes, there was 'Sharpe's Devil', a story set six years after Waterloo in 1821, but there was no mention of the Chosen in the novel. To be ready for when the Sharpe door closed, I would need to concentrate on getting my face seen in other projects.

Sean had always said five series was the optimum number, just enough to get everyone appreciating the product or hooked, then leave them wanting more; I was anticipating that a fifth tour would be our last stand. I knew the siren call of *Sharpe* would soon have me pricking up my ears for future news. What I didn't expect was a letter from Malcolm Craddock's lawyers requesting I assist in a court case brought by Equity on behalf of Paul McGann and the original cast of 'Sharpe's Gold'. I placed the letter on my desk with no intention of replying, hoping the whole matter would simply go away; my hopes were quashed a week later with a phone call from Paul McGann. He was asking if I wouldn't mind having a chat with the lawyer representing Equity; nothing wrong with a little chat I thought and agreed to a meeting on 15 March.

I pitched up at the lawyer's office where we talked chiefly about the two incidents that had exacerbated his knee injury and watched footage of Paul as Sharpe, skilfully managing to avoid mentioning I had instigated the football match that started all the trouble in the first place. Once the meeting was over, I signed an affidavit verifying what I'd just told him was true, then went on my way home totally oblivious as to the significance of what I had just done. Less than a week later a letter bearing some very official stamps and seals arrived; once the letter was open, I realised exactly what I had done. Call me naïve, but at no time did the lawyer say I would be required as a witness, but in my hand was a summons stating just that. The timing was terrible; if *Sharpe* did run to a fifth series, my agent would be negotiating with producers who would consider me the enemy. I was disappointed with Equity's lawyer for not being straight with me; I was angry at myself for not fully questioning what I was signing. I thought I was helping out a friend who had been hard done by; I should have been more circumspect when putting my name to paper, especially in a lawyer's office. I hoped I wouldn't experience any blowback from this down the road.

A call to Daragh was in order, both to see if he had any advanced news and to see what he thought about the legal action taken against Sharpe Film. He told me he had also considered helping Paul but, as he was in Los Angeles, he hadn't met with Equity's lawyer yet. He might soon have a reason of his own to consult the actors' union. Apparently, Sharpe Film had declined to pay for any ongoing medical fees to fully fix Daragh's cheek beyond the care he had received in Turkey; he said he would have no choice but to sue Malcolm. Join the queue, I guess. Daragh was short on advanced news but understood one episode could be shot in England, which made sense as there was peace for a hundred days before the Battle of Waterloo commenced.

Speaking with Big D kicked off a flurry of Sharpe-related interactions; I got a call from Sam Craddock letting me know a couple of our stunt team were visiting London. I asked him about Sharpe. He replied that he had done his last tour and wouldn't be returning for a fifth. This was shocking news to say the least; Sam was a stalwart member of the Sharpe family, a true veteran and major contributor to the Sharpe spirit, not to mention a prime source of intelligence about future developments. But I knew Sam had a tense relationship with his dad at times, so it didn't come as that much of a surprise. It brought home to me that the next tour could have a very different look and feel and that I was probably correct in trying to concentrate on a world without Sharpe, a feeling that went completely counter to how I'd operated for the last four years.

I CAN SEE CLEARLY NOW

At 8 p.m. on Wednesday 1 May our efforts reached the screens with 'Regiment' achieving the highest ratings with just over ten million viewers. 'Mission' was obviously very good for Harris and 'Siege' wasn't bad either, even though some nice stuff didn't make it to the final cut. Meanwhile, Sharpe's tom-tom beat got louder; at my agent's annual party I was very surprised to see Tom Clegg as one of the guests. Never one to make anything other than small talk with me, I wasn't expecting any great revelations about the upcoming campaign. Ultra-cagey Tom did divulge he had stayed with John Tams while scouting locations up north. I assumed this was for the one episode to be shot in the UK; I signed off our conversation by saying 'Hope I'm in it!' Tom just shrugged, leaving me genuinely fearing for my part in the English shoot.

I supposed bumping into Tom absolutely settled the question as to whether there would be a fifth series of *Sharpe* this year. Further verification of this had recently been revealed in the tabloids covering the regrettable news of Sean's divorce from Mel; in an article Sean confirmed he'd be donning the uniform one last time this year. I had learned of their split while partying chez Bean. Sean had gone upstairs briefly leaving me alone with Mel; in hushed conspiratorial tones she had said, 'Sean is divorcing me.'

Just as Mel uttered the last words of her sentence, Sean came back into the room. At first I thought it was some sort of joke, but Sean had a look on his face that said he knew exactly what had just gone down and he wasn't laughing. It was a terribly awkward moment. I had no idea what to say; my loyalties were torn between my work colleague, the man I considered a friend, and Mel, whose warmth and hospitality had been instrumental in forging our bond through the regular soirées at their home. It was the end of their marriage and, as awful as it is when a long relationship breaks up, I also knew it signified the end of an era in more ways than one.

EVERYONE HAS A PLAN TILL THEY GET PUNCHED IN THE FACE

Confirmation of the Bean divorce was depressing. Even more miserable for me was the kick in the teeth followed by a slow stab to the heart in the form of an availability check from *Sharpe*'s casting directors. This wasn't the offer of a contract, merely a call to my agent to find out if I have any other work commitments during the time I would be needed on *Sharpe*. On the first three tours I was required for the full sixteen-week shoot, on year four it was eleven weeks; this fifth and final campaign would only require my services for five weeks. At first, I thought it had been a mistake; a five-week stint would mean I was only in one episode. How could that be? I'd been in every episode of *Sharpe* to date. Something wasn't right. Would Harris go missing after one episode like Cooper in the third series?

I called John Tams; he hadn't been contacted yet but mentioned that an early treatment of the episode set in England had both Hagman and Harris in the story. The following day, my agent called confirming my contract offer; I would only be required for one episode: my contribution to the last hurrah was being reduced by two-thirds. It was a bombshell I didn't quite know how to process; was this a drastic way to reduce the acting budget or a decision based on retribution? It dawned on me, it could only be the latter; I was being punished for ignoring Malcolm's lawyer's letter and instead taking the side of McGann. I again called John, who told me he'd been offered a two-episode contract, one in England and one in Turkey, which would possibly indicate that our reduced contribution was a cost-cutting exercise. Then it all became clear once I had attended my physical at Dr Gaynor's office, as I had done these past four tours. On this occasion I was examined by a different doctor; I remembered then that Dr Gaynor's name was on the list of defendants in the McGann case. He either didn't want to be accused of witness tampering or he thought I was perfidious scum and couldn't bear to be in the same room as me.

I felt there was no alternative but to call Malcolm in the hope that he could provide some words of comfort, which I knew was a fool's errand as unpopular decisions were usually his and Muir's. I began by asking why Harris wasn't in the episode shot in England, 'Sharpe's Justice'. Malcolm countered with: Harris comes from the south and couldn't possibly join up with the gang's adventures in the far-off land of Yorkshire. Hagman hails from the north, that's why he features in the episode. I was almost speechless listening to such a spurious argument. Harris had followed Sharpe across Portugal, Spain and on to France, yet the journey from Oxfordshire to Yorkshire would be too much for him? And why does Harris appear in early treatments for 'Justice', but not in the final script? When I mentioned this to Malcolm, he plunged the knife deeper into my heart with the following words: 'Jason, you've done well to make it this far.'

I had suddenly become a mere figure on the balance sheet they needed to be rid of. On my four tours of *Sharpe* I had literally shed blood, sweat and tears in trying to make the show as brilliant as possible. I had returned twice on frozen wages and was a chief instigator in forming the team spirit that kept the unit going in those early dark days in the Crimea. I wanted to ask the reason I was being left out of the majority of the last series. Was it because I took Paul McGann's side in the court case? But by the end of the conversation I had no fight left me. I seriously considered turning down the offer, to petulantly cut all ties, to move beyond *Sharpe*'s all-enveloping bosom and on to bigger and better things; but I loved the show too much, had vowed to see it through to the end and knew, deep down, that *Sharpe* for me might possibly be as good as it was going to get.

I was beyond hurt; it was like your lover, your best friend and your parents all suddenly turning their backs on you. It was the worst possible end to my tenure on *Sharpe*. The *coup de grâce* came quite unexpectedly one day. Jules Chapman, our Australian hairdresser, came over for tea one afternoon; during a lull in the conversation Jules turned to me and said, 'Oh, Jason, I'm really sorry Harris gets killed this year.' I wasn't sure if I wanted to laugh or cry; not content with freezing me out of two-thirds of the series the powers had decided to kill me off as well. All there was left for me to do was call Sean to let him know the news; I knew he had a lot on his plate domestically, but he still offered to say something to Malcolm about my situation. I thought about it but declined the offer. My pride was hurt, I was angry, but I didn't want to appear like I was begging. I would take my punishment and try to reassure myself that all was for the best in the best of all possible worlds.

The weeks leading up to our fifth tour couldn't have been more different from the lead-up to all previous *Sharpe*s. Before I would be brimming with anticipation, looking forward to getting the uniform back on, reuniting with 'family' members and continuing to add to the *Sharpe* canon. This time I felt I was counting down the days until my execution, in some ways literally. I was so angry with the powers for deciding I was an expendable component of our show, I was afraid of what I would say when I got on set; this would be my last *Sharpe*, soon there could be no retribution for revolutionary acts committed while on location.

As the days crept closer to embarking upon our swansong campaign, I still couldn't shake off the nagging sense of injustice. Not eight months earlier everything had looked rosy. I was hoping Harris's contribution to 'Mission' and 'Siege', episodes that showed his versatility, might have earned the right to a juicy involvement across all three episodes of our last season. As always on Sharpe, harbouring high hopes was the swiftest and surest route to heartbreak. My spirits were crushed, but at the same time Sharpe had lodged in my consciousness and was ticking all the right boxes in terms of career satisfaction, so no matter how miserable I was feeling I had to see Sharpe through to the end.

5

HEAVEN KNOWS
I'M MISERABLE NOW

I had never felt so conflicted at the eve of departing for a tour of *Sharpe* and I was dreading meeting up again with the people who had caused my malaise. Natasha and I decided my stay in Turkey wouldn't be long enough to warrant her and Daniel joining me on tour; instead I packed them off to Yalta for the duration of my stay. On 19 August 1996, I headed to Turkey for my final *Sharpe* campaign. After a two-hour bus ride from Istanbul, we approached the Adapazarı region and our base while shooting 'Waterloo', the Elmas Hotel; the other Turkish episode, 'Sharpe's Revenge', would be shot down in Silifke. Adapazarı, in the centre of north-western Turkey's industrial heartland, wasn't far from the southern shores of the Black Sea. Heavier rainfall up there made it a lot greener, hopefully making it look a bit more like Belgium. Information on the area contained the priceless sentence 'Adapazarı grew out of a weekly market on an uninhabited site and there is little of interest in the town.' Looked like production had found us the Turkish version of Simferopol; thankfully our proximity to Istanbul could provide possible avenues of entertainment.

Later that evening a welcome party was held in the function room. I managed to busy myself with unpacking and getting drunk in my room, only dropping in on the party when I knew Malcolm wouldn't be there. I was aware I couldn't avoid him for the entire shoot, but for now I wasn't sure I would be able to hold my tongue. I was hurting big time, but while out there on location I had to force myself to put on a happy face to fool the public and to avoid potential eruptions.

At lunch the following day, Daragh appeared after his marathon flight from Los Angeles; he drove from Istanbul with Muir, who he informed at every opportunity how unhappy I was with the way I'd been treated. Good old Big D, he'd got my back. Somewhat optimistically he felt there'd be an eleventh-hour reprieve for Harris in 'Justice' as the script had barely been written yet and they'd need to fill it with a familiar face. Not if they wanted to do it cheaply, I retorted, trying not to get my hopes up. I found out 'Justice' was scheduled to shoot for three weeks in London with only a couple of weeks up north in Yorkshire, allowing ample scope for soft-southerner Harris to feature in the story. Not only had I been denied what I felt was my rightful place in an episode of *Sharpe*, I had been deprived of five weeks' wages and the comfort of waking up in my own bed before heading out to location.

DEAD MEN WALKING

August the 21st saw the first call sheet of our final campaign and soon my five-year odyssey would be at an end. It was a fairly easy first day for John and me; Sean hadn't arrived in-country yet and Daragh wasn't on set, so Tom concentrated mainly on Hagman and Harris.

Ridiculously enough, in 'Waterloo' we'd been promoted to sergeant; of course, had I read the script I might have known this. Discovering Charles Wood had been commissioned to write the screenplay, my heart had sunk, and I didn't even bother to pick up the script other than to pack it in my bag. Having said that, that day's two-hander was quite a nice one. In the woods we watch a cuirassier riding away with the colours, discussing who should have the honour of shooting the flag-snatching Frenchman; in the end it was decided to let him be shot tomorrow. A very satisfying scene to kick off with; we even got to shoot three takes, which was highly unusual as Chosen Men.

There were definitely more crew on set than usual, more costume people, more horses, more hardware; our special effects chaps, five-year veterans of *Sharpe*, Gobi and Dima, had been augmented by a couple of UK crew equipped with two incredibly impressive smoke machines. I hoped production was happy spending the budget on more smoke and less Harris. Speaking of production, Malcolm had slithered up to our motorhome as John and I were changing that morning, taking me completely by surprise. I had no time to deploy my defensive shield; I almost replied to his greeting with a perfunctory 'It's good to be back' but instead nodded in his direction, managing to hold back all the bitterness and hurt I was feeling inside. Johnny recognised I'd been caught off guard and complimented me for not blanking Malcolm or lashing out. It was the truth, though; I was happy to be back in the Sharpe fold, just bitterly upset at my reduced contribution.

A showdown was avoided, but at some point on this tour I was sure the elephant in the room would have to be addressed. John and I left location for our hotel, and I ventured into Adapazarı in search of a beer shop; getting one inside at the hotel wasn't a problem, outside it was. In Adapazarı strict Islamic law was adhered to, prohibiting the widespread sale of alcohol. After investigation we learned that one of the only places in town to buy a can of beer was a furtive little hole-in-the-wall shop across from our hotel, obviously there to serve infidels from the Elmas. The transaction was very exciting; the chap behind the counter nervously passed the beers to me like a Harlem crack dealer handing me a bag of rocks. I hid the beer in my jacket for fear of being spotted crossing the road with immoral contraband.

After a strenuous first foray into work, the schedule had thrown up a five-day break. In happier times I'd be exploring the local environs, cadging a lift to set for lunch and shooting a few photos. Daragh seemed to have the right idea: he'd gone off to Istanbul for a couple of days. My spirit of adventure had all but died, suffocated by self-pity and anger. I just stayed in my room watching telly. John Tams told me Malcolm came up to him in the bar the night before expressing concern about my state of mind; I laughed, likening it to an arsonist worrying about the house he's just set ablaze. Don't worry, Malcolm, remember 'I've done well to get this far.' At least it was Saturday and the ritual of tuning into the BBC World Service sports report took my mind off my Sharpe situation. While I was listening, Lyndon called, lightening my mood considerably; he more than anyone knew exactly what I was going through. As we chatted the hotel room phone rang; it was Beano freshly arrived; I was touched that the first person he decided to call was me.

Fairly soon, Sean descended from his suite to crack open an illicit beer and we proceeded to have a two-man welcoming party, blabbing about everything except the two main issues preying on our minds: my despair at being left out of two episodes and the much more serious matter of Sean's divorce. It was, of course, mentioned, but neither of us was ever prone to divulging our innermost feelings, so we didn't delve deeply. I could see it was weighing on his mind, though, so I didn't want to bring the mood down as I was all too aware these could possibly be among the last occasions where we would be relaxing together like this. We'd been close for five years now both on and off screen, tackling every sort of hardship, and I knew I would miss times like this. We wisely decided to truncate our party, as Sean had horse-riding practice in the morning. After a quick tour of the bar, I returned to my floor, where Giles Butler was hosting a massive party in his room; just like old times! Next morning Beano knocked at my door in need of toothpaste. It seemed Sean had only so far learned where my room was, knowing he could rely on his Chosen Man for supplies.

I had a lovely late lunch at the hotel with Daragh, who regaled me with tales of his trip to Istanbul and news that the morning's equestrian practice hadn't gone well for Sean. As soon as he was in the saddle, some of the horses freaked out, causing Beano's nag to rear up and almost unseat the Yorkshire Lad. Not fancying a session of Buckaroo, Sean simply dismounted and motioned to Gary to take him back to the Elmas, ending the grand practice session before it began. Hanging out with Sean and getting the lowdown from Paddy World News started to make me feel as if I actually belonged on this show, lightening my gloom considerably.

THE FAB FOUR RETURN

On 26 August the four longest-serving actors on *Sharpe* commenced shooting the final episode of this great show. We were shooting

William of Orange's staff galloping along a lane fleeing French cannon fire, Paul Bettany playing the foppish, incompetent Orange to a tee. For much of this episode Sharpe and Harper were on horseback, hence the need for extra riding practice. This forced the newly promoted Hagman and Harris to jog along behind the two horsemen as they raced around the Waterloo area, which seemed ridiculous.

Tom looked ecstatic at having all the big pieces of his jigsaw at his disposal, ready to create an epic last episode. I decided to take a leaf out of his book and try to be less doom-laden; then again, I remembered production once suggested Tom shouldn't direct all three episodes, which he had opposed vehemently, so I Imagined he wouldn't be so gleeful in my position. Overall, the day went well, and we were back at the hotel by early afternoon; at the bar that evening both Daragh and Sean said they felt very nervous being back on set, which I thought was extremely endearing.

After two days in the fields, we moved location to another incredibly convincing construction of La Haye Sainte, site of Harris and Hagman's death. Andrew Mollo and his team had done an amazing job as usual; the set looked so realistic. The next couple of days were spent skirmishing in the woods outside the farmhouse as a huge French column advanced on our position, the sheer weight of numbers giving me an authentic feeling of terror. Tom still felt he might have to 'borrow' a few battle scenes from 'Eagle' to edit into 'Waterloo'; I'm not sure why as we had way more extras here that day than we ever had while shooting 'Eagle'. In those days the extras had to switch from British red coats to French uniforms at lunchtime in order to shoot the battle scenes. Four years later we'd got plenty of bodies to fill out both armies at the same time.

YOU'VE DONE WELL TO GET THIS FAR

So far, I had managed to avoid Malcolm's gaze and any entreaty to initiate conversation. During a tea break I was chatting with Sean and Daragh when Malcolm walked over, causing my hackles to rise. Sean and Daragh looked on nervously as we exchanged pleasantries and made small talk; somehow the conversation turned to well-loved Sharpe characters. I was in no mood to be diplomatic and mentioned what an injustice it was leaving Ramona out of the final series, which Malcolm rightly took as a dig at him. It also got me thinking that her absence from this year's campaign could be punishment for letting slip production's plans to axe Daragh from Sharpe. Of course, my anger wasn't about leaving out Diana, it was pure displaced rage at the shabby treatment I felt was meted out to me.

That evening Malcolm arrived at my door looking very nervous with his eyebrows twitching, a habit he had when he was concerned about something. The showdown I had been avoiding was about to materialise in the comfort of my sanctuary from Sharpe politics. Malcolm opened saying he thought I was steaming mad on set today, which was a tad exaggerated; if I had been grumpy it was down to having to endure the bloated waiting times due to cack-handed scheduling rather than at Malcolm. That said, I was even madder at Malcolm than I was at having to endure waiting around, which, after all, was commonplace on a film set. He tried to explain more fully the reason for my absence from 'Justice': Sharpe gets posted up north as part of a militia. Our hero is assigned to take charge of the Yorkshire Yeomanry, which just so happens to be Hagman's neighbourhood despite him being from Cheshire. One evening, by chance, they meet up at a tavern where Hagman gives Sharpe intelligence about the local area. Hagman doesn't get into uniform, they don't reform the band and they don't head over the hills together at episode's end. Harris, meanwhile, is cobbling in London's Soho or being a wastrel in Oxfordshire, blissfully unaware of what's occurring with his old chums.

It was a pretty weak explanation; as I was fully resigned to my fate and two weeks from leaving *Sharpe* forever, I saw no point in fully airing my grievances. I had lost the will to fight and it was too late to make a difference anyway; that ship had sailed. I should have demanded a genuine explanation of my partial exclusion after appearing in every episode to date. What was the lame excuse for leaving the Chosen Men out of 'Revenge' completely? Wouldn't our deaths at the end of 'Waterloo' be even more heartbreaking if we had both been in all three episodes of the final campaign? I just wanted him to admit I was being punished for taking Paul McGann's side in the court case. I felt it was my right to know; but what did I think Sharpe Film was, a democracy? A reference to one of Harris's first lines in the premier episode, 'Rifles'.

THE END IS NIGH

The countdown to our deaths had begun. Far from a sense of dread, I was feeling quite curious about how it would be handled as I had never shot a death scene. Before the fateful blows were struck, the last Chosen Men standing desperately defended the farmhouse now inundated by the vast French force outside, firing through loopholes, throwing roof tiles at the enemy and running to protect William of Orange. Tom had directed the action so convincingly I had no problem imagining my life was in danger.

On the afternoon of 4 September, the time had come to film what I was hoping would be the saddest scene of the whole *Sharpe* series, the senseless killing of not one, but two Chosen Men. The premise of their deaths for me was slightly ridiculous. Sharpe and Harper leave the farmhouse just as it's about to be overrun, Harris and Hagman deciding for the first time ever not to join them, electing instead to stay and protect William of Orange. After Silly Billy and his staff suddenly flee the farmhouse on horseback, Hagman and Harris follow on foot into an overwhelming mass of French troops. In past episodes we had been in total control, brushing aside numerically superior forces; this time, without Sharpe by our side, our charmed lives came to an abrupt end. As I said, it was a preposterous scenario in which to meet our deaths; I had known for some time that Hagman meets his death, shot through the lungs (page 342 of Bernard's novel *Waterloo*). Harris wasn't a Cornwell invention, so Harris's death was purely a decision and the invention of the producers, which strictly I was okay with; the fact that I was being left out of the other two episodes of the series – that was a true stab to the heart.

I was betting Sharpe fans would find it one hell of a moving scene, not that the scriptwriter or the producers made much of it. There was no graveside scene, nor was much said, barring Harper's cold, rational, unemotional assessment that Harris and Hagman were soldiers, they knew it could happen one day; he might as well have said we 'had done well to get that far'. Tom told me that on one of the takes a fly landed on my hand as I died; I hoped that would make the final edit.

Well, that was that then. Except it wasn't. The following weekend, due to the bizarre out-of-sequence world of filmmaking, we were winding back the clock to the beginning of the script where the Fab Four re reunite for the first time. Until then I had a four-day bereavement break. Adjacent to our location lay a sprawling graveyard reminiscent of the Crimean cemeteries we'd seen with little white fences around low-lying graves; how appropriate, I thought, production thoughtfully easing us into the idea of our characters' deaths.

I used my time off for a couple of days in Istanbul before completing the final days of the Salkey era on *Sharpe*. At a newsstand I bought a few British papers to take back to the unit; it seemed the paparazzi had found their way to Adapazarı. A two-page spread in the *News of the World* talked about the *Sharpe* shoot, Sean's divorce, his new barmaid 'girlfriend' and the possibility of him taking over Bond when Pierce Brosnan retired. The most prominent photo in the article was of Beano walking through the lobby of the Elmas with can of beer in hand, a photo John Tams claimed would reinforce Sean's man of the people credentials in the eyes of the public.

My last days on location with *Sharpe* were close at hand with John Tams and I filming a bit of skirmishing in the woods and the scene where Sharpe is reunited with his men at a tavern; unfortunately Charles Wood had rendered Harris inarticulate, reduced to forced, awkward exchanges with Sharpe. Hagman and Harris, virtually fused at the hip on this episode, had also become long-distance runners, being seen taking off on foot every time Sharpe and Harper arrived or exited a location; preposterous! What a way to bow out from the Sharpe story.

September the 12th, and the last day shoot with my name on the call sheet; I was scheduled to return for one night shoot at the end of the month, thus elongating the pain of separation from Sharpe. I so wished we could have done that night shoot in this first trip out, but it was to be shot at a completely different location. I supposed it took the emotional sting out of saying goodbye to everyone after this day was done, knowing I'd be back in a couple of weeks. Not that I was feeling emotional about my exit, far from it; I just wanted to get it all over and on the plane to Simferopol to see Natasha as soon as possible. Gosh, how times had changed. Four years ago I would never have had a longing to fly to Simferopol. On Friday 13 September that's exactly what I did, took a plane from Istanbul to the Crimean capital to be reunited with my Sharpe-generated family in Yalta, where it all began.

Since Sharpe moved base from Yalta, I had noticed improvements making it more comfortable for western tourists with a proliferation of bars and eateries; including some ridiculously priced high-end restaurants where only oligarchs and mafia dons dined. Our weekend was spent bidding farewell to Natasha's parents and grandmother; with Sharpe no longer bringing me to this part of the world who knew when we'd be back as a family. I was hoping one day a direct flight from London to Simferopol would open up, but in the five years since becoming an independent state there still seemed to be no sign of that happening. Our trip back to reality was through Istanbul, staying overnight in the Hilton, where the thought of no more *Sharpe*s began to hit me. Would my five-year stint on Sharpe help my career? Surely it must! Would I ever get a job as good as Sharpe again? Was this as good as it gets? Only time would tell.

HOME IS WHERE THE HEART IS

I was relieved to be back in London with the whole family in tow, with one more day to shoot then I could put a full stop on the whole saga. Or so I thought. Not long after returning from Turkey I got a letter from a Sharpe fan who had formed an appreciation society and wanted me to write the foreword for the latest newsletter. I wasn't sure what she was expecting, but I turned it into a bit of a vent against the powers, expressing how after all these years the Chosen Men were finally being appreciated. I wondered if the newsletter would have been read by anyone on set before I was due to arrive back to work.

Just as I had settled into life back in London, I prepared to rejoin the unit in Turkey, thus prolonging the pain of my 'break-up' from Sharpe; the more I thought about it, the more I realised what a cruel bit of scheduling it was to have me back for one day. It was a fucked-up way of saying goodbye to a five-tour veteran. On 30 September I boarded BA flight 677 to Istanbul; aboard the plane with me was Alexis Denisof, who plays Rossendale, the man who steals Sharpe's wife. At the Elmas, production had laid on a farewell party for me; I couldn't think of anything worse. I started the evening in Sean's suite having a few beers; Beano gave me the best farewell present I could ever ask for: his manager's jacket from his appearance on BBC's *Fantasy Football League* with the name of his team, the Chosen Men, on the back. Good old Sean: he knew what Sharpe meant to me, he knew this wasn't just another job, he knew how committed to the cause I was. It was the perfect send-off and I was humbled and touched at such a gift. I was happy to stay in Sean's room all evening, but he persuaded me I should go upstairs to at least show my face, which I did reluctantly. Production hadn't exactly pushed the boat out for this party, so I didn't feel obliged to stay too long and drifted back to Beano's suite for a bit of bacchanalian excess; my last session while still on the Sharpe payroll.

The following evening, I donned my costume one last time for a couple of two-handers with the man who had been by my side since day one in the basement of St Saviour's Church on Warwick Avenue, John Tams. One scene covers us boarding a wagon for the long trip back to re-enlist; the other a scene that would open the great debate about Harris's first name, not that we'd ever wondered about my character's Christian name. Yes, we had joked about it, especially Lyndon who mused it could be Anita, Rolf, or Keith, after the ventriloquist with the pale green duck dressed in a nappy on his arm. Never had there been a debate on screen regarding Harris's first name, so it came as a bit of surprise that they should be making an issue of it at this late stage in the series; at least it would provide a neat TV trivia quiz question in the future. The scene was shot inside a dilapidated wooden shack in a tiny village just outside Adapazarı. As we set up, a large group of children crowded behind the camera to witness the strange goings-on. Having the village munchkins hanging about took the sting out of the sad finality of my last take on *Sharpe*. Tom called cut, followed by 'and that's Jason wrapped on *Sharpe*'. Just like that, it was done, never to be repeated; the absolute end of an era.

WHO NEEDS SHARPE?

Shortly after getting back home to London I was resolved to draw a line under Sharpe, put it in my past and move on to other, if not better, things. Not helping me put Sharpe in my rear-view mirror, an invitation arrived from the steadily growing Sharpe Appreciation Society to attend a signing of Bernard's Sharpe novels at W. H. Smith in Nottingham. It was comforting to be reunited with Lyndon and John Tams again, even though it hadn't been that long since I had last seen them. It was a sort of Sharpe reunion before the show had even finished production. The turnout of fans eagerly purchasing Sharpe novels and VHS tapes was quite impressive, so maybe I wouldn't be able to shake Sharpe out of my life that easily.

December rolled around and *Sharpe* wrapped in Turkey and moved back to the UK to commence shooting 'Justice' in Fitzroy Square, just around the corner from Muir's office. Looking for activities to keep my eighteen-month-old Chosen Man occupied, we visited the set; the first person I saw was Daragh kitted out in Harper's best dress uniform. It was so very incongruous to see Big D standing on a London street dressed as Harper. I took Dan into one of the splendid Georgian houses on the square being used as Jane Gibbons' London home to sit with Abigail as she was being made up for the scene. She made no reference to the bombshell fact that she had started a relationship with Sean Bean. I found out when Natasha and I went to visit the unit up on location in Yorkshire a couple of weeks later.

While completing the 'Justice' shoot the unit was based in a Bradford hotel. We arrived to find Sean and Abigail deep in conversation at a secluded table in the bar; this struck me as somewhat odd. Beano customarily preferred the company of John Tams, his driver Gary or other male *Sharpe* lifers when winding down after a shoot, so it was mighty bizarre to see Sean in almost intimate tête-à-tête with a woman. I just assumed they were rehearsing a scene for the next day; when enquiring with Daragh about the state of affairs he just said, 'We've got a real "turtle dove" brewing there' – 'turtle dove' being cockney rhyming slang for 'love'. I was flabbergasted. It was the most unlikely Sharpe liaison. I couldn't think of two people who were more different in personality; when had this all started? She hadn't been in Turkey while I was shooting 'Waterloo'; had their relationship started last year when we were in Antalya? These were questions that only the two of them could answer and I certainly wasn't going to ask them.

Absolute confirmation of their relationship came a couple of weeks later back in London as I made my way to the *Sharpe* wrap party; as I was coming out of the tube station at Temple I bumped into Sean and Abigail walking hand in hand, having left the party early. Hopes of a mini session dissolved as it seemed Sean's priorities had shifted; I wished them well and headed to the 'party', where I was berated by Tom Clegg for the foreword I had penned in the Sharpe Appreciation Society newsletter. The central theme addressed how we, the Chosen Men, were never properly appreciated by the powers; underused, underpaid and generally treated like dirt. So, it was nice finally to get the appreciation we deserved with the formation of the society. It was a rant but not really a pop at Tom, even though he admitted he wouldn't have cast us in the roles and often accused us of whinging when we were standing up for our basic rights.

OLD SOLDIERS FADE AWAY

We were on the cusp of 1997; the entire *Sharpe* cycle had almost come full circle. Soon the off-screen politics would no longer concern or affect me, and I would have hopefully moved on to different if not better projects. The first audition of 1997 promised to take me into a completely new orbit as I auditioned for a job on *Lost in Space*, just the kind of job that would thoroughly banish *Sharpe* into the recesses of my mind; however, reality dawned as I was only being asked to read in the part of the older Will Robinson who was unavailable at the time. My agent kind of made it sound like I might be considered for the role if Jared Harris didn't sign on time; in my heart of hearts I knew that would be too good to be true, but actors live in hope.

The year kicked off with important life milestones: our second wedding anniversary and, at the grand old age of thirty-five, the time had also come to apply for my first mortgage. Scary, as I was an actor at the end of a five-year pay bonanza, but I could thank *Sharpe* for being financially in the position to purchase my first home. More Sharpe Appreciation Society events (from here on referred to as the SAS) came along and on the employment front I secured a little role in an ITV detective drama, *Wycliffe*, starring Jack Shepherd; I played a hippy traveller who possibly fits the bill as a murderer but turns out to be innocent. It was great to get a job outside *Sharpe*, though it seemed being in *Sharpe* hadn't significantly increased the quality or amount of castings I was getting; I wondered if I would experience some sort of *Sharpe* backlash at being too associated with the show, or being at the heart of too many 'industrial disputes' while on location. Time would tell.

In a letter from Equity's lawyer dated 27 March 1997, I was informed the McGann case had been settled out of court. I was relieved I wouldn't be required in court and happy for Paul and the other plaintiffs in the case. At the same time, I felt slightly hard done by; did they really have to name me as one of their witnesses? Surely my signature on the affidavit and the potential evidence I could have given hadn't swung the case? Johnny and Daragh told me they had both communicated with Paul's lawyer but probably on the phone or by letter and hadn't signed anything, possibly because they weren't

London-based; or maybe they were far savvier than me, refraining from signing anything that could bite them in the arse down the line.

Paul had won his damages, but I had damaged my *Sharpe* legacy. I felt like a bitter war veteran, loyal to the core, used in my prime then discarded at the roadside like a bag of dog shit. Instead of being elated at having contributed to one of the finest television shows of the era, I was sore and indignant at going out like that. Eight months later, it still rankled that I wasn't included in 'Revenge' and 'Justice'. What was I to do, though, when faced with the choice of helping the friend I'd known before *Sharpe* or taking sides with producers who had continually denied pay rises and overseen the marginalisation of the Chosen Men? What if I hadn't ignored Malcolm's lawyer's letter and hadn't answered Paul's plea for my assistance? What if I had accepted Sean's offer to lodge a protest with Malcolm at leaving Harris out of 'Revenge' and 'Justice'? What if I hadn't been an active participant in all industrial action down the years? At this point of the final *Sharpe* cycle, I would never know; there were so many 'what ifs', so much to ponder.

On 9 April Carlton Television held 'A Celebration of Sharpe' at the Royal Society of Arts, on John Adam Street just off The Strand. The very posh evening at a very exclusive location kicked off with a champagne reception followed by a showing of 'Sharpe's Waterloo'; many of the leading players were there, Sean notable by his absence. As I stood surveying the room with Daragh, he turned to me saying, 'Well, that's closure on *Sharpe* for you.' After a second's thought I replied that there was not much chance of that, living under the same roof with my two flesh and blood reminders of our time on *Sharpe*. The realisation had dawned, for better or worse, that I would never have closure on *Sharpe*. With that thought turning over in my mind,

I declined to watch the screening of 'Waterloo', choosing instead to take advantage of the free bar with Lyndon and Sam Craddock. At the end of the screening I could hear 'O'er the Hills' blaring out through the now open doors to the theatre and saw many of the audience were in tears. I jested with Lyndon that they were tears of disappointment at a sub-standard instalment, but soon remembered Hagman and Harris snuffed it near the end of the episode, which must have jerked a few tears.

Aside from realising I would never have closure on *Sharpe*, the screening showed me how much our deaths moved the audience. I wondered if the same would happen when the episode was broadcast the following month. Until then, I had plenty to keep my mind occupied with more SAS events, taking twenty-month-old Dan to his first football match, a change of government after nineteen years and my beloved Chelsea winning their first trophy in twenty-seven years. So, when 'Revenge' was broadcast on 7 May I just set the timer on my VHS and got on with anything other than watching *Sharpe*, ending a tradition started when 'Rifles' was first aired four years and two days earlier. I followed the same protocol for the broadcast of 'Justice', committing it to video for possible viewing at a later date, which eventually came twenty-three years later.

At ten in the evening on Wednesday 21 May 1997, as the credits rolled on 'Sharpe's Waterloo', my final *Sharpe* cycle officially came to an end. What a journey, what an odyssey, what a long, undulating, life-changing trip it had been; now it was all over, no powers to remonstrate with, no one to strike or withhold labour from. It was done. The pain of rejection was still raw. The way I was feeling, I was happy to see the back of *Sharpe*, never to be referred to or mentioned again. Or so I thought.

AFTER THE BALL IS OVER

Well, that was certainly an interesting and life-changing five years spent at the coalface of television legend; a period at the time I assumed would receive a full stop with the broadcast of the final episode. Looking back, with the benefit of almost three decades of hindsight, I can't help but notice what a moaning malcontent I sounded like. Other actors would have been lining up to give their right arm to have been a regular on *Sharpe*, but I'm sure that, if they didn't succumb to the physical illness or psychological stress so prevalent on the Crimean *Sharpe*s, their experiences would have been summed up in the much the same way. And, yes, the diaries do have a high whinge factor, but I assure you nothing within these pages has been concocted or exaggerated. Experiencing what we suffered on *Sharpe*, particularly during the first three campaigns, it's hard not to have a little bitch about what occurred. Coming out intact from a Crimea tour was a true badge of honour; surviving three should surely merit the film industry equivalent of the Victoria Cross, *Légion d'honneur* and a Purple Heart rolled into one. And without conflict there is no drama; if life on *Sharpe* had been a bowl of cherries tied up with a pretty silk ribbon it wouldn't have made for an interesting read.

They were the best of times and the worst of times, but, had *Sharpe* been shot close to home on easy street, it would have given the show a completely different feel; the dearth of edible food, the mistreatment, infirmity and the boredom all served to give us the look of soldiers who had fought a long, attritional campaign. So, I'm of the opinion that the Crimea made *Sharpe* the realistic, engaging, compelling show it is. With the passage of time, the painful memories began to recede. I came to realise that *Sharpe* was far more high-profile than even I could have imagined and truly what a lucky boy I was to have landed the part of Rifleman Harris.

So how did I get from desiring to put a massive full stop to my *Sharpe* existence to all these years later writing a book about my adventures? I suppose the rekindling of my love for *Sharpe* arrived once I had received global fan mail, met legions of *Sharpe* fans at related events and experienced the sharp pain of extended unemployment. It appeared that Britain, many of our ex-colonies and quite a few of our European neighbours had been bitten by the *Sharpe* bug.

It took me about four years after my final *Sharpe* campaign to stop feeling sorry for myself; cantankerously, I tried to consign *Sharpe* to the dustbin of negative experiences, but as Burns's old 'mice and men' saying goes, my best-laid plans to fully separate myself from Sharpe never quite came to fruition. In that time, I had attended the first Sharpe convention, appeared at various historical events, meeting fans and signing location photographs provided by Carlton Television. I was still determined to purge myself of *Sharpe* memorabilia I had kept hold of, peevishly selling my cartridge belt and powder horn at the second Sharpe convention in 2001. I thought I'd better get rid of the stuff while *Sharpe* was still hot in the eyes of the public just in case it was a passing fad that would run its course and peter out in time.

That attitude was directly counter to my initial assumption that *Sharpe* was destined to be one of Britain's most iconic television shows, establishing itself in the same league as *Dad's Army* and *Doctor Who*. After a passage of time that, funnily enough, saw Paul McGann become the eighth incarnation of Doctor Who, the release

of the first Harry Potter novel, the death of Diana, Princess of Wales
– ITV broadcast 'Sharpe's Eagle' to soothe a grieving nation making
me very proud – 9/11 and our little Chosen Man starting school,
the scales fell from my eyes and I accepted *Sharpe* had been damn
good for me. Around the end of 2001 it started to dawn on me what a
treasure trove for *Sharpe* fans I possessed sitting in my loft: hundreds
of photographs, scores of videocam tapes and a written diary of each
of the five series of *Sharpe*.

Then it occurred to me that I could create a *Sharpe* documentary,
turning the location video footage I had shot into a video version
of *The Recollections of Rifleman Harris*. Trawling through the footage,
it rekindled my love for the bond we had formed on *Sharpe*; I was
regretting the sporadic contact I had with the main cast, so I made a
conscious effort to get back in regular touch with the main guys.

In May 2002 I released the first volume of the *Harris Video Diaries*;
soon a website followed and an entire Harris industry was spawned.
At the tailend of 2003, I found myself back in Russia shooting a
TV movie in Moscow, playing an Englishman married to a Russian
woman, a case of art imitating life. In the New Year Honours list Pete
Postlethwaite was awarded an OBE, a year that saw another trip back
to Yalta, where I visited Dimerdji for the first time in ten years and
ate at Yalta's bustling new McDonald's situated directly opposite the
statue of Lenin.

In late 2004, Ukraine underwent an Orange Revolution after
the pro-Moscow president rigged the election, sparking civil
disobedience and a re-vote, which the president lost. With a more
western-looking government in charge, visa-free travel was granted
to westerners, sparking hopes that Ukraine was moving towards
being admitted to the EU along with almost all other ex-Warsaw Pact

countries. The ugliness in the aftermath of the Balkans conflict was also being resolved with the imminent trial of Slobodan Milošević as part of Serbia's attempts to be admitted to the EU.

In 2005 an event was held celebrating twenty years of Bernard's Sharpe novels, which coincided with the first murmurings of a new Sharpe television episode; Doctor Who had just been resurrected, so why not Sharpe? Bernard had recently written two new stories set in the peninsula, Escape and Havoc. I was praying they would be the novels turned into television shows. I was disabused of that fantasy by Stuart Sutherland, son of Muir, who told me there would be no turning back the clock, arguing we'd lose credibility with viewers if previously dead Chosen Men showed up on screen and, anyway, we were all too haggard and old to look like our former selves. I reasoned it was only pressure from fans that compelled ITV to do another Sharpe so original fans of the show would love seeing expired Chosen walking beside Sharpe and new fans wouldn't know. In the end part of the old 'Sharpe's Curry' script was resurrected to form the basis of the new story which categorically meant Harris wouldn't be reincarnated in India when they started principal photography on another Sharpe in late 2005.

The year 2006 opened with Russia seemingly displeased with Ukraine's west-leaning administration cutting off gas supplies. The year went on to be heavily Sharpe-related; all twenty-eight hours of Sharpe were sold to BBC America and I met up with Beano again at the 'Sharpe's Challenge' press screening. I noticed the first half-hour of 'Challenge' was a flashback to before the peninsula; so much for not turning back the clock. In May the tenth anniversary of the SAS was celebrated at the Chelsea Army Museum, a fantastic event attended by many Sharpe campaign veterans, but not Sean. In June,

Sean also declined a large sum of money to appear in a reunion with Harper and all the Chosen Men at Autographica '06; I began to realise that attending *Sharpe*-related events wasn't high on Sean's agenda.

As the decade progressed, I started attending events without the SAS; at the Kelmarsh Festival of History, I met up with Richard Moore for the first time in years, not this time dressed in his Rifle green, but still totally dedicated to bringing history alive for today's generation. Living history festivals like Kelmarsh and another called Military Odyssey were full of dedicated people like Richard who immerse themselves in the period they are representing. The Sealed Knot Society, which brings the English Civil War to life, is Britain's oldest re-enactment group and there are always lots of Roundheads in attendance. But you'll see halberdiers and hoplites sharpening their weapons, Viet Cong strolling past Union and Confederate soldiers from the American Civil War and, of course, group upon group of 95th Rifleman and redcoats, their numbers swelled by the popularity of *Sharpe*.

And *Sharpe* was indeed living beyond the original five series, with ITV sufficiently happy with 'Challenge' to commission another Indian episode not based on a novel, so it would be an original story like 'Sharpe's Gold', our most ridiculed episode.

In August 2007, our family returned to the Crimea, this time taking my mum to the scene of the crime and the place that changed my life. Yalta was humming with holidaymakers all enjoying the new bars, restaurants and nightclubs that have proliferated since *Sharpe* was last based there; apart from the still tortuous journey to get there, it was just like any resort town in the summer.

As the second great financial crisis unfurled, *Sharpe*'s popularity showed no sign of abating; proving as popular with the Yorkshire

Lad as marriage, as Sean embarked upon his fourth wedding early in 2008. Sharpe's Chefs also sprung up, a group raising money for charity with a cookbook of recipes provided by *Sharpe* veterans; it was a good cause, but also a chance for me to be reunited with my fellow Chosen Men as we did at events held at Waterstone's bookshops across England.

In spring the Sharpe unit started shooting 'Sharpe's Peril'. I'm entertained by regular updates from PWN by email; it seems not a lot has changed. Daragh, moved by the plight of young people in India, had decided to start a charity called Sharpe's Children; fellow cast members have been mobilised to help the cause by signing photos and other *Sharpe*-related items. In June a diverse collection of *Sharpe* cast gathered at Firepower in Woolwich; as usual there was no Sean in attendance, but Muir, Daragh, Lyndon, Hugh and Tim Bentinck, plus a smattering of other cast, showed up. As 2008 progressed, I recorded an audio book of *The Recollections of Rifleman Harris*, adding to *Sharpe*-related merchandise I'm making available to fans. The year end saw 'Sharpe's Peril' broadcast; it received one of the worst reviews of a television show I think I've ever read. The late A. A. Gill, formerly a big fan, wrote: 'It was a dire travesty of the *Sharpe* we once loved.' I was aghast to think the powers had let this happen to *Sharpe*. Hadn't they learned that if you deviated too far from Bernard's template, as with 'Gold', the results wouldn't be favourable?

In early 2009 came news of the premature death of Chris Clarke, founder of the SAS; Paul Trussell and I attended her funeral, where the *Sharpe* theme was played as her body was interred. I had held it together until that point but hearing Johnny's violin strokes brought tears to my eyes. With Chris gone, it was up to me to be the de facto Appreciation Society, serving fans with the wealth of *Sharpe*-related goodies I had at my disposal. In the summer I received an invitation to a major war-gaming convention in America for which I created a lecture with slideshow about my life on *Sharpe*. I followed this in 2010 with a trip to a living history festival in Chicago; it was great to see first-hand how popular *Sharpe* is across the pond.

Returning to London, I was met with a pleasant surprise: Sean was filming on my street, directly in front of my house. He popped in for a brief chat before he was needed back on set. The year 2010 proved to be one for bumping into *Sharpe* icons near my home; out of the blue I saw none other than Pete Postlethwaite standing alone on the pavement. I hadn't seen him for sixteen years but there was no mistaking that face; I gave him my phone number and told him we should hang out and chat about the old days. A few short months later I realised why I never got a call from Pete. The year ended on a *Sharpe* note with the launch of Daragh's charity, Sharpe's Children, at Apsley House, otherwise known as Number One London. The Fab Four were in attendance, along with many other *Sharpe* luminaries; the highlight of the evening was John Tams leading cast members in a rendition of 'O'er the Hills'.

In January 2011 every news channel reported Pete Postlethwaite's death from pancreatic cancer. I was shocked to the core and terribly saddened. The nation had lost one of its best-loved actors and *Sharpe* had lost one of its legends. That year, the Harris roadshow continued its assault on the USA with two trips, one to Lancaster PA and Williamsburg VA, in between which the Arab Spring kicked off, *Game of Thrones* was released, the final Balkan baddie Ratko Mladić was arrested, and Obama got Osama. All of this unknown to us as we made our last journey back to Yalta, where I took a trip down memory lane with visits to Baidar Valley and Polikur studios. In September, cast members and re-enactors embarked upon Sharpe's

March, a sponsored walk that took us through Reading as part of a fundraising drive for Sharpe's Children.

London 2012 was Olympic year. Vladimir Putin changed the constitution so that he could be president for a third term and Beano was arrested after a bust-up with his new wife. The same year saw Ukraine co-host the UEFA European Football Championship; I was hoping events like this meant Ukraine joining the EU would be just a formality. In July of the following year, Croatia, the scene of recent horrific warfare, joined the European Union. At the end of 2013 we got some idea of what had been keeping Ukraine from being offered EU membership. Inexplicably, pro-Moscow Viktor Yanukovych, ousted in the 2004 Orange Revolution, was president again and in the autumn turned down signing an association agreement with the EU, a precursor to the formal process of joining.

The citizens of Kiev recognised they had been sold short and hit the streets, resulting in weeks of increasingly violent protest culminating in the death of more than a hundred people. Natasha and I watched with horror as events unfolded. Putin seized the opportunity, putting into action what some say was planned way in advance of the protests: the illegal annexation of the Crimea. Seeing 'little green men' surrounding the terminal at Simferopol airport was beyond a shock; we began to worry about the safety of Natasha's parents, but the violence in Kiev wasn't replicated on the peninsula. My mind swung back to the fears Natasha had expressed when we were first married, that the communists would take over again, and this seemed just as bad if not worse.

These fears were manifested when Russian-backed separatists started fomenting trouble in eastern Ukraine, on the Russian border, in what was recognised as a flagrant attempt to join Russia to the

Crimea with a land corridor. Separatists then shot down a commercial airliner, turning an already serious situation deadly. Putin met all accusations with the Bart Simpson defence 'It wasn't me,' as he did with the Polonium assassination of Alexander Litvinenko and the Novichok attack on Sergei Skripal in Salisbury years later. Natasha started raising money to aid the ever-increasing number of wounded soldiers returning to Kiev from the front. She started pressuring her parents to sell up and move from the Crimea to Kiev as she had vowed never to return to Yalta again, thoroughly disgusted with former neighbours and schoolmates for falling for Putin's propaganda in the referendum. In 2014 there was also sad news on the *Sharpe* front with the death of executive producer Malcolm Craddock from cancer; it had been a few years since I had seen him, when he came to dinner at my house, but this came as a real shock. We had at least put behind us any residual enmity from our fifth and final campaign.

Attempts to calm the conflict raging in eastern Ukraine came, with France and Germany arranging a ceasefire which was broken within the first day. In early 2016 Radovan Karadžić, architect of many of the atrocities in the Balkans war, was sentenced to forty years in prison for genocide and crimes against humanity. One day I long to see Vlad the Annexer in the dock, alongside the now vanished Yanukovych. I shan't hold my breath, though. On 23 June the whole point of wanting Ukraine to join the EU became moot with the Brexit vote. In the summer of 2016, as Pokémon Go fever transfixed the world, I attended a living history show called War & Peace, where some of the *'Allo Allo'* cast were signing autographs and posing for photos. I proposed a *Sharpe* event to the organisers for the following year which just so happened to be twenty-five years since we'd started shooting the show.

By early 2017, it was apparent there was not much appetite within my band of brothers for a *Sharpe* event so I quietly shelved all plans, sad in the knowledge there might never be another reunion. At least Natasha and I got to see Daragh, who was performing in the West End; neither of us knew that Beano was about to get married for a fifth time. In July I was invited to the Chalke Valley History Festival where I delivered my Sharpe lecture, attended by many TV historians and their literary agents, one of whom told me 'there's a book in that lecture'.

In August another *Sharpe* titan, Tom Clegg, died; he had remained fit and active, so his death was a very unexpected. Along with the theme tune from *The Sweeney*, they played 'O'er the Hills' as Tom's coffin disappeared through the curtain to be cremated; I guess that will have to be my exit music one day. Afterwards veterans of past campaigns raised a glass to Tom at his local pub.

Shortly after that, we travelled to Kiev in September to visit Natasha's parents now permanently moved from Yalta and by November Unbound agreed to publish my *Sharpe* memoir.

Russia's bad behaviour towards Ukraine progressed with cyber-attacks, clashes in the Kerch Strait and, of course, the continuing conflict in the east of the country; with Russia's sham democracy putting Putin back in power for a fourth term, there appears to be no end in sight. In May 2019 the mercurial Ukrainian electorate voted out President Porochenko and elected an actor/comedian with no political experience other than playing the Ukrainian president in a TV show, a bit like like putting Sean Bean in charge of the British armed forces. To new President Zelensky's credit, by the end of 2019 he had initiated prisoner swaps with Russia, though many fear that he'll cede autonomy to the separatists, which only means they'll be puppets ruled from Moscow. That would suggest Zelensky has little appetite for reversing the annexation of Crimea and no chance of me returning to the scene of so many crimes.

But what of *Sharpe* and me and the way forward into the future? *Sharpe* hasn't quite reached *Dad's Army* or *Star Trek* status – shows that have had quite a head start – but it is still very popular around the world. In August 2019 the *Washington Examiner* asked: 'Looking for a TV series full of great writing, acting and swashbuckling adventures? Look no further than *Sharpe*, starring Sean Bean.' As 2019 closed, Muir Sutherland, the last of the big three responsible for *Sharpe*'s success, died. There were times many years ago when I didn't see eye to eye with this powerful Sutherland/Craddock/Clegg triumvirate, so caught up was I in what I perceived to be ills perpetrated against me by them.

I lost sight of the fact that they were all under intense pressure to make the show a success while maintaining the high quality expected by the viewing public. I wrongly focused my ire on them when, really, they provided the platform for five of the best years of my life. So, it is Muir, Malcolm and Tom who I must thank for my part in the amazing legend of *Sharpe* and their memory I'll always respect. Particularly Muir, whose friendship with Bernard Cornwell, association with ITV and dogged tenacity in seeing *Sharpe* to screen, was chiefly responsible for making this great show a reality.

And as the *Sharpe* television incarnation enters it fourth decade, I'm sure you'll find me at military and Napoleonic-related events right up until the *Sharpe* theme tune plays at my funeral or for as long as I have the strength to carry on as *Sharpe*'s unofficial ambassador.

ACKNOWLEDGEMENTS

With thanks to:

Bernard Cornwell, Trevor Dolby, Daragh O'Malley, Stuart Sutherland, Alejandro Sutherland, Sam Craddock, Tim Bentinck, Michael Mears, Lyndon Davies, Paul Trussell, Christian Abomnes, Scott Cleverdon, Assumpta Serna, James Purefoy, Hugh Fraser, Phil Elton, Paul McGann, Michael Cochrane, Colin Thurston, Ivan Strasburg, Robin Sayles, Anna Wilbraham, Igor Dymitirev, Valentina Lakhmaniuk.

In memory of:

Malcolm Craddock, Tom Clegg and Muir Sutherland, the Holy Trinity of Sharpe Film.

Unbound is the world's first crowdfunding publisher, established in 2011.

We believe that wonderful things can happen when you clear a path for people who share a passion. That's why we've built a platform that brings together readers and authors to crowdfund books they believe in – and give fresh ideas that don't fit the traditional mould the chance they deserve.

This book is in your hands because readers made it possible. Everyone who pledged their support is listed below. Join them by visiting unbound.com and supporting a book today.

A Splendid Day Out Steampunk
  Festival
Kristin R. Adams
Antoinette Adkins-Riepl
Mark Aldous
Mark Alger
Jack Allen
Jon Allen
Sam Allo
Jamie Allonby
Irene Ambrose
Libby Anderson
Vanessa Anderson
Ste Applegate

Stuart & Sarah Archibald
Mr Philip Atherton
Robert M Atwater
Robert Morrisson Atwater
Atef Awad
Daniel Baber
Thomas 'Major Tom' Baggaley
Chris Bailey
Peter Baines
Laurence Baldwin
Drew Bale
Kathleen Balem
Nathan Ball
Anthony Barker

James Barker

Sam Barker

Adam Barnes

Stephen (Titch) Barrett -
    A Coy - 3 RGJ

Colin Bassett

Robert Bateman

Glynis Baxter

Alan Baxter 84 1-95

Anthony Beachey

Joe Beer

Max Beeson

Christopher Bell

Oliver Bentley

Bonne Beste Bejan

Buzz Beurling

Bev

Mark Beyer

Gary Bezant

Tim Bickerdike

Alastair Bickerstaff

Jon Birnie

Austin Bishop

Andrew Bizley

Martin Blagoev

Andy "Chosenman 44" Blake

Jennifer Blazek

Graham Blenkin

Joshua Blythe

Boakesey (Liz Boakes)

Stephanie Bognar

John Bone

Matthew Bone

Paul Bonnici

Charles Boot

Peter Boulton

Pete Bounous

Rob Bracewell

Becca Bradford

Chris Bradshaw

Marcus Brain

David Branfield

Nick Breeze

Mickaël Bretin

Jonathan Broad

Samantha Brodeur

Andrew Brooker

Brian Brooks

Sam Brotherwood

Kevin Broughton

Ann Brown

Ben Brown

Jamie 'Wagonmaster' Brown

Margaret Brown

Matt Brown

Paul Andrew Brown

Scott Brown

Valerie Brown

Wilma Brown

Fergal Browne

Chelsea Brownridge

Adam Brunskill

Sue Brunt

John Bull

Nairn Buntain

Jeremy Bushnell

Christopher Callow

Judi Calow

Callum Campbell

Daniel Cane

Freddie Capper

Ambrose Carey

Robert Carlysle

Tim Carroll

Richard Carson

Svetlana Carsten

Pete Carter

Tom Carton

Isabel Casamassa

David Casserly

Dympna Cassidy

Andy Cater

Shaun Catton

David Challoner

Michael Chamberlain

Ron Chamberlain

Ruth Chamberlain

Michael John Chandler

Paul Chandler

Becky Chantry

Rob Chester

Paul Child

Ryan Chittenden

Sarah Chivers

Juan Christian

F. Alistair Christie-Henry

Njal A. Christie-Henry

Alexandra Churchill

Stuart Churchman

Teri Cilurso

Claire Clark

Jamie Clark

Paul Clark

Ryan Clark

Ryan Clarke

Claire Claydon

Luke Cleaveley

Sean Clonch

Tony Cole

Rudi Colman

Duncan Connell

Ian Connell

Jason Cook

Jack Copeland

Elizabeth Coppes

Jonathan Coppock

Lee Cordingley
Christian Cornforth
Michael Cosgrove
Dr. Ed Coss
M. Denise Costello
Sue Couldwell
Marius Coulon
Jane Coward
Adele Cox
David F Cox
Alfred Crane
Stefan Crawford
Neil Creaton
Marcus Cribb
Daniel Cruttwell
Iain Cullen
Stuart Cullen
Mark Cumberbatch
Malcolm Cuming
Michael Cyster
Kam Dale
Jim Dallas
Mike Dallison
Daniel & Kaitlin
Andrew "Beastie" Davidson
Andrew Davies
Alice Davis
Andrew C Davis
Precious Davis

Russell Davis
John 'Funky JD' Dawson
Phil Dean
Bob Dee
Bev & Jeff Delacruz
Jared Delacruz the
    History Teacher
Joseph DeLory
Adrian Deluce
David Dent
Mike Dent
Stephen Dicey
Robert Dickson
Matthew James Didier
Diane Dixon
Hal Dixon
Matt Dobson
Andy and Michelle Dolan
Linda Dombrovska
Georgie Donald
Mark Donald
Keith Downey
Jeanie Dubberley
Derek Dubery
Sarah Duffy
Corky Duke
Natasha Durlacher
Thomas Duvernay
Claire Dwyer

Deann Malonnie Dwyer
Daniel Earnshaw
Colin Eden-Eadon
Matthew D. Edson
Angela Eismann
James Ekberg
Karen Eley
Chani Elkin
Andrew RI Ellis
Pete Emmett
Philip Espinosa
Mark Etienne
Shane Evans
Christopher Evans RAMC
George Evans-Hulme
Emma Everson
Phil Eyden
Nataliya Fafrunyk
Harley Faggetter
Robert Fanning
James Farrow
Stuart John Faulkner, B#st#rd
Featherston Public Library
Mark Fewtrell
Steve Fielding
Dawn Figgis
Evi Finsterer
Ellie Fisher
Bob Flanagan

Joy Flannigan
Edward Fleming
Eric Fleming
Molly Fletcher
Anke Fontaine
Allie Ford
Glen Ford
James Anthony Ford, B#st#rd
Sam Foresha
Mark Forsyth
Alan Foster
Jake Fountain
Gary Fowler
Raymond Frandsen
Eddie Franklin
Anne Fredrickson
William Frewin
Ian Furey-King
Felicity Gale
Peter Galloway
Oli Game
Nikki Gates
Gino Gatti
Matt Geary
Ian Gelsthorpe
David Gerhard
Stephen Gibbons
Viv Gibbons
Bob Giglio

Chris Gilham

Stephen Gillen

Gillian & Simon

Carlo Giovale

Susan Godfrey

Sterling Godwin

Rachel Gollub

Jane Goodenough

Mark Goodman

Philip Goodyear

Peter Gordon

Roy Gore

Richard Gott

Alec Graham

Barry Dominic Graham

Hannah Helena Margaret Graham

Helen Frances Graham

Jonathan Christopher
  James Graham

Tom Graham

Anthony Gray

Thomas Gray

Dan Green

Jack Green

Rob Green

Steven Gregory

Mark J.T. Griffin

Rob Griffith

Mary Grinch

Blake Guion

Sean Guy

Sue Haga

William Hagan

Simon Haines

Damian Haire

Leslie Hajdu (SAS #146)

Jay Hall

Martin Hall

Rob Hall

Terry Hall

Kyle Hall-Brown

Phyllida Hallidie

Alison Hamilton

Allen Hammack

Edina Hancock

Dave Harding

Gary Harding

Paul Harding

Sophie Harley

Craig Harris

Guy Harris

Matt Harris

Frederic Harry

Steven Hars

Barry Hart

Gael Harvey

Michael Harvey

Tim Harwood

Donald Hauser

Ben Haworth

Robert Hayes

Tim Heale

Andrew Heathcote

Craig & Lauren Henderson

James Henderson

David Hensley

James Hepplestone

Sam and Steve Hewlett

Andy Heys

Richard Hicks

William Patrick Hide

Alison Higginbotham

Andrew Michael Hill

Hilltop Florist Limited

Bobbie Hindman

Nicholas Mark Hine

Nicholas Hodges

Ray Hodson

Lisa Holdsworth

John Holland

Will Holland

Peter Hollander

Dean Hollisey

Wendy Hooker

Alan Hooson

Marc Hope

John Hopkins

Karen Hopkins

Paul Horton

Martin Hough

Lucy Houghton

Lucy Hourahane

Henry Howard

Wendy P. Howard

Lord Robert J Howlett

Andy Hudson

Joshua Hudson

Alison Hull

Alan Hume

Alan Hunt

Richard Hyman

Elaine Jackson

Adele James

Anneli James

Stuart James

Alpini Jeff

Gary Jeffery

Martin Jeffery

Jo

Brian M. Johnson

Owen Johnston

Denis W Jones

Derek Jones

Gareth Jones

Harry Jones

Kelly Jones

Stanley Jones

Tony Jones

Jay Jordan

Stella Kane

James Kearney

Brad Keller

James Kellett

Mark Kelly

Simon Kelly

Sinéad Kelly

Stephen Kendrew

Jonathan Kenny

Paul and Cheryl Kenny

Winona Kent

Dan Kieran

Julie Kimpton

Michael Kirkby

Stewart Kitching

Heather Klem

Steve Knight

Tim Knight

Anne Knowles

Scott Knox

Carolyn Koh

Juliana Korver

Richard Kovacs

Valerie Krueger

Jeff Labow

Arron Lace

Paul Ladhams

Alex & Valentina Lakhmaniuk

Lyosya Lakhmaniuk

Dave Lamb

Stephen Lancaster

Roni Landis

Gerard Lavigne

Elizabeth Lawton

Kelly Bolster Leach

Jonathan Leafe

Karl Lechmere

Myriam Lechuga

Keith Lee

Mark Lee

Michael Lentz

Jack Leonard

Pete Lever

Ellis Lewis

Aldona Likus

Karen Lilley

Martin Lindsay

Tracy Lindsay

Jana Lindström Shepard

Billy Frodo Little

Jeff Livy

David Llewelyn Egan

Hugh Logan

Stuart Logan

Gerald & Aileen Loney

John Lønnum

Elliot Lowe

Trevor Lowes

Samuel Ludford

Robert "Frankie" Lunn,
   aka King Mong

Lemuel Lyes

Philip Lyes

Chris Lynch

Stephen Lynch

Ian Macallan

Alison Macintosh

Andrew Mackay

John & Nikki MacKenzie

Keegan MacKinnon

Gill MacLaine

Bonnie MacPherson

Richard Macpherson

Daniel Magill

Philippa Manasseh

Joe Mansfield

Charlie Marsden

Lawrence Marsh

Phil Marsh

John Martin

Abbie Mason

Samuel Matthews

David Maxwell

Tim May

Helen Mayer

James McAnich

Craig McConnell

Davinia McDonnell-Wilson

Susan McDowell

Daniel McEvilly

Greg McGee

Andrew McGregor

Colonel (retired) Michael S.
   McGurk

William F McHardy

Nicky Mckenna

Nick McLean

Joshua McManus

Beth McMillen

Harry McNally

David Mcwhirter

Nancy Meacham

Michael Mears

Steve Medlock

Dorothea Mellor

Jonathan Mellor

Leslie Ernest Mellor

Memorial At Peninsula Limited

Llyr Mercer

Paul Middleton

Thomas Middleton

Tom Milburn

Duncan Miles

Wesley Ann Miles
Richard Miller
Andy 'Machete' Mills
Charles Mills
Derek Milton
Darren Mitchell
Michael Mitchell
John Mitchinson
Duncan Moffat
Steve Mollison
John Molloy
Alastair Monk
Laura Monroe
Malcolm Montanaro
Guy Montgomery
Daniel Moore
Mark Moraghan
Anthony Morgan
Craig Morgan
Patrick Morgan
Ben-Ged-Bentovin Morley
Richard Morley
Julie Morrison
Robin Morrison
Inge Müllejans
Janet Munin
Letitia Munson
Robert Murphy
Jake Musil

Dan Nathan
Carlo Navato
Christopher J. Navetta
Tom Newey
Roo Newton
Merry Niewojna
Sylvie Nixon
Kim Noad
Garrett Noel
Andrew Norley
Andy Noyce
Sam Nuckolls
Conchobhar Ó Súilleabháin
Joe O'Bannon
Drew O'Connor
John Oakley
Angelina Olding
Sharon Oley
Alex Oliver
Anthony Oppe
Sophia Oppe
Gareth Oram
Victoria Organ
Hugh Osborne
Bindi Ouston
Emlyn Owen
Mark Page
Rick Parkhurst
Jamie Parmenter

Sarah Paul

Martin Peake

CPL Tony Pearce 4 Rifles

Mary Ann Peden-Coviello

David Peebler

Marie Pepper

Mark Peters

Jacky Pett

Jacquelyn Phillips

Karl Pielorz

Sanz Piroth

David Platt

Edward Plowman

Marek Polívka

Justin Pollard

Jack Potter

Colin Poulton

Adam Powell

Char Powell

Mark Prescott

Charlotte Pritchard

Heather Pritchard

Steve Pritchard

Annie Pye

Nick Pyfrom

Sean Raffey

Jeremy Ramsey

Phillip Ratcliffe

Axel Harris Ravera

Thomas Raymann

Andy Rayner

Nathaniel Reade

Ian Reed

Dan Rendell

Ali Rex

Simon Rhodes

Steve Ridgewell

Philip Rietti

Matthew Ring BEM

Holger Rinke

Ian Roberts

Peter M. Roberts

Rosemary Roberts

William Roberts

Gareth 'Form Square' Robinson

William Robinson OBE

Ken Rodger

Stefanie Roessner

Callum Rogers

Elizabeth Rogers

Robert Rogers

Steve Rogers

Geoff Rose

Trudy Rosevink

Jon Roskill

Julie Ann Rosser (Hampshire
  Ambassador)

Andrew Rowland

The Royal Green Jackets and
   their Successors
Zachary Rumney
James Rushmer
Christopher Ryan
John Ryan
Adrian Saich
Dan Salkey
Eliot Salkey
Joe Salkey
Natasha Salkey
Alexander Salmon
Rachael Salsbury
Lyndon Sanderson
Shawn Sando
Kiran Scholl
Greg Scott
Anna Scott-Mathieson
Roy and Marcelle Scrivener
Dan Sharpe
Robert Sharpe
David Shayler
Eleanor Sheehan
Jana Shepard
Clare Shepherd
Pete Shepherd
Keith Sherratt
Johnny Sherwin
Catherine Simpson

Bradley Sinfield
John and Holly Skittrell
Dr Katherine Slinger
Toni Smerdon
Colin Smith
David Smith
Ian Smith
Kate Smith
Mark C Smith
Paul Smith
Simon Smith
Alexandra Smithson
Andrea Smolla
Derrick W Sole RGJ Band
   and Poet
Christopher A. Sorensen
Neil & Jenny Spalding
David Sparke
Melissa Speed
Jason Spencer
Jack Stabler
Neil Stabler
Thomas Stabler
Philippa Stainton
Chris Starling
Jason Stechele
Kevin Steele Parker
John Stephens
Neil Steward

Stewart

Carolyn Stiegler

Adrian Stillwell

Neil Stocks

Ronnie Stocks

Alison Stokes

Jordan Stone

Peter Stone

Mandy Stubbs

Thomas Styring

Rich Sutton

Taz Szulc

Edward Taberner

John Talbot

Brian Taylor

Christopher Taylor

Jon Taylor

Richard Taylor

Robert Tedders

Rick Thomas

William Tidmarsh

Nancy Timmer

Andrea Tisdale

Mike Tittensor

Owen Toms

Guy Travers

Keiron Trebilcoe

Paul Trussell

Abby Turner

Julia Tyler

Caroline van der Velde

Olaf van Hoften

(Byzantine) Peter Vella

James Vella-Bardon

Henry Venable

John Verden

Dominic Verheije

Mark Vernon

Sarah Vernon

Eltjo Verweij

Gareth Virr

Donna Visiers

Gordon Von Krafft

Kirt Wakefield

Wallye Walcott

Greg Walden

Enola Walker

Kelly Georgiana Walpole

Brian Walters

Paul Ward

Steven Ward

Adam Warne

Tim Warrener

Dean Waters

Aynsley Watson

James Watson

Malcolm Weavers

Michael Webb

Michael Webster

Lesley Wells

Andrew Wells-Gaston

Barrie I. Wells, CD

Danny Westall

Ciaran Westland

Niall Westland

Richard Westran

Simon Westwood

Richard Whitaker

Chalky White

Laura Whitfield

Ian Whitlock

Mike Widdrington

Fraser Wilkes

Beate Wilkesmann

Claire Wilkins

Ian Wilkins

Marc Wilkinson

Mirjam Willems-Breen

Charlotte Williams

Gary Williams

Paul Williams

Crystal Williams Brown

Andy Wilson

David Wilson

Samuel 'The Pious' Windle

Chris Woodall

David Woodman

Gavin Woods

Joseph Woolf

Tom Woollam

Peggy Wynn

Malcolm Yates

Josh Young

Michael Young

Celena Yussen

Angharad Zafar

Larisa Zubkova

Илья Дмитриев

THE HARRIS VIDEO DIARIES

On the final three series of Sharpe, I kept a video log, pointing the camera everywhere and anywhere my unique access took me.

The Harris Video Diaries pre-date my written account of life on Sharpe in this book but derive from the same urge to emulate the original Harris from the book *The Recollections of Rifleman Harris*.

Using footage shot on location in Crimea, Portugal and Turkey a remarkable visual insight into the epic adventure of Sharpe's production has been achieved. The video diaries are a brilliant accompaniment to the book and slot perfectly between episodes when binging on Sharpe marathons.

You can go to my website www.riflemanharris.co.uk for more details or YouTube for promo clips. Alternatively drop me a line at jason.salkey@ntlworld.com